The International Hospitality Industry

Structure, characteristics and issues

Edited by
Bob Brotherton

OXFORD   AMSTERDAM   BOSTON   LONDON   NEW YORK   PARIS
SAN DIEGO   SAN FRANCISCO   SINGAPORE   SYDNEY   TOKYO

Butterworth-Heinemann
An imprint of Elsevier Science
Linacre House, Jordan Hill, Oxford OX2 8DP
200 Wheeler Road, Burlington MA 01803

First published 2003

British Library Cataloguing in Publication Data
A catalogue record for this book is available from the British Library

Library of Congress Cataloguing in Publication Data
A catalogue record for this book is available from the Library of Congress

ISBN   0 7506 5295 0

For information on all Butterworth-Heinemann publications
visit our website at www.bh.com

Printed and bound in Great Britain by MPG Books, Bodmin, Cornwall

Contents

Contributors

Adee Athiyaman
Adee is an Associate Professor of Marketing in the School of Business, James Cook University, Australia. His research and teaching interests include tourism marketing, buyer behaviour, marketing research, and marketing communications. Adee's work has appeared in a number of journals such as the *European Journal of Marketing, Marketing Intelligence & Planning, Tourism Management, Leisure Studies* and the *Academy of Marketing Studies Journal* – to mention a few. His present research focuses on advertising carryover effects.

Stephen Ball
Stephen is a Reader in Hospitality Management at Sheffield Hallam University and Vice Chair of the Council of Hospitality Management Education (CHME). He has over 20 years' experience as an academic in higher education and previously worked in operations management within the hospitality industry. He has published extensively in the area of hospitality operations management and has written or edited books on fast-food operations and their management, food supply chain management and hospitality systems. He has collated and compiled information for the British Hospitality Association's: Trends and Statistics annual reports. His current research interests include operations and productivity management in the hospitality industry, small hospitality business management and research leadership in universities.

Paul Beals
Paul Beals was raised in the resort community of Saratoga Springs, New York and worked in the hospitality industry for 14 years before commencing his career in academe. He is currently a Professor at the University of Denver's School of Hotel, Restaurant, and Tourism Management, where he is responsible for two MBA programs in hospitality real estate. Professor Beals's research, primarily in the area of hotel development and finance, has appeared in *The Cornell Quarterly, Real Estate Review, The Journal of Real Estate Finance, l'Hôtel Revue,* and *Le Monde.* He holds both masters and doctoral degrees in hospitality management from Cornell University.

Bob Brotherton

Bob is a Principal Lecturer and the Director of postgraduate programmes in Hospitality and Tourism Management at the Manchester Metropolitan University. He teaches comparative hospitality studies, research methods and operational management. Bob has been involved in hospitality management education for nearly 20 years, and has undertaken a number of consultancy assignments in the UK and overseas during this period. He has published a wide range of conference and academic journal papers, book chapters, and edited three books. He is currently undertaking research concerned with the 'nature' of hospitality and the critical success factors associated with various types of hospitality operation.

Judie M. Gannon

Judie has several years' experience in the hospitality industry, mainly in hotels and contract catering. She joined the School of Hotel and Restaurant Management at Oxford Brookes University in 2000 and contributes to a wide range of courses at undergraduate, postgraduate and post-experience levels. Previously she taught human resource management to hospitality and transport and logistics students at the University of Huddersfield. Her research interests lie mainly in the area of people management and international issues and she is currently in the process of writing up her doctoral thesis on the development of managerial resources in the international hotel industry.

Alex Gibson

Alex is a Senior Lecturer in Marketing and the Course Director of the BSc (Tourism Marketing) course at the Dublin Institute of Technology, where he teaches marketing communications, international marketing and business tourism. He is a Visiting Professor at IMHI (Cornell ESSEC, Paris). Alex has held a number of marketing positions in food and hotel companies and has published a wide range of conference and academic journal papers and co-authored a tourism marketing textbook. He is also a consultant to several international hotel chains and the Vice-President of the Irish Chapter of the Hospitality Sales and Marketing Association International (HSMAI). He presents a weekly local radio programme on marketing issues.

Frank Go

Frank Go is the Bewetour Professor of Tourism Management at the Rotterdam School of Management, Erasmus University, The Netherlands. Prior to his present post he worked in the USA, and served within faculties of management at universities in Canada and Hong Kong. His current research focus is on creating value through managing interfacing processes within networks. He is on the editorial board of six learned journals addressing themes that reflect major strands of interdisciplinary research, thinking and practice, has co-authored and co-edited several volumes, including: *Entrepreneurship and Innovation in Tourism* (in press) Sagamore, Illinois; *Towards interactive tourism: capitalising on virtual and physical value chains, Human Resource Management in the Hospitality Industry*, Wiley, New York (1995) and *Tourism and Economic Development in Asia and Australasia*, Pinter, London (1997 and 1998).

Michael Haywood

Michael Haywood is Professor in the School of Hotel and Food Administration, University of Guelph, Guelph, Ontario, Canada. Currently he is in charge of their Tourism Management program, and teaches courses at the undergraduate and graduate levels in strategic management and tourism development. Michael is widely published with over 150 articles to his credit; and serves on the editorial boards of Canada's *Hotelier* magazine and six hospitality and tourism journals. Michael was a recipient of the John Wiley Award for lifetime achievement in hospitality and tourism research. His current projects include a detailed analysis of the hotel development process, the application of intellectual capital and knowledge management to tourism businesses and enhancement of competitiveness for the Caribbean tourism industry.

David Litteljohn

Professor David Litteljohn has been publishing in hospitality management for over 15 years. His work spans strategic and economic aspects of the industry, with an orientation to internationalization and corporate strategy. He also nurtures an interest in policy as it affects the hotel industry and the dynamics of the Scottish hotel and tourism industry. He leads the Tourism, Travel and Hospitality staff in the Division of Management, Caledonian Business School, Glasgow Caledonian University.

Peter O'Connor

Peter is an Associate Professor at the Institut de Management Hotelier International (IMHI), ESSEC Business School which operates an MBA programme specializing in international hospitality management that is jointly administered by the Cornell School of Hotel Administration and the ESSEC Business School. His primary research, teaching and consulting interests focus on the use of technology in the hospitality and tourism sectors. He has developed expertise on the use of electronic channels of distribution in tourism, and on how information technology can be used to enhance both the management and operational effectiveness of hospitality organizations. Based on his work, he has authored two leading textbooks on hospitality technology, as well as numerous articles in both the trade and academic press. Peter has taught professional seminars on information technology management for a variety of leading international hospitality companies, and he is also a regular speaker at academic and industry conferences on hospitality technology-related issues and trends.

Gabriele Piccoli

Gabriele is an Assistant Professor of Information Technology in the School of Hotel Administration at Cornell University. Gabriele's research has been published in the *MIS Quarterly*, *Cornell Hotel and Restaurant Administration Quarterly*, the *International Journal of Hospitality Information Technology* and *Information Technology and Management*. His research and teaching expertise is in the use of Internet technology to support customer service, organizational relationship and internal operations such as virtual teaming and Web-Based Training (WBT).

Michael Riley

Michael Riley is a Professor of Organizational Behaviour in the School of Management at the University of Surrey, Guildford UK where he is also the Director of Postgraduate Research. Initially trained in hotel management he studied labour economics, industrial relations and human resource planning at the University of Sussex, UK and was later awarded a doctorate at the Department of Sociology of the University of Essex, UK. He became an academic after a career in the hotel industry. His work over two decades centres upon the labour aspects of tourism and hospitality and he has written extensively on human resource management and labour market issues. His current research interests are concerned with pay, knowledge accumulation and with managerial cognition.

Linda Margaret Roberts

Dr Linda Roberts is an Associate Professor in the School of Hospitality, Tourism and Marketing at Victoria University in Melbourne, Victoria, Australia. Linda is the Hospitality Discipline Leader within the School and is also Course Director for the postgraduate Hospitality programmes. She has over 25 years of lecturing experience in hospitality at both undergraduate and postgraduate levels in higher education in both England and Australia. Linda's teaching interests include contemporary issues in hospitality and tourism, foodservice industry trends, food safety, environmental management as well as the supervision of postgraduate research students and aspects of marketing. Her research interests include new product development, new product adoption, food safety and foodservice industry trends.

Geoff Wilson

Geoff Wilson is President of Geoff Wilson and Associates Inc., a Canada-based consulting firm specializing in business strategy for clients in the foodservice, hospitality and support services industries. The company's clients include attractions, institutions, managed services providers, restaurants, hotels, food manufacturers and trade associations. The company's services include sector and concept market research, business case analysis and strategy development, optimum concept and location identification, performance enhancement, partnership development assistance, bid strategy development and preparation, litigation support, valuations and transactions.

Geoff is a graduate of the University of Guelph's School of Hotel and Food Administration and has 13 years of operations and marketing experience in the foodservice industry. His work experience covered fine dining, casual dining, accommodation food and beverage, managed foodservices and trade and convention centre foodservices. From 1989 to 1999, Geoff led foodservice consulting practices at two major professional services firms – first Price Waterhouse and then KPMG. Geoff holds the designation of Credentialed Food Executive through the Canadian Food Service Executives Association.

Roy C. Wood

Professor Roy Wood holds the Chair of Hospitality Management at the University of Strathclyde from which he is currently on leave of absence as Principal and Managing Director of the IMI/ITIS Institutes of Hotel and Tourism Management, Lucerne, Switzerland. The author, co-author, editor and co-editor of some 14 books and many academic journal articles, his current interests are in multicultural education, teaching and learning.

Editor's preface

This text is aimed at undergraduates, postgraduates and practising managers studying the international hospitality industry. In addition, similar students following international tourism courses may also find it to be of value. Though the text is not specifically designed to be a companion volume to my previous book on the UK Hospitality Industry (Brotherton, 2000) it does complement this in that students who use the UK text early in their courses may view this international text as one that can help to develop their breadth and depth of understanding and analytical skills in the wider international context. In this sense the two texts may be seen to be complementary and mutually supportive. On the other hand, the prior use of the UK text is in no way regarded as an essential prerequisite for this one.

One major reason for producing this book now is that, although there are a number of other 'international hospitality industry' texts available on the market, many of these were published some time ago and also tend to concentrate on the 'issues and perspectives' aspect of international hospitality alone. What is generally absent within the other literature available at present is the sectoral aspect and an up-to-date collection of chapters discussing pertinent contemporary issues relating to the international hospitality industry. Hopefully this text addresses these deficiencies in the extant literature and provides much needed material for students trying to grapple with the contemporary nature of the industry.

I hope you enjoy reading this book and find it helpful in your studies. I am immensely grateful to all the contributing authors for taking time out of their busy schedules to write the chapters and for their good humoured, timely and positive responses to my numerous editorial requests for amendments etc. during the process of producing the book. I am not sure that I have survived the 'conductor of the orchestra' role as well as these individual virtuosos!

Once again I must record my thanks to my wife, Penny, who has had to endure my preoccupation and time spent on the word processor for such a venture for the third time now. I, and she most certainly, hope that this will not be repeated for some time to come. However, such are the vagaries of academic curiosity and interest that neither of us would regard this as a safe bet! My thanks must also go to Sally North at Butterworth-Heinemann who has supported this project from the beginning and provided immense assistance in numerous ways. In particular, my thanks must go to Sally for her patience and cool-headed professionalism in helping to steer the project through some choppy waters and bringing it to a successful conclusion.

Finally, having applauded, quite correctly, my co-conspirators for their contributions to this book I must record that, as the Editor, I alone remain culpable for any errors, omissions etc. in the book. If any of these exist I hope they are minimal in nature and significance and do not detract from your enjoyment of the book or the valuable contributions of my hospitality management colleagues.

Bob Brotherton (July 2002)

Reference

Brotherton, B. (ed.) (2000) *An Introduction to the UK Hospitality Industry: A Comparative Approach*. Butterworth-Heinemann, Oxford.

Structure and characteristics

Overview

The three chapters contained in Part One are designed to provide you with an analysis of the key sectors of the international hospitality industry, namely *Hotels, Restaurants and Contract Foodservice*. Unlike other texts that seek to provide a similar analysis of the hospitality industry within one country, the range of sectors dealt with here is narrower in some respects. The reason for this being that, although there are other forms of hospitality provision that can be identified as discrete sectors within given national parameters, this diversity becomes more difficult to sustain within the international environment. For example, many countries can identify pubs, clubs and bars as a discrete sector within their indigenous hospitality industries. However, at an international level this is not possible as the number/size of any international operators in this field is extremely limited. There are major international, if not global, brewing/drinks companies, but these are essentially manufacturers and/or distributors. They do not really own international estates of pubs, bars or clubs, and certainly not on any appreciable scale.

There are also sectors identifiable within national contexts, such as self-catering accommodation, that cannot be mirrored in the international arena as these types of businesses tend to be small, fragmented, and operate under local/national ownership. Conversely, other hospitality activities often identified as discrete sectors in particular national contexts, such as Welfare or Educational Catering, are represented here as they occur in the context of the *Contract Foodservice* sector of the international hospitality industry.

It may be argued that chapters concerned with activities such as Timeshare/Holiday Ownership, Resort Complex and Cruise Line operations should be present as identifiable sectors of the international hospitality industry in this part of the book and this may be a reasonable argument. On the other hand, all these activities are essentially engaged in accommodation provision and face many of the same strategic and operational issues as international hotel companies, some of whom are involved in one or more of these activities. Therefore, in the interests of producing an affordable student text focusing on the key sectors of the industry and a range of pertinent issues it was decided not to include any of these as discrete chapters.

Each of the three chapters follows a similar format beginning with a brief *Historical overview* of the sector. This is designed to give you an awareness of the key historical developments and influences associated with the evolution of the sector to assist your understanding of its contemporary nature. A major part of each chapter is then devoted to providing you with an understanding of the *Structural characteristics* of the sector. Here you will find information, analysis and discussion on the size distribution, ownership types and patterns, and the main companies operating within it. However, given the pace of change and consolidation evident in the international sphere, you should review this material carefully as the situation described by the author/s may have changed by the time you read this material. Although correct at the time of writing the extent of merger, takeover and collaborative venture activity in the international hospitality industry is such that it is highly likely the detail of this material will have changed in the time between writing and publishing the chapters!

Following the historical overview and the structural characteristics you will then find material on the nature of the sector's *Products and operations*. This is designed to provide you with a critical understanding of the types of product/s and operational formats existing in each sector. To complete the analysis, each of the chapters also contains material relating to the sector's *Market dimensions and conditions*. This material will enable you to develop an appreciation of the scale and value of the sector's output, and contemporary trends and competitive conditions prevailing in the market/s served by the sector in question.

How you choose to use the material in the three chapters will of course be largely determined by the reasons you are accessing it in the first place. If your interest is in a particular sector, or perhaps a particular type of product/operation, you are likely to focus on the relevant chapter. On the other hand, you may wish to consider the extent to which the structural characteristics, strategic directions, product and operational formats/practices across the sectors are similar or quite different. The common format adopted for the chapters facilitates this type of comparative analysis. Therefore, if you wish to analyse whether the structures of the sectors are essentially the same, or not, this can be done. Similarly, if you want to take a particular perspective to compare the operational nature of the sectors this can also be achieved. For example, you may wish to ask; to what extent are the operational systems similar in hotels, restaurants and contract foodservice? Alternatively, are the issues associated with logistics, capacity utilization, market reach, customer relationship management etc. the same in each sector? Indeed, if you are interested in identifying some recurrent, or over-arching, themes you will find that I provide some thoughts in this respect in the concluding chapter of the book.

CHAPTER 1

Hotels

David Litteljohn

Introduction

This chapter sets out a broad context for discussing the nature of the hotel sector of the international hospitality industry. Fuelled by increases in personal incomes and, in particular, the availability of mass short- and long-distance travel, international hotel suppliers have responded vigorously in a number of ways. These changes bring up important issues for hotel organizations and managers as they meet new challenges.

When you have studied this chapter you will be able to:

- Recognize the nature and size of the international hotel sector of the international hospitality industry.

- Assess differences in regional distribution of international hotel demand and supply.

- Discuss the underlying factors affecting the supply of hotels in the international hospitality industry, in particular those relating to capital funding and affiliation.

- Analyse the nature of growth and of integration forces in and across the hospitality and tourism sectors.

- Provide evidence from a selection of international hotel operators on the nature of products and operations.

- Explain possible structural developments in the hotel sector of the international hospitality industry.

Problems in commonality of definitions and types of measures for hotels in different countries must be acknowledged when gaining an international perspective of hotels. While this chapter does use internationally gathered and collated figures, no attempt should be made to use figures in this context as precise and comparative measures, they must always be used carefully and with the appropriate *caveats*. The chapter uses the Western (European/USA) conventional view of hotels. These are establishments that offer meals and drink together with accommodation to travellers and local markets, in return for financial exchange. They vary from those offering only basic levels of comfort, security and service to luxury hotels. Establishments at any service level may also provide a range of additional amenities and services – such as swimming pools, gyms and other recreational facilities.

Overview: hospitality and hotels in an international context

When tracking a phenomenon as varied as hospitality it is difficult to agree the size of the industry and its role in different communities. Indeed the term 'industry', conventionally seen in economic literature as being 'the set of all firms making the same product', could be called into question, though utilization of the term underlines the perspective of commercial, rather than personal/domestic hospitality. Even given the focus on hotels in this chapter, it will be realized that analysis covers different types of businesses, e.g. from large resort hotels catering for beach and leisure customers to small city centre low-spend business travel hotels.

Hotel provision falls within the general context of hospitality, an aspect of human activity which has important social dimensions, as well as meeting physiological requirements of shelter and body comforts. The actual term *hotel* is originally French and was commonly applied to commercial hospitality establishments in the mid- to late eighteenth century. By 1780, for example, the concept had crossed from France with the founding of *Nero's Hotel* in London (Taylor and Bush, 1974). This and other similar establishments catered for the affluent sectors of the population who were becoming increasingly mobile in their personal and work lives.

From an international perspective it is important to understand that *hotel* may be considered as a culturally bound phenomenon. This is because customs that govern hospitality provision and the ways that hospitality providers operate have an in-built set of assumptions. For example, in the case of hotels, locations are often chosen carefully to appeal to certain types of user; establishments offer particular combinations of meal and drink services to accompany a range of private and public accommodation facilities; hotel customers and staff operate to given social codes (e.g. certain behaviours are considered acceptable while others are discouraged). Many of these factors centre around notions of hospitality and hotel keeping current in Europe and latterly the USA during the main epochs of their development. However, both within the European/USA or Western hospitality axis, and internationally, there are many variants to this configuration of service.

Thus, different cultures and groups view hospitality in various ways and have a range of commercial accommodation establishments. For example, other common terms for commercial accommodation establishments include: inns, (youth) hostels, guesthouses, pensions, boarding houses, bed and breakfast operations, taverns, lodges, hydropaths, sanatoria, apart-hotels and holiday camps/villages. Thus, while there is a ubiquitous acceptance of conventional hotel product/service configurations, there is a wealth of options that serve similar functions to hotels, though they work differently.

In addition, commercial accommodation establishments can be treated differently both legislatively and administratively. Common variants across countries include the methods by which registration, licensing, classification and grading of commercial accommodation establishments are carried out. For example, some countries demand compulsory registration/licensing of all commercial accommodation establishments. In practice, national approaches towards the need for central, national systems to exist as well as the agreement on the mechanics of current systems (classification of accommodation sectors and quality grading measures) show little standardization. This means that statistics covering the international nature of the hotel sector will often suffer because they are drawn from data that are not strictly comparable.

A selection of factors that influence the dynamics of tourism, and therefore impact on the hotel sector of the international hospitality industry, is shown in Table 1.1. The table is by no means complete, but attempts to illustrate some of the factors that could affect local and international business and leisure travel market characteristics at a given destination. The examples put forward are sufficiently diverse to show that there is such a range of factors to ensure that the characteristics of hotel environments at any location will consist of a complex interplay of factors drawn from the local environment and, if experiencing international demand, more globally.

While these factors only sketch the complexities that impinge on hospitality demand and supply, they underline intercultural and policy dimensions which affect hospitality at any destination. Intercultural factors emerge at general, social levels. In relation to international travel, for example, there may be great differences in wealth and social customs between foreign travellers and indigenous hospitality staff. Further, bearing in mind the Western culture of many international tourists, perceptions between tourist and hospitality employee reflecting master/servant relationships

General environment	Variable – general level	Local/national population	International markets
Economic	Levels and type(s) of economic development Distribution of income	Propensity to take trips away for home: business and leisure Amount of income devoted to consumption in leisure, tourism and hospitality	Economic attractiveness of destination for leisure and business purposes (e.g. relative cost levels, including cost of travel)
Social	Social customs and habits	Propensity to travel home and/or abroad Accommodation preferences when travelling	Appeal of national hotels to international markets attracted
Political	Provision of stable political environment	Legislation towards tourism movements/trips Attitude and legislation to foreign travel	Legislation affecting provision and operation of hospitality Safe environment Currency exchange/ restrictions Travel visa/entry requirements Attitudes and policies to foreign investment Attitudes and legislation re national and international transport operators
Technological	Transport facilities and services	Public transport infrastructure Levels of car ownership	Availability of international transport facilities (airports/seaports etc.)

Table 1.1 An indication of influences on markets for hotel consumption at a given location

may take on a master/slave dimension or similar feelings reflecting colonialism. Thus, cultural issues need to be carefully considered by both tourists and those planning to provide facilities with international appeal to travellers.

As the examples above, and many other issues relating to hospitality provision, imply, government policies are important to mould hospitality supply characteristics at any destination. Hospitality specific areas of government policy include legislation affecting the location, density, design and operation of hospitality facilities. Socially and culturally sensitive issues include rates of pay/minimum wage policy, the role of female labour, legislation relating to gambling and alcohol, attitudes towards entertainment and subsidies/financial incentives for investment in hotels and/or for promotion of tourism.

An introduction to the changing nature and characteristics of international hospitality supply

The main physical measures of hotel size are units, rooms and bedspaces. Each measure has different advantages and disadvantages. Measuring the size of the hotel sector of the international hospitality industry by units has the benefit of being the most simple to count (particularly if hotels are required to be registered or licensed by government and records are centrally kept). However, the measure provides no clear indication of industry *capacity* as it does not calculate the number of persons that could be accommodated by hotels at any one time. Capacity measures may be obtained by counting either rooms or bedspaces. Information on rooms is usually available from a range of sources such as accommodation guides and directly from the establishments themselves. However, due to property alterations, seasonal closing, refurbishments and opening policies, the measure can change seasonally and annually. These characteristics also can be applied to a bedspace measure. In addition, the number of bedspaces available can change even when the room capacity remains the same (e.g. twin rooms being used as family rooms). Room capacity is often the most popular measure due to its reliability, together with the fact that many larger operators will charge a standard price per room type, regardless of the number of occupants. However, these figures are not always available.

The World Tourism Organization (as quoted in Finnie *et al.*, 2000) states that there were 29.4 million bedspaces in hotels and similar establishments worldwide in 1997. For comparative purposes below the figure used refers to hotel units. The dynamism of the hotel sector internationally is evidenced by a growth of over 25% in the number of units in the period 1990–1998, to nearly 15.5 million units. Table 1.2 also shows a variety in growth trends across global regions from the lowest figure of 20.8% to a high of 54.1%.

As the table shows the lowest growth rate belongs to Europe, the region with the largest share of hotel units. To an extent, this reflects the maturity of many traditional hotel markets in the region. Another area facing elements of market maturity is the large North American market (shown as a sub-region in Table 1.2) which grew by only 13.2% though, given the limitation of the data and the safe assumption that hotels in North America are larger than those in other parts of the world, it may be inferred that the absolute increase in room capacity is significant. Other regions, admittedly growing from much smaller bases, record higher growth rates. For example, the number of hotel units in Western Asia grew by 54.1% and in the Eastern Asia and Pacific Asia region the number grew by 45.4%.

This analysis emphasizes the regional locus of international hotel development. While similar factors across the world may

Region	Number of hotels* 1990	1998	Change from 1990 to 1998: 000s; (%)	Share of world total (%) 1998
Africa	333	428	95 (28.5)	2.8
Americas				
(North America)	*(3652)*	*(4133)*	*(481 (13.2))*	*(26.8)*
Total Americas	4308	5164	856 (19.9)	33.5
Eastern Asia and Pacific	2399	3487	1088 (45.4)	22.6
Western Asia	111	171	60 (54.1)	1.1
Europe	4912	5935	1023 (20.8)	38.5
Middle East	160	221	61 (38.1)	1.4
World	12 223	15 406	3183 (26.0)	100

* Hotels and similar establishments
Source: World Tourism Organization (2001) Trends in tourist markets, published by the World Tourism Organization, Madrid, Spain.

Table 1.2   Size of the international hotel industry, units* (000s), 1990–1998

mould the nature of the hotel sector of the international hospitality industry, it is important to recognize that the way these express themselves in any particular area or location will often be particular, as a reflection of local sociodemographic factors, stage of economic specialisms and stages of development, international communications and specific tourism/hospitality resources. These factors can be illustrated by a discussion of the nature of demand characteristics faced by hotels in the international hospitality industry.

The changing nature and characteristics of international hospitality demand

When measuring hotel demand there are even greater definitional and comparability problems than those discussed in relation to supply. These revolve around definitions and measures used for stays away from home, the purpose or motivation for travel, whether travel is national or international and, finally, the use of hotels (rather than other forms of accommodation) by travellers.

There are several ways to collect this type of data. The first method is to have a consumer or traveller-based system of collecting data. Here information is collected directly from travellers or potential travellers. The second method is to collect data on travel movements at certain points of the supply chain, e.g. at hotels or from transport operators. Thirdly, there exist certain major transport points or nodes (e.g. airports, seaports, road border crossing points) where it is possible to track international travel movements. In all these methods anything but a cursory head count usually involves obtaining information from only a sample of travellers. While bodies like the World Tourism Organization have helped in the development of standard definitions and approaches to measuring demand, the complexity of the issues involved means that international comparability of demand is something for the future. Indeed, many countries lack either the methods or desire (or both) to collect data that can be used to provide a reliable guide for visits away from home or stays in hotels. Currently the data that have been collected for the longest period, and on the most reliable basis, are those relating to international travel movements. Naturally, this does not plot directly the change in national markets for tourism and hotels. However, given difficulties in gaining internationally compatible data available in collating national/local demand, no such attempt is made here.

By 2000 it was possible to record a global total of nearly 700 million international tourist arrivals (Table 1.3). This represents an increase of 241.5 million over the 10 preceding years, with an annual growth rate of 4.9%. The most popular region was Europe, though at 4.5% average annual change overall market growth was much less dynamic than the Middle East (10.7%), Western Asia (8.8%), Eastern Asia and Pacific region and Africa (both averaging 6.6% growth).

The unequal impact of international travel can be illustrated by examining the relative shares of international tourism to countries. Table 1.4, again based on figures produced by the World Tourism Organization, presents the shares of international tourism, by grouping, by the main receiving tourism destinations over the

Region	Number of international tourists		Share of world total (%)		Average annual change: 1995–2000 (%)
	1990	2000	1990	2000	
Africa	15.0	27.6	3.6	4.0	6.6
Americas					
(North America)	(71.7)	(92.0)	(14.6)	(13.2)	(2.7)
Total Americas	92.9	128.0	19.8	18.5	3.4
Eastern Asia and Pacific	54.6	111.9	14.8	16.0	6.6
Western Asia	3.2	6.4	0.8	0.9	8.8
Europe	282.7	403.3	58.8	57.7	4.5
Middle East	9.0	20.6	2.2	2.9	10.7
World	457.3	698.8	100	100	4.9

Source: World Tourism Organization (2001) Trends in tourist markets, published by the World Tourism Organization, Madrid, Spain.

Table 1.3 International tourism trends, 1990–2000, by international travel to major regions (millions)

Grouping	1950 Countries (world share of international tourists, % by grouping)	1970 Countries (world share of international tourists, % by grouping)	1990 Countries (world share of international tourists, % by grouping)	2000 Countries (world share of international tourists, % by grouping)
Group A: Top 5 international tourism destinations/ countries	USA, Canada, Italy, France, Switzerland (71%)	Italy, Canada, France, Spain, USA (43%)	France, USA, Spain, Italy, Hungary (38%)	France, USA, Spain, Italy, China (35%)
Group B: International tourism destinations/ countries 6–10	Ireland, Austria, Spain, Germany UK (17%)	Austria, Germany, Switzerland, Yugoslavia, UK (22%)	Austria, UK, Mexico, Germany, Canada (19%)	UK, Russia, Mexico, Canada, Germany (15%)
Group C: International tourism destination/ countries 11–15	Norway, Argentina, Mexico, Netherlands, Denmark (9%)	Hungary, Czechoslovakia, Belgium, Bulgaria, Romania (10%)	Switzerland, China, Greece, Portugal, Malaysia (11%)	Austria, Poland, Hungary, Hong Kong, Greece (11%)
Group D: Other destinations/ countries	(3%)	(25%)	(33%)	(38%)
Total international tourists (millions)	25	166	457	699

Note: Countries shown are listed in order of the magnitude of their international tourist numbers.
Based on figures provided by the World Tourism Organization (2001) Trends in tourist markets, published by the World Tourism Organization, Madrid, Spain.

Table 1.4 Share of international world tourism by groupings of destinations 1950–2000

fifty years to 2000. Changes in the relative importance of destinations can be related to the overall volume of international tourism. First, the significance of China as a world player is emphasized: while it is not among the top 15 countries in 1950 by 2000 it the fifth most important country in terms of international travel.

More generally it is interesting to note the extent to which this type of tourism has become much more dispersed since 1950 when the top five receiving countries accounted for 71% of all international tourism. Fifty years later the top five countries (which consisted of three of the destinations in the 1950 group, together with Spain and China as entrants and Canada and Switzerland having exited this group) accounted for a share of 35% of the global figure. In other words, the relative share of the top five countries has reduced by half over the period.

As previously stated these figures deal only with international travel. In cases such as the USA and Canada, national demand will be very important and, indeed, play a primary role in hotel demand. Furthermore, this broad look does not segment travel markets by tourism motivation. An understanding of the international hospitality industry and hotel sector dynamics at particular destinations requires consideration of the types of tourism demand it deals with and the subsequent requirements this puts on accommodation, e.g. the balance of motivations between leisure and business travel and the reliance on large group travel (e.g. mass market package tours and/or conference/congress/exhibition markets) or on independent travellers.

Influences on the international hotel sector's structure

To understand the nature of supply in the international hotel sector it should be remembered that:

- It is a sector that has high fixed investment costs.

- It is possible to divorce ownership of assets from their operation.

In other words, it is important to understand that supply may be influenced by two important components: first, the capital structure of the sector that relates to the sources of capital for funding the buildings or fixed resources of the sector; and, secondly, the type of management arrangements that are used to operate hotel establishments. This latter arrangement is known as the types of affiliation arrangements. Figure 1.1 summarizes the main sources of capital and property arrangement and, below these, the main type of affiliation in the sector. These are then discussed in greater detail.

Given the capital-intensive nature of hotel investment, availability of capital is a key driver in the development of the international hotels and hotel companies. Historically, the main sources of capital for international hotel development are:

(i) private finance through personal savings etc.
(ii) loan capital through banks and other sources, often secured on property assets
(iii) finance provided by specialist investment companies
(iv) through stocks and shares (equities) in a company: these can be traded in the stock market
(v) government.

In some cases there may also be tourism/hotel accommodation financed by local cooperatives – sometimes known as the voluntary or not-for-profit sector – or special interest organizations such

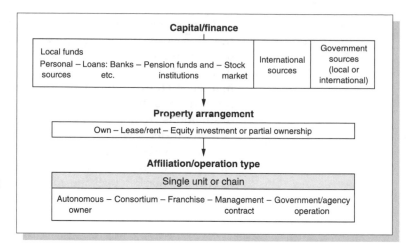

Figure 1.1 An indication of the main sources of capital and types of property arrangements and affiliation types in the international hotel sector

as conservation/historical/ sporting trusts and associations. Major financial arrangements can be illustrated as follows:

- Privately financed: invariably these are businesses where ownership and operation come under the direct control of one main party. Many operations may be small units operating autonomously or only partly devoted to tourism/hotel accommodation, e.g. where hospitality/room letting makes up only part of a family's income which could also include earnings from other activities such as agriculture and/or fishing. However, there is no intrinsic reason for these operations to be small. It largely depends on personal access to large amounts of capital. Thus big businesses of either single or multiple hotels may arise when asset and income distribution is such that it allows sufficient concentration of wealth. Personal ownership will be favoured when capital markets are relatively less developed. In most cases these types of business draw on indigenous sources of capital including, for example, banks. It is also feasible that international capital is involved if a local business decided to accept a partnership with a foreign national who was willing to invest capital transferred from abroad.

- Finance provided through limited liability companies. These are recognized by the term 'incorporated' in the USA, 'PLC' (public limited company) in the UK and 'SA' in many other countries (*Societe anonyme* in French). While privately financed operations have to rely on their own resources (and loans they may be able to secure on their property), limited liability companies can raise capital on the stock market. The availability of this type of capital facilitates the expansion of hotel chains. It is a feature of many economically developed countries, which support large hotel organizations, that the limited liability company often becomes a significant phenomenon.

- Government funding can occur through a number of different means. Governments may own assets outright or take a direct share in their ownership. This form of government involvement might occur in economies where the government wants to plan its economy to grow in very specific ways. On the other hand, governments may assist private sector development through packages of financial incentives to cover building, furnishing and equipment costs. In these cases, the government (or their agency) is likely to impose conditions on trading (e.g. purpose of building, annual period of trading, type of service offered, conditions for resale of business). Direct government involvement in hotels through ownership and operational control became less popular at the end of the last and the beginning of the twenty-first century (e.g. the dissolution of state-owned enterprises with the collapse of communist systems of government in Eastern Europe during the 1990s). However, there are still examples such as the paradores of Spain. Also, when governments wish to encourage the growth of tourism in less developed regions they may well consider direct investment in hotels to provide the necessary commercial stimulus for tourism expansion.

Many hotel operations, as stated, find their capital through a mix of the above factors. In a survey of capital sourcing among PLC/SA hotel companies, Slattery (1996) divides hotel capital into categories: *Hotel chain capital* where funds come from the stock market and bank debt and *Hotel capital* which encompasses direct equity from financial institutions, property development companies, (local) governments, local entrepreneurs, private individuals and syndicates. The results of his survey are shown in Table 1.5.

Slattery comments that hotel chain capital is particularly popular in the UK and is also significant in the USA and Western Continental Europe since hotel chains have been more willing to invest their own capital when they wished to expand. On the other hand, hotel investment in Eastern Europe and Asia has relied more on individual and business partnerships rather than external funding sources.

Another important structural variable in the hotel sector, shown in Figure 1.1, relates to the form of affiliation hotels operate under. In this context an important feature of the sector has been the development of hotel chains. Hotel chains may be defined as,

> multi-unit service organizations in which units operate under a system of decision-making permitting coherent policies and a common strategy through one or more decision-making centres, and where hotel units and corporate functions are linked to add value to each other by ownership or contractual relationships (Peng and Litteljohn, 1997).

Region	Rooms funded by hotel-chain capital (%)	Rooms funded by hotel capital (%)
UK	90	10
Western Continental Europe	35	65
Eastern Europe	6	94
Asia	10	90
USA	6	94
Total	33	67

Source: Slattery (1996).

Table 1.5 Regional patterns of capital access (1995)

Through attaining size, chains will target the possibility of gaining economies of scale in their operations. While some chains are a product of direct connection between ownership, control of capital assets and the direction of hotel operations, different affiliation modes show that capital–operational relationships may be more complex.

As Figure 1.1 illustrates, other affiliation modes cover consortium membership, franchising and management contracting. A final variant may be where governments or their agencies directly operate hotels. The characteristics of each of these modes are discussed below.

- Consortium member. This is a mechanism whereby hotels (or indeed a wider set of tourism organizations) agree to cooperate in order to gain corporate benefits, which raise revenue and/or cut costs in ways the business could not achieve on its own. For example, benefits could accrue from joint purchasing or marketing activities. The consortium approach can operate in tandem with other forms of affiliation – i.e. include independently/autonomously owned hotels as well as units which are members of chains. In addition to cost efficiency possibilities, consortium membership may appeal to hotels because of their locational needs (e.g. marketing a specific destination during periods of slack demand/overcapacity), market niche/branding purposes (reach new custom due to branding national/international benefits together with joint services such as central reservations and joint representation. Membership is considered on the basis of the fit of the applicant to the objectives of the consortium and their ability to meet subscription and operational requirements (such as maintenance of a given standard/style of operation). It is also a feature of most consortia that members are represented on the management board of the organization.

- Franchising. In this situation the hotel owner 'buys-in' a specific style of operation from a parent/owner of the operation format. The format parent or *franchisor* owns the business format, the trading name and all proprietary aspects of the operation – the formula or design of the business. It may also provide a range of resources and support activities such as central reservations, training, advertising and technical advice. The operator, a franchisee, is given a licence to operate in the franchisor's name, in return for the payment of a royalty fee.

- A franchising licence may be granted to an operator (or franchisee) for one or several operations. A licence which gives an operator exclusive rights in a particular territory is called a master franchise. As exchange for the payment of the royalty fee, the franchisee will receive a standard operating format and the necessary back up to launch and maintain the business.

- Management contracting. Here asset ownership and operation are separated. This might happen where the hotel owner is, for example, an investment company that has no expertise in hotel management, and enters into an agreement with a hotel operator to run the hotel on their behalf, in return for a management fee. In these arrangements there is clearly an expectation that the owners expect that the contractor will be able to run the operation more effectively than they could themselves.

- It is possible that a government, or its agencies, may operate hotels. However, even when governments played a more active part in hotel ownership (see above), the operation was often put out to management contract and the current decline in direct hotel asset ownership in many countries has further decreased government operation.

The attractions of belonging to a hotel chain largely hinge on the ability to gain economies of scale. While hotel units may operate more effectively as they grow in size, economies of scale for hotels largely express themselves at corporate levels of the organization, as well as through the enhanced risk of diversification gained by the possession of a geographically dispersed portfolio of properties. In many cases the popularity of branded operations has both pushed established operators to develop and internationalize their chains further, while also providing smaller operators with a clear rationale for giving up an element of independence through joining consortium membership or franchising agreements.

Table 1.6 shows the extent to which patterns of affiliation alter by region of the world. Franchising is common in its 'parent' of the USA (where, for example, there are developed brands) and markets that are currently in the throes of development or re-development (i.e. Eastern Europe). On the other hand the UK showed,

Region	Affiliation type			
	Franchised (%)	Leased (%)	Managed (%)	Owned (%)
UK	4.1	9.3	6.2	80.4
Western Continental Europe	23.3	12.9	31.9	31.9
Eastern Europe	55.9	1.0	38.2	4.9
Asia	14.9	0.6	74.9	9.7
USA	70.8	1.8	20.5	6.9

Source: Slattery (1996).

Table 1.6 Regional patterns (%) of hotel affiliation (1995)

in 1995, the extent to which it still relied on direct investment by owner/operators.

Issues in international hotel sector structure

Industry structure literature often proposes clear relationships between supply, demand and major economic variables affecting an industry in order to explain the nature and the working of an industry and/or its constituent sectors. The economics literature indicates that organizations will tend to expand (perhaps through takeovers/amalgamations with similar organizations) if there are considerable economies of scale to be gained. An example of possible economies, as discussed above, might lie in gaining corporate efficiencies for hotel chains. In addition, pressures for integration may come from other organizations across different stages of the supply chain, if there are market or supply-based benefits to be gained by working very closely together (e.g. improved relationships with final customers, benefits in cost and quality arising from security of supply). These latter relationships are termed vertical links, or vertical integration. In tourism and hospitality they can be illustrated in tie-ups between tour operators, transport providers, hoteliers and so on. As pointed out by Lafferty and van Fossen (2001), Sainger (1990) found that larger firms are more profitable because they both exploit market power (e.g. ability to negotiate price discounts from suppliers) and because these larger firms are able to garner efficiencies through scale economies.

Reviews of the international hotel sector confirm two main factors: a preponderance in the large number of independent/small business units (important in numbers if less so by share of total industry business: see Slattery, 1992) and secondly, an increasing penetration of chain units. Thus Todd and Mather (2001: 17) point out that 'despite the expansion of branded hotel capacity and the plethora of mergers, acquisitions and take-overs during the last decade, Europe's hotel sector remains dominated by individually-owned properties or small hotel companies. As a result, it is estimated that no more than 20% of Europe's hotel capacity is branded.' Todd and Mather (2001) also point out that in 1990 the top 20 corporate hotel chains (listed in *Hotels* magazine) controlled a total of some 1.8 million rooms, while by 2001 the number of rooms belonging to the top 20 had increased to 3.6 million rooms. It is clear, therefore, that horizontal integration and hence consolidation in the international hotel sector has been a major feature over the recent past. In establishing important drivers for change in industry or sector structure it should be borne in mind that many other sectors of tourism, as well as hotels, are characterized by heavy initial capital costs and low marginal/variable costs for carrying each additional customer. Further, as reflected in the commentary above, branding and market presence obtained by growth will, in themselves, confer marketing advantages leading to higher financial returns.

In a review of integration strategies in the tourism industry covering the half century to 2000, Lafferty and van Fossen (2001) conclude much vertical integration has failed, largely due to the differences in capital and organizational/operational characteristics in activities (e.g. the differences between providing hotels to running airlines). These authors point out that horizontal integration strategies have been more successful, though they indicate that there are important issues of consumer choice that should be considered if this is diminished. Based on this work, therefore, it is likely that the growth of large hotel chains will be a significant feature of the international hospitality industry.

Another view is put forward by Poon (1993). In her study of trends affecting the tourism industry, she highlights the role of information in the industry supply chain (e.g. information on consumer requirements, distribution and availability of capacity among different suppliers) and the wealth, or value, creating process of organizations. She goes on to say that: 'It is no longer relevant whether a company is an airline, a travel agent, hotel or tour operator. As the boundaries among players are re-defined, what becomes relevant are the activities along the value chain that they control' (Poon, 1993: 215) and concludes that information management and consumer proximity (through knowledge of and relationships with customers) will drive that nature of the supply/value chain in the future.

Poon's information technology, futures-based work (1993) indicates a dynamic, changing set of structural relationships for hotels. This contrasts with Lafferty and van Fossen's (2001) review. They suggest that businesses concentrating on developing their core operations – and hence integrating horizontally – are more likely to succeed. Neither of the cited works discusses – or intended to – separation between hotel ownership and operation evidenced by franchising and management contracting options. In finalizing this survey of hotels a review of the strategies adopted by international companies is useful, to gain a view of their product/service offerings and their international presence.

A review of current product trends and operations in the international hotel sector

This section presents data gathered from a selection of major international hotel organizations over the winter of 2001/02. The selection of organizations chosen, while representing a number of the major players, is not exhaustive. Operations have been chosen on the basis that they reflect important trends internationally and regionally. Examples of corporate trends are illustrated within three main regions: North America, Europe and Asia.

The period when the USA hotel market and companies alone shaped the characteristics and the nature of the international hotel industry has passed. This period, which perhaps extended until the early 1980s, ended with the advent of European and then Asian companies developing international portfolios on a significant scale. Major international hotel operations by the three main generating world regions are discussed below. Table 1.7 shows companies that are based in North America.

North American companies, mainly from the USA but also showing a Canadian presence, have developed a multifaceted range of hotel brands. Providers have adopted a tiered or product segmentation approach to hotel markets, aligning service offerings to different travel purposes and different customer requirements (e.g. long stay rather than overnight visitors in relation to suite/residence properties) as well as by market-service level. It is a feature of many companies' tiered/segmented operations that most of their brands are currently designed for North American consumption rather than for export from the region. Hotel companies also operate a sophisticated approach to expansion using a mix of ownership/operating methods. Internationalization, as judged by countries covered, has been particularly successful for the following companies: Carlson, Choice, Four Seasons, Hyatt, Marriott and Starwood. One company from the USA not shown in Table 1.7, but owning hotels abroad is Blackstone that owns the small, but exclusive, Savoy chain in the UK. Like Felcor (which operates the brands of other groups as a franchisee) and Starwood, a major motivation for its ownership in hotel assets is for investment in property assets, facilitated by the development of international capital markets.

The table does not bring fully into view the extent of joint activity or joint ventures that may exist. For example, close relationships may be developed between parent franchisors and key franchisees. Thus Hyatt has very close relationships with Park Plaza Kemayan (licensee for 35 countries in Asia-Pacific),

Company	Type	Domicile	Main international brands	Main modes of ownership and operation	International representation (countries)
Carlson	DHT	USA	Country Inn, Country Suites, Park Inn, Park Plaza, Radisson, Regent International	F	57
Cendant	D	USA	Days Inn, Knights Inn, Ramada, Super 8, Travelodge, Villager, Wingate Inns	F	C 95% room in USA; Days Inn is the main brand operating outside NA
Choice Hotels	H	USA	Clarion Hotel, Comfort Inn, Comfort Suites, Econo Lodge, Mainstay Suites, Quality Inn, Quality Suites, Rodeway Inn, Sleep Inn, Sleep Suites	F	42–83% of units in NA
Fairmont	H	Canada	Fairmont, Princes	D, M	6
Felcor	H	USA	Operates franchised brands	Owner/franchisee	NA
Four Seasons	H	Canada	Four Seasons, Regent	M	25
Hilton Hotels Corporation	HT	USA	Conrad (operated jointly with Hilton International), Doubletree, Embassy Suites, Hampton, Harrison Conference Centres, Hilton, Hilton Garden Inn, Homewood Suites by Hilton, Red Lion Hotels and Inns	D, M, F	Mainly NA
Hyatt Hotels/ Hyatt International	D	USA	Grand Hyatt, Hyatt Park, Hyatt Regency	D, M, F	80
Marriott International	H	USA	Courtyard by Marriott, Fairfield Inn, ExecuStay by Marriott, Marriott Executive Apartments, Marriott Hotels Resorts and Suites, JW Marriott Hotels, Ramada International, Renaissance Hotels, Residence Inn by Marriott, Ritz Carlton, SpringHill Suites, TownePlace Suites	F, M	64
Omni	H	USA	Omni	D	3 (NA, Mexico)
Orient Express	D	USA	Orient Express	D	15
Starwood Hotels and Resorts	H	USA	Four Points by Sheraton, The Luxury Collection, Sheraton, St Regis, W, Westin	D, M, F	80

Abbreviations: DHT = Diversified hospitality and tourism conglomerate; D = Direct owner/operator (may only have equity stake); F = Franchise; H = mainly hotel focused company; M = Management contract; NA = North America; nsi = not sufficient information.

Table 1.7 Examples of major North American hotel companies with international holdings (2001/02)

Marriott works closely with its UK licensee, Whitbread, as does Choice with Friendly Hotels. It is also the case that many of the larger companies have diversified into vacation ownership/time-share management. Radisson, too, has marketing arrangements with Edwardian Hotels in the UK and Scandinavian Air Systems (SAS).

In the past there were close links between some North American airlines and hotel operators: e.g. between Pan American Airlines and Intercontinental and Trans World Airlines and Hilton International. Both airlines have now ceased operations, though they divested themselves of their hotel investments well before their downfall. Contemporary relationships between the sectors rely more on integration through IT-based booking systems and partnerships that confer favoured customer benefits via joint loyalty schemes.

A selection of European companies is shown in Table 1.8. Given that this region has the largest number of hotels (see Table 1.2) it is notable that, in comparison to North America, it does not support as many large and sophisticated international hotel chains. This reflects the fragmented structure of the hotel sector in Europe where, as already noted by Todd and Mather (2001) much opportunity for consolidation exists. The European hotel company Accor exhibits many of the traits of established and successful North American hotel companies in its tiered approach to the market, though it has also kept specific brands for some areas (All Seasons in Australia, Motel 6 and Red Roof in North America and Orbis in Poland).

The UK's presence in the international hotel arena has been largely built on the acquisition of USA brands (Hilton, Holiday Inn). With the exception of these brands and Accor, the extent of international representation is less than is exhibited by the major North American chains. In addition, there is a healthy growth of companies at national level: e.g. the Husa Hotel chain in Spain and the existence of chains in the UK such as De Vere, Macdonald, Queen's Moat and Thistle. Spain, since the 1970s a major recipient of incoming international tourists, has now begun to internationalize its indigenous hotel industry though only Sol Melia is shown in this analysis. Table 1.8 also does not show the extent of joint venture/partnership agreement that is occurring. For example, Accor has, since 2002, allowed the German Rema hotels group to market 15 hotels under its Mercure brand. Finally, the IT-driven nature of the market was underlined by a tie-up between three major European hotel groups in October 2000. Accor, Forte (now re-organized) and Hilton International have collaborated to develop a web-based electronic distribution system. As in North America, hotels and airlines (and other tourism suppliers such as car rentals) join together for marketing purposes. For example, SAS not only has a marketing agreement with the North American Radisson, but also an agreement with a UK property

Company	Coy type	Domicile	Main international brands	Main modes of ownership and operation	International representation (countries)
Accor	D	France	All Seasons (Australia), Coralia, Etap, Formule1, Good Morning, Ibis, Jardins de Paris, Liberotel, Mercure, Motel 6 (NA), Novotel, Orbis (Poland), Parthenon, Red Roof (NA), Sofitel, Suitehotels, Thalassa	D, F, L	81
Club Mediterranee	D	France	Club Med Resorts	D, M	40
Dorint	H	Germany	Dorint	L	9
Golden Tulip	H	Netherlands / Spain*	Golden Tulip Hotels, Tulip Inns	D, F	42
Hilton International	D	UK	Hilton International	D/equity stake, M, L	69
Jurys Doyle Hotels	H	Eire	Jurys Hotels, Jurys Inns	D	3
Kempinski	H	Germany	Kempinski	M	16
Movenpick	H	Switzerland	Movenpick	M	10
Six Continents (formerly Bass plc)	H	UK	Crowne Plaza, Express By Holiday Inn (also Holiday Inn Express), Holiday Inn, Intercontinental, Staybridge	D, F, M, L	circa 100
Sol Melia	H	Spain	Melia Hotels, Paradisus Resorts, Sol Hotels, Tryp Hotels	D, M	32
Societe de Louvre	H	France	Bleu Marine, Campanile, Concorde, Cote a Cote, Kyriad, Premiere Classe, Nuit d'Hotel	D, M, F	Mainly Europe with a presence in USA and Japan

Abbreviations: DHT = Diversified hospitality and tourism conglomerate; D = Direct owner/operator; F = Franchise; H = mainly hotel focused company; M = Management contract; L= leases property.

Table 1.8 Examples of major European hotel companies with international holdings

developer/hotel owner to operate and manage Malmaison Hotels (currently UK-based).

Europe also hosts a number of vertically integrated hotel and tour operators of scale. For example, Club Mediterranee has a successful tour operating arm (though a previous foray into airline ownership was not successful). Similarly, operators such as Preussag, C&N, Iberostar all have a degree of hotel ownership.

As a region growing in international travel and leisure business Asia would be expected to increase its indigenous chains as well as attracting foreign entrants. Further, it is interesting to add to the data in Table 1.9 that some chains now operate hotels in developed economies (e.g. Mandarin Oriental, Nicco). Also, that there are Western chains which have been taken over by Eastern companies: for example Normura's acquisition of Le Meridien is shown in the table. In this vein it may also be noted that there is a substantial Singapore investment in the UK's Thistle hotel group.

Table 1.10 indicates some of the consortium activities which act to supplement the relationships discussed above. The examples below illustrate two types of consortium arrangement:

- Location-based consortia: Connoiseurs Scotland and Legends of IndoChina, while covering areas of very different size and characteristics, both provide a distinctive marketable infrastructure for, in particular, developing international tourism

- Market standard niche consortia: the remainder of the organizations in the table are of these types though they have differing market levels and geographic coverage.

While consortium membership may appeal to independent organizations, most also have chain membership. Two of the examples shown (Connoiseurs, Legends) also show affiliation with other tourism suppliers as part of their core membership indicating the flexibility of consortium arrangements.

Conclusions

Partly because of its focus on hotel companies this review highlights consolidation through strategies of horizontal growth, though it also recognizes a divergence between asset ownership and operation. It appears that the twin needs to raise substantial amounts of capital and to develop branded operations have particularly favoured the development of chains. It has also been shown that different regions possess different industry structures, characteristics and organizations at different stages of their international profile.

Company	Coy Type	Domicile	Main international brands	Main modes of ownership and operation	International representation (countries)
Dusit	DHT	Thailand	Dusit	Nsi	4
Century International Hotels	H	Hong Kong	Century	M	7
Mandarin Oriental	D	Hong Kong	Mandarin Oriental	D/M	12
Marco Polo	H	Hong Kong	Marco Polo	M, JV	4
Meritus	D	Singapore	–	Nsi	4
Japan Air Lines Coy Ltd	DHT	Japan	Nikko	D, M	14
New Otani Group Hotels	H	Japan	New Otani	Nsi	4
Normura*	D	Japan*	Le Meridien	D, M, L, F	52
Oberoi	DHT	India	Oberoi, Trident	nsi	7
Pan Pacific	D	Singapore	Pan Pacific	M	11
Peninsula Group – Hong Kong and Shanghai Hotels	DHT	Hong Kong	Peninsula	nsi	4
Raffles International Hotels	D	Singapore	Raffles, Swissotel	D, M	17
Shangri-La Hotels and Resorts	D	Hong Kong/China	Shangri-La Hotels, Traders Hotels	D, M	10
Taj Hotels	DHT	India	Taj (Luxury, Business, Leisure)	D, M	9

Abbreviations: DHT = Diversified hospitality and tourism; D = Direct owner/operator; F = Franchise; H = mainly hotel focused company; M = Management contract; nsi = not sufficient information.

Table 1.9 Examples of major hotel companies in Asia with international holdings

* Normura International plc acquired the hotels in 2001

Consortium	Domicile	Main international brands	International membership
Connoiseurs Scotland	UK	None – members are 7 hotels, 1 cruising boat and 1 train – accent is on luxury travel	None
Best Western International	USA (with country affiliates)	Best Western	84 'countries and territories'
Leading Hotels of the World	USA	Leading Hotels of the World, Leading Small Hotels of the World	75
Legends of IndoChina	SE Asia	Up market accommodation and train	5 (SE Asia)
Minotel International	Switzerland	Minotel	30 countries (Europe)

Table 1.10 Examples of international consortia

While the predominance of horizontal growth has been empha-sized, Poon's (1993) work implies that the nature of relationships among suppliers will be more fluid and variable than was pre-viously the case. The experience of the international hotel sector would seem to favour a dynamic scenario and evidence pointing in this direction comes from the existence of hotel consortia (a more temporary alliance of different suppliers in tourism which may transcend sector boundaries) and the diversification of hotel organizations into different areas of operations (e.g. gambling, timeshare) and tour operator ownership of hotels. Another initial conclusion from the review undertaken is that former organiza-tional relationships are not so much replaced by the development of new forms of rationale and relationships, instead the old rela-tionships are supplemented by newer forms of alliance between organizations.

In a globalizing world, where a major feature is the integra-tion of economies through private capital on a worldwide scale (Jary and Jary, 1991), it will be interesting to explore further change in international hospitality industry structure and opera-tions. It must be recognized that organizations are not passive in these changes: 'the combined activities of all kinds of organiza-tions *stimulate, facilitate, sustain and extend* globalization' (Parker, 1996 – emphases added). The extent to which these will adopt conventional views of industry development, repeating the les-sons of change from the USA as opposed to new looser types of arrangement and alliances, will have significant effects on the nature of hospitality organizations and the environments they operate in.

Summary

This analysis of the international hospitality industry has focused on hotels. The chapter has traced the growth in the size of the sector.

In particular it has stressed:

- Growth and regional variations in international hospitality supply.

- The dynamic, and changing nature of international hospitality demand.

- A perspective on hotel operations that stresses its capital intensive nature and possible separations between asset ownership and affiliation.

- Benefits of chain as opposed to independent operations, in relation to branding and different affiliation modes.

- Rationale for changes in market structure that alternatively stress horizontal, vertical and diagonal integration.

- Corporate developments in hospitality that highlight market segmentation.

- Corporate developments that highlight separation between ownership of hotel assets and ownership of brands.

- The development of new corporate operators in areas of economic growth such as Asia.

- The development of alliances and partnerships (e.g. consortia) across the hotel industry and more wisely across tourism industry suppliers.

Review questions

1. To what extent is the term hotel a culturally bound phenomenon? You may find it helpful to discuss this topic with examples drawn from Tables 1.7, 1.8, 1.9.
2. Discuss the implications for corporate hotel development of the changes in international travel to destinations between countries 1950–2000.
3. To what extent do different forms of capital sourcing for hotel investments spring from the needs of hotel operators?
4. Discuss the extent to which corporate economies may arise through international branding (of hotel chains).
5. Indicate in what supply/management areas corporate advantages may arise in chain operations.
6. Discuss the different advantages that may occur through horizontal and vertical integration for hotels – provide examples.

7. Why is Poon's notion of diagonal integration appropriate as the potential for IT data storage and linkages increase?
8. Distinguish between corporate activity in North America, Europe and Asia.

References

Finnie, M., Champion, S., Holden, J., Collyer, G. and Noble, S. (2000) *Pan European Hotels,* January, Deutsche Bank, London.

Jary, D. and Jary, J. (1991) *Dictionary of Sociology.* Collins, Glasgow.

Lafferty, G. and van Fossen, A. (2001) Integrating the tourism industry: problems and strategies, *Tourism Management,* **22**, (1), 11–19.

Parker, B. (1996) Evolution and revolution: from international business to globalization. In Clegg, S. R., Hardy, C. and Nord, W. R. (eds), *Handbook of Organisation Studies,* Sage, London, pp. 484–506.

Peng, W. and Litteljohn, D. (1997) Managing complexity: strategic management of hotel chains, paper presented at the *Hospitality Business Development Conference (EuroCHRIE/IAHMS),* Sheffield, UK.

Poon, A. (1993) *Tourism, Technology and Competitive Strategies.* Cab International, Wallingford.

Sainger, M. (1990) The concentration-margins relationships reconsidered. In *Brookings papers on economic activity special issue,* Brookings Institution, Washington, pp. 287–335.

Slattery, P. (1992) Unaffiliated hotels in the UK *Travel and Tourism Analyst,* No 1, Economist Intelligence Unit, pp. 90–103.

Slattery, P. (1996) International development of hotel chains. In Kotas, R., Teare, R., Logie, J., Jayawardena, C. and Bowen, J. (eds) *The International Hospitality Business,* Cassell, London, pp. 30–35.

Taylor, D. and Bush, D. (1974) *The Golden Age of British Hotels,* Northwood, London.

Todd and Mather, S. (2001) The structure of the hotel industry in Europe. In Hall, L. (ed.), *New Europe and the Hotel Industry,* PriceWaterhouseCoopers Hospitality and Leisure Research, London, pp. 16–26.

Further reading

Alexander, N. and Lockwood, A. (1996) Internationalisation: a comparison of the hotel and retail sectors. *Service Industry Journal,* **16**, (4), 458–473.

Dicken, P. (1998) *Global shift: transforming the world economy,* Paul Chapman, London.

Go, F. M. and Pine, R. (1995) *Globalisation Strategy in the Hotel Industry*. Routledge, London.

Litteljohn, D. and Roper, A. (1991) Internationalisation of hotel groups. In Teare, R. and Boer, A. (eds), *Strategic Hospitality Management,* Cassell, London, pp. 194–212.

Litteljohn, D., Go, F. and Goulding, P. J. (1992) The international hospitality industry and public policy. In Teare, R. and Olsen, M. (eds), *International Hospitality Management Corporate Strategy in Practice*, Pitman, London, pp. 36–66.

Litteljohn, D. and Watson, S. (1992) Multi and transnational firms – the impact of expansion on corporate structure. In Teare, R. and Olsen, M. (eds), *International Hospitality Management Corporate Strategy in Practice*, Pitman, London, pp. 135–159.

Litteljohn, D. (1993) Western Europe. In Jones, P. and Pizam, A. (eds), *The International Hospitality Industry – Organisational and Operational Issues*, Pitman, London, pp. 3–24.

Litteljohn, D. (1997) International hotel development. In Foley, M., Lennon, J. J. and Maxwell, G. (eds), *Strategy & Culture – Current Themes in Tourism, Hospitality and Leisure*, Cassell, London, pp. 229–246.

Slattery, P., Ellis, S. and France, D. (1998) *European Quoted Hotel Companies, Rethinking Cyclicality*, Dresdner Kleinwort Benson Research, London.

Restaurants

Stephen Ball and Linda Roberts

Chapter objectives

When you have read this chapter you will be able to:

- Explain the nature and structural characteristics of the international restaurant sector.

- Provide an insight into the historical development of the industry and some of the influencing factors upon this development.

- Discuss the types of products and operational formats that exist in the sector.

- Analyse the size, some of the key trends and competitive conditions in this market and its main segments.

- Critically evaluate the future outlook for the sector.

Introduction

Dining out in restaurants is a ubiquitous, significant and growing international phenomenon. Everywhere one travels people from all ethnic backgrounds, nationalities, ages, socioeconomic groups and both genders can be observed eating and drinking out in independent, locally owned and operated establishments or in strongly branded multiunit chain outlets. The international restaurant market is benefiting from a number of trends, including rising personal disposable income and a leisure environment in which many consumers eat out more frequently. Future growth though is not guaranteed with uncertainties and threats omnipresent. Among these currently are those associated with international terrorism, reductions in international travel and the global economic slowdown. However, being optimists, in the longer term restaurant dining seems set to become increasingly popular with the corporately-owned restaurant chains expanding further, and at the expense of the independents who currently hold the predominant market share.

Contemporary restaurants take many forms and have developed considerably from their humble origins in eighteenth century France. This chapter begins with an insight into the historical development of restaurants and the factors that have influenced the development of the sector. Space mitigates against this being more comprehensive. However, from this analysis an awareness of the historical antecedents associated with the evolution of restaurants will be possible. This review also makes a contribution, later in the chapter, to an understanding of the contemporary nature of restaurants and to a vision of the future of restaurants. Such an approach was echoed by O'Connor (2000) who said; 'history is the raw material from which understanding of the present might be gleaned and from which future scenarios might be constructed'.

The basic restaurant concept today is identical to its predecessors and can be defined as an establishment where refreshments or meals can be obtained, usually for money, by the public. However, this general definition of a restaurant conceals a diversity of restaurant types. It is possible to segment the types of restaurants in various ways. For example, distinctions can be made according to characteristics of consumers including age, gender, ethnicity and lifestyle; elements of the concept such as geographic location, menu, service style and price; and according to ownership structures which for restaurants usually follow one of three patterns: independents, chains or franchises.

This chapter draws upon the universally accepted body of knowledge related to international restaurant products and operations developed for Western countries notably USA, UK/EU and Australia. It also discusses trends and concepts of applicability to the broader international restaurant sector. Particular reference is given to US restaurant businesses due to their influence upon the contemporary international restaurant sector and also to the high profile of a number of US restaurant chains around the world. The reference to Australia and the UK also reflects the geographical bases of the authors.

Historical overview

Restaurants in their various forms are conspicuous and well-established features of the worldwide contemporary hospitality industry. Conflicting views surround the date and place of their origin. Some claim that they existed in Italy around 50 AD: 'Restaurants unearthed from the tons of ashes from Mt. Vesuvius that buried Pompeii in the year 62 show not only that restaurants existed, but that they catered to different budgets and needs. Some were set in amiable surroundings; others consisted of dim little rooms' (Chon and Sparrowe, 2000: 205). However, while establishments existed in ancient civilizations serving food and drink they were almost certainly not called restaurants. This was true in the middle ages when inns and other hostelries provided food to paying guests from the host's table, or table d'hôte, and coffee-houses, which gave later rise to the café, evolved selling beverages (Medlik, 1978; Lattin, 1997).

The term 'restaurant' has been attributed to the French. In the beginning a restaurant appears to have been a thing to eat rather than a place to eat. According to Spang (2000) a restaurant was a kind of restorative, semi-medicinal 'bouillon that formed an essential element of pre-revolutionary France's nouvelle cuisine'. Gradually this bouillon or soup started to be served in public eating places. Lattin (1997) records that probably the first restaurant proprietor was a soup vendor called A. Boulanger, who opened rather modest premises for the sale of *restaurants,* or soups and broths, in Paris in 1765. The first luxury restaurant, La Grande Taverne de Londres, opened in Paris in 1782. Soon public eating places began to adopt the word 'restaurant', or variants of this word, as the name of their establishment and offered diners a menu offering a choice of dishes.

A complex and heady mix of factors contributed to the transition of this representation of the restaurant to the emergence of other restaurant forms and types.

Spang (2000: 3) describes a shift influenced by 'restaurant reviews and political banquets, fashionable innovation and Enlightenment science, revolutionary zeal and aesthetic hierarchies, adulterous dalliances and medicinal concoctions'. With the restaurant came the development of the modern culture of food, which not only reshaped the social life of the French but of people globally.

Restaurants first appeared in Britain in the late nineteenth century. The dining rooms of large hotels, which quickly developed in London and subsequently in other provincial cities and towns, following the arrival of the railways, often became known as restaurants. These invariably provided sophisticated standards of cuisine. The chef, Georges Escoffier, was one of the prominent figures who emerged during this period. He commanded the cuisine for the luxury hotels, including the Savoy and the new Carlton in London, owned by Cesar Ritz. Escoffier stamped his talent on everything he touched and was responsible for creating numerous classical dishes, many of which were included in his *Guide to Modern Cookery*. He also perfected the partie system and influenced the organization of kitchen practice.

Towards the end of the nineteenth century the term 'restaurant' was also applied to a few large, separate high-class establishments, which provided formal meals and refreshments to the more critical diner. Diners of these early British restaurants were expected to dress formally and women were seldom seen in public restaurants (Jones, 1996a). Most of the clientele were wealthy and from the upper end of the social scale. To many, eating out was regarded as an expensive luxury.

Gradually a taste for dining out in restaurants in Britain developed and new concepts and operators entered the market aiming to attract and cater for other customer types. One development from the traditional restaurant was the 'grill room' that had less formality and which, according to Taylor (1977), 'emerged from the desire of American tourists to avoid the dining ceremonial each night'. Cafés and tea shops providing cheap refreshment, and later more substantial meals, emerged to cater for the less well off. Some of these, like the Aerated Bread Co. shop, which opened in London in 1884, and the Lyons teashop, which first opened in 1894, later grew into chains.

Elsewhere, as Lattin (1997) documents, many other contributions to the development of the restaurant were taking place. These specialized in particular foods and local dishes or had innovative service delivery systems, such as in the USA where the self-service cafeteria originated in San Francisco in 1849. This was essentially a quick-eating place. In the twentieth century, and with the arrival of the car, restaurants became more widespread and, continuing an earlier trend, started to target particular markets. In France, for example, three categories developed: bistros or brasseries, which are simple, informal and inexpensive establishments, mid-priced restaurants and the more elegant higher priced restaurant. Similar groupings can be identified in other countries.

Perhaps the most significant phenomenon in recent years has been the global development and growth of fast food and of fast-food, or quick-service, restaurants. McDonald's, KFC and Pizza Hut epitomize this expansion. The fast-food sector, like the contemporary restaurant sector more generally, has been significantly influenced by US-generated ideas. Ball (1992) details the origins, influences (including those from North America) and historical development of fast food in the UK. The fast-food sector is operating at different stages of development around the world but fast food remains big business and currently represents over 25% of the world consumer catering market. Buying from fast-food restaurants has become more popular because of a combination of social and other factors. According to Ball (1996) these include greater average real personal disposable incomes, the desire to trade down, less formal eating patterns, more women workers, more one-person households, better access to private transport, increased international travel and efforts of the operators themselves. Similar factors have also contributed to the development of other restaurant types during the mid- to the end of the twentieth century. A consideration of this development in the UK is provided by Jones (1996b).

To summarize the development of the restaurant we turn to Spang (2000: 3) who says with particular reference to the French scene that:

> In the past 230 years, the restaurant has changed from a sort of urban spa into a 'political' public forum, and then into an explicitly and actively depoliticised refuge. Throughout, these transformations have been not so much a progression through a series of clearly defined stages as an ongoing and contestatory process.

Structure of the international restaurant sector

The restaurant sector represents an important constituent of the international hospitality industry. Using a global sample of 103 countries the International Hotel and Restaurant Association (1998) estimated that, in 1997, the total number of restaurants was 8.1 million and that these generated US$704 billion and employed 48 million people. Table 2.1 details the population per restaurant unit by global region in 1997. While the sector has developed at varying rates in different countries, in general, expansion appears to have been especially substantial over the last two to three decades.

A restaurant is basically defined here as an establishment where refreshments or meals can be obtained, usually for money, by the public. Fisher (1993) offers a similar definition when he says a restaurant provides food and beverages prepared outside of the home for public consumption. However, these basic definitions are very broad and conceal a diversity of restaurant types. Consideration of a few variations will serve to illustrate this point. Refreshments or meals are normally supplied for consumption on the premises in restaurants but sometimes a take-away service may also be available where refreshments or meals are supplied for consumption off the premises. Many ethnic restaurants, such as Indian and Chinese restaurants, and fast-food restaurants offer both an on-site and take-away service.

Ball (1996) states that many conventional fast-food restaurants offer prepared food for take-away as a means of diversifying and increasing trade. Restaurants range from up-market, full service gourmet restaurants to self-serve establishments and some may have elements of both. They may or may not be licensed to provide alcoholic liquor with meals. Factors such as these make the distinction between restaurant types increasingly blurred.

Global region (HRA classification)	(A) Population total	(B) Number of restaurants	Ratio (A/B) population per unit	Number of countries covered
European Economic Area	384 947 550	625 367	616	20
Rest of Europe	319 268 900	659 747	484	14
Middle East	147 357 100	168 739	873	12
The Caribbean	39 059 060	56 678	689	12
Central America	33 680 300	33 583	1003	7
North America	388 426 000	1 022 823	384	3
South America	288 111 500	1 193 329	241	10
Northeast Asia	1 395 532 200	3 490 200	400	5
South Asia	382 448 530	188 182	2032	7
South East Asia	483 191 000	578 886	757	7
Australasia	27 713 380	59 689	464	6
Totals	3 844 735 520	8 066 233	477	103

Source: International Hotel and Restaurant Association (1998: 5).

Table 2.1   Population per restaurant unit by global region, 1997

In most countries the restaurant trade is extremely fragmented and comprises a wide diversity of outlets and food types providing for different markets. A variety of different criteria can be used when analysing the structure of the restaurant sector. These include analysis by ownership, by branded or unbranded operations and by market, concept and menu.

Restaurant ownership

Despite some of the difficulties referred to above, different types of restaurants can be segmented according to one of three patterns of ownership structure: independents, chains or franchises.

Independent restaurants

Independent operators, running small single establishments mostly in secondary locations, dominate the worldwide market for restaurant food. This dominance is noted by Jones (1996b) who states that 'restaurants tend to be owned and operated by individuals and individualists'. In the USA, which is often perceived to be dominated by large corporate chains, most restaurants are, in reality, small businesses with annual sales less than $US 500 000 (Chon and Sparrowe, 2000). Similarly in the UK independents and small restaurant groups dominate the market (Mintel, 2000a). Figures for the size of the small business sector within the restaurant sector are provided later in this chapter.

Individuals or proprietors who are also involved in the day-to-day operation of the business mostly own independent restaurants. If the proprietors have more than one property then it is often the case that each property operates independently and has little or no formal relationship with other properties under their ownership.

Chain restaurants

The multiunit restaurant chains have captured, and at the expense of the independents, an increasing share of the total restaurant market. In the USA, Chon and Sparrowe (2000) claim that this has been particularly the case since 1950. In other countries this trend has been more recent. In the UK, for example, this trend dates back only 20–30 years.

A chain restaurant is one of two or more restaurants normally owned by a company and marketed on a corporate basis. The individual restaurant in the chain is virtually identical to the others in the chain in terms of its target market, concept, menu, design and name. McDonald's, KFC, and Burger King are examples of fast-food, or quick- service, international restaurant chains. Hard Rock Café, Planet Hollywood, Rainforest Café and T.G.I. Friday's are examples of international theme restaurant chains offering moderate upscale concepts and operating in the casual dining market.

Chains may be owned by franchise or management companies while others may be family-owned. Small and adventurous chains have been predicted to perform much better in the UK up to 2010 than their big corporate rivals (Frewin, 2000).

Table 2.2 shows a variety of competitive advantages and disadvantages of small independents and chain restaurant businesses. It should be recognized that these are general and may vary in their importance to individual businesses (Ball, 1999).

Franchises

Franchising has been a major factor in the growth of many fast-food and some other restaurant concepts (Ball, 2000). Franchising has been commonly utilized by chains. The largest fast-food companies are involved with franchising and, according to Entrepreneur International, six of the top ten international franchisors in 1999 were in the restaurant sector, with McDonald's in top position.

A restaurant franchise is a form of restaurant ownership where the parent company, the franchisor, allows other people, the franchisees, to operate clones of 'the business' under the same name, and using the same systems and operating procedures in return for an initial fee and an ongoing management services fee. Both the franchisor and its franchisees have contractual obligations to one

	Competitive advantages	Competitive disadvantages
Independents	Flexible	Limited bargaining power
	Specialized offerings	Few economies of scale
	Direct control of strategy, image	Reduced media access
	Consistency and independence	Over-dependence on owner
	Entrepreneurial drive	Limited planning
	Close to customer	Inertia
		Often lack specialist retail expertise and capital to expand
		Offer greatest risk
Chains	Bargaining power	Inflexibility
	Multiunit efficiencies	High investment costs
	Greater use of sophisticated technologies	Reduced managerial control
	Well-defined management capital	Limited independence
	Often able to attract expansion	
	Specialist expertise	
	Long-range planning	

Table 2.2 Competitive advantages and disadvantages of small independents and chain restaurant businesses

another (see Acheson and Wicking, 1992). Business format franchising is the most common form of franchising arrangement. It has been utilized by many leading international restaurant businesses to grow their businesses. Much franchising activity in the UK occurs in the restaurant market that has about a quarter of all franchises. Table 2.3 shows that there were over 1700 franchisee-owned catering establishments in 1991; an increase of nearly 500

Total number of establishments within franchised businesses	1989	1991
Company owned	229	548
Franchisee owned	1297	1735
% of Franchisee owned to total establishments	85	76
	1990	
Company owned sales (£000)	154 280	
Franchisee owned sales (£000)	636 880	
% of Franchisee owned sales to total establishments sales	80	

Source: Based on data from Power, M. In Horwath International and Stoy Hayward Franchising Services (1991).

Table 2.3 Business format restaurant franchising in the UK

compared to two years earlier. In catering franchise systems 76% of all establishments were franchisee owned in 1991.

To many, fast food is the home of the franchise. It certainly has made a key contribution to the popularization of the concept with its simple menus, quick product finishing and service times, standardized production methods and service delivery systems and heavily branded chains. These factors have made it easier for the fast-food concept to be rolled out across the world and has attracted entrepreneurial financing through franchising. This has enabled businesses with sound fast-food concepts to achieve rapid distribution independent of having to raise extra capital funds. Fast-food giants such as McDonald's, KFC, Dunkin' Donuts, Burger King and Subway, household names worldwide, have all developed their chains through franchising. For non-fast-food restaurants chaining and groups are less prominent and therefore so is franchising. Nevertheless, there are some well-known corporate-owned non-fast-food restaurant chains, which have used franchising to expand their concepts, including T.G.I. Friday's and Harry Ramsden's. While food may be produced and served less quickly and be relatively highly priced compared to fast-food products they are still standardized and themed restaurant branded concepts. These factors along with the desire for geographic expansion, often on an international scale, have facilitated franchising.

Restaurant franchising effectively began in the USA in the 1950s, with McDonald's, Kentucky Fried Chicken and the Burger King franchise system called at that time Insta Burger King. In the UK Wimpy opened their first franchised outlet in Ramsgate in 1957. Wimpy grew on a franchise basis to over 1200 outlets in 37 countries over the next 20 years. However, unlike the USA where fast food and franchising became dominant forces, in the UK there were, with the exception of KFC in 1965, few new entrants to the market until the mid-1970s with the arrival of McDonald's and Burger King. Since then restaurant franchising activity has increased in the UK. Indeed, Acheson and Price (1992) claim that most American fast-food franchisors regard the UK as the 'gateway' to Europe with there being more American franchise units in the UK than the rest of Europe combined. In Britain the restaurant sector contributes an average of 18% of sales to the total franchise sector, whereas in the USA by comparison this is 11% (Price, 1992).

Multiunit restaurant businesses

Multiunit restaurant businesses are another ownership type. These are most commonly a single company that owns and operates a number of restaurants, each with a different concept, menu and target market. In the UK, City Centre Restaurants plc and Groupe Chez Gerard plc are examples, whereas in the US

McDonald's has diversified through the acquisition of Chipotle Mexican Grill and Donatos Pizza. Some multiunit companies may be completely responsible for the management and operation of restaurants but do not own them. Multiunit restaurant businesses may benefit from some of the economies of chain restaurants such as centralized human resource functions. However, there may be risks associated with them as each concept is different and will have to prove itself in the market.

The structure of the restaurant sector can also be analysed according to concept, menu and market. Chon and Sparrowe (2000), for example, distinguish the following categories using these criteria:

- Fine dining restaurants

- Theme restaurants

- Casual dinner houses

- Ethnic restaurants

- Family restaurants

- Grill/buffet

- Quick-service or fast-food restaurants.

A similar categorization approach is employed by the *Restaurants and Institutions* publication in its annual ranking of the top 400 restaurant concepts with their corporate headquarters in the USA. Table 2.4 presents the percentage shares of each of its categories of the top 400 in July 2001.

Such a structural analysis presents a number of issues. One relates to the ease of categorizing certain restaurant types due to the increasingly mixed menus and target markets of certain operations. Another issue for some relates to identifying certain categories, e.g. sandwiches/bakery and coffee/snacks as restaurants. However, when these categories are considered in relation to the

Table 2.4 The category percentage shares of the top 400 in 2001

	%		%
Dinner houses	0.3	Steak/barbecue	4.5
Asian	0.5	Sandwiches/bakery	6.2
Retail	0.7	Coffee/snacks	6.6
Cafeteria/buffet	1.4	Chicken	6.8
C-stores	2.2	Family dining	8.0
Seafood	2.3	Casual dining	8.1
Italian	2.5	Pizza	10.2
Mexican	4.5	Burgers	35.2

Source: *Restaurants and Institutions* (2001: 90).

definitions of restaurants set out earlier in this section then it is clear that these are restaurants. Table 2.5 shows the 20 top ranking restaurant chains according to *Restaurants and Institutions* in July 2001.

Restaurants can also be distinguished according to whether they are branded or not. A restaurant brand is a name, design or symbol (or a combination of these) used to identify the offering provided by a restaurant. Branding has become even more important in the eating out market in recent years. In the UK, for example, 'many operators have sought to not only strengthen their existing brands, by emphasising quality of service and pricing, but they have also established new brands which are helping to further change the eating habits of UK consumers' (Mintel, 2001). The City Centre Restaurants group has done this in the UK. It has three brand categories: developed, developing and new brands. In 1998 new brands under trial included Wok Wok and Rick Shaw's. Downbeat financial announcements from leading UK operators have caused companies to focus heavily on brands and particularly upon the development of flagship brands to the provinces outside of London, which has been claimed to be oversupplied with restaurants (Buckingham, 2000).

	Sales US$ (millions)	Units	Category
McDonald's	39 576.0	27 699	Burgers
Burger King	11 400.0	11 340	Burgers
KFC	8649.0	11 388	Chicken
Pizza Hut	7960.0	12 084	Pizza
Wendy's	6400.0	5792	Burgers
Taco Bell	5300.0	7200	Mexican
Subway	4072.0	14 681	Sandwiches
Domino's Pizza	3540.0	6977	Pizza
Dairy Queen	2780.0	5953	Coffee/snacks
Applebee's Neighborhood Grill & Bar	2669.0	1286	Casual dining
Arby's	2410.0	3153	Sandwiches/bakery
Dunkin' Donuts	2300.0	5000	Coffee/snacks
Denny's	2230.0	1822	Family dining
Hardee's	2130.0	2660	Burgers
7-Eleven	2122.2	5756	C-stores
Outback Steakhouse	2091.0	664	Steak/barbecue
Red Lobster	2000.0	655	Seafood
Jack in the Box	1921.0	1634	Burgers
T.G.I. Friday's	1893.7	646	Casual dining
Little Caesar's	1852.0	3900	Pizza

Source: *Restaurants and Institutions* (2001: 40).

Table 2.5 The 20 top ranking restaurant chains, 2001 (N.B. These all have their corporate headquarters in the USA)

In 1999 the Hotel and Catering Research Centre at Huddersfield University (UK) identified 347 companies in the UK operating 713 brands in 22 859 restaurants. The 20 leading operators represented nearly 62% of all the branded restaurants. However, as mentioned previously, the sector is fragmented and no operator dominates the restaurant market.

The significance of branding in the restaurant sector can be explained by four factors:

1. Repeat business represents an important source of restaurant income, and repeat business depends on satisfied customers and a recognizable brand name. So product acceptance is improved by popularizing brand names.
2. The number of different restaurant brands and the rapid rate of new brand introduction complicates choice for customers and emphasizes the need to obtain customer brand recognition.
3. The choice of brand has implications for the company's marketing mix.
4. Customer loyalty in restaurants is difficult to obtain and hence branding is very important.

The Hotel and Catering Research Centre has also analysed the structure of the branded restaurant sector in the UK using a similar concept-menu-market model discussed above (see Table 2.6). Interestingly this found pub restaurant brands are the most notable having 192 brands and nearly 10 000 units.

Classification	Brands	Units	% Market share
Quick Service Restaurant – Ethnic	4	5	0.02
Quick Service Restaurant – Global staples	75	4439	19.4
Quick Service Restaurant – Peripherals	18	581	2.5
Casual Dining – Bar	79	835	3.7
Casual Dining – Café bar	16	266	1.2
Casual Dining – Dinner house	74	340	1.5
Casual Dining – Ethnic restaurants	59	225	1.0
Casual Dining – Family dining	87	2457	10.7
Casual Dining – Pizza/pasta	16	1212	5.3
Casual Dining – Pub	192	9949	43.5
Casual Dining – Pub restaurant	46	2440	10.7
Fine dining	47	110	0.5
N	713	22 859	100.0

Source: Hotel and Catering Research Centre (1999).

Table 2.6 Market share distribution of branded UK restaurant market segments

Nature of the restaurant product and operations

The principal component of any restaurant operation is the menu. However, products may be composed of both tangibles and intangibles. For a restaurant the most significant intangible component is the service but the product is much more than just food and service, it is a 'complete meal experience'.

With the diverse range of restaurants that has developed over the past two centuries there have been several approaches to the classification of restaurants, which have attempted to define more clearly the product and its mode of delivery. Some have focused upon the product itself utilizing the menu, service style and price as significant variables in determining the levels within the classification (Spectrum, cited in Jones, 1996a), while others (Powers, 1979) have viewed them from a system's perspective utilizing 'complexity' and 'innovativeness' as essential criteria (see Figure 2.1). Most of these classifications have been derived from studies of restaurant operations in the USA. While the Spectrum classification produced eleven restaurant types, the Powers classification showed the restaurant typology in matrix format plotting complexity of delivery against innovativeness of the system. Thus the least complex and most traditional format would be for example, the hamburger stand in the USA or a street vendor in Hong Kong. The most complex and innovative format would include theme restaurants, a popular form of which is a theme derived from other cultures. For example, a Thai restaurant in Australia in which an atmosphere is created by means of artefacts, furnishings, traditional dress and menu items reflecting the unique ingredients and tastes of Thailand, all of which contribute to 'transport' the diner to Thailand.

The ideal classification would combine factors from both of these classification types and also incorporate the nature of the business, whether independent stand-alone or multiunit chain restaurants. In the typology used to describe independent restaurants (Goldman, 1993), three segments have commonly been identified, quick-service, midscale and upscale restaurants. However, Muller and Woods (1994) argued that this typology is inadequate for the multiunit chains. These authors added two more segments, moderate upscale and business dining, to produce their 'Expanded Restaurant Typology'. The five resulting segments may be summarized as follows:

- Quick-service restaurants, which provide a consistent product with fast service at a low price, like McDonald's

- Midscale restaurants, for example Denny's family restaurants, which offer comfortable surroundings, value for money, convenience and greater selection of menu items with table or counter service

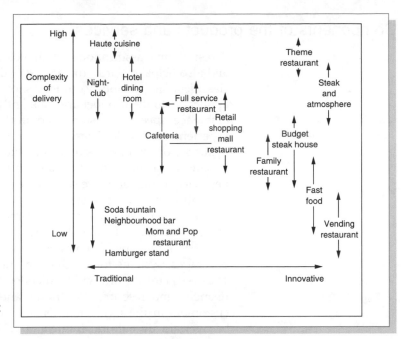

Figure 2.1 A restaurant typology. Source: Powers (1979: 49)

- Moderate upscale 'casual-theme' restaurants, like T.G.I. Friday's, which make a 'fashion statement' where customers identify with the restaurant's concept and where there is more concentration on ambience and flexibility of use by key customer segments

- Upscale restaurants, often independently owned but include chains like Outback Steakhouses, which offer a higher priced product with the greatest emphasis on the dining experience, relying more on personalization, image, quality, style and ambience

- Business dining, often provided by contract caterers like Serco Ltd in corporate locations, which places emphasis on value for money, price – whether subsidised or discounted – convenient location of the operation and changing menus to satisfy regular business clients within the 'captive market'.

However, even this typology was not seen to be entirely applicable in other countries. Jones, (1996a) identified midscale, moderate upscale and upscale restaurants as types that could be matched to UK restaurants. Goldman (1993) has also noted that further subdivision of the three of these, quick service, midscale and upscale, into concept groups by the American National Restaurant Association and CREST (Consumer Reports on Eating Share Trends) has facilitated clearer definitions of these segments.

Components of the products and services

A restaurant classification system aids the ordering of restaurants and also helps to clarify the nature of the restaurant product. The classifications previously outlined show a number of terms directly applicable to the product are constantly recurring: menu, service, ambience, speed, consistency, comfort, quality, flexibility, dining experience and style. These terms, almost in themselves, reflect a hierarchy of components of the product as the restaurant attempts to satisfy consumer needs from the most basic of physiological needs to the higher, more social levels of the need for self-respect, reputation, prestige and status.

The system for delivery of the product will be determined by the combination of tangibles and intangibles it comprises. For delivery of the tangible components of the product, the food and beverages, systems for production and service will be required. These systems in turn will be dictated by organizational policies, financial and resource constraints and also by the demands of customers in the target market. Furthermore, these factors will be overlaid by cultural influences within each country. At one end of the scale customer needs may be very basic, with food and beverages of consistent quality, served quickly and at a low to moderate price while, at the other end of the scale, there may be greater emphasis on an extensive, high quality and creative menu with ambience, comfort and style contributing to the total experience offered at a much higher price. For quick, efficient service, delivering a consistent product at a moderate to low price, a totally different system is required than for the highly creative and expensive menus in the most exclusive establishments.

The role of technology

Advances in information and catering technology over the past two decades have enabled foodservice systems to be developed which have revolutionized the delivery of food and beverages in restaurants. These developments have also produced an unprecedented increase in the productivity of foodservice operations, which consequently has led to intensification of competition within the sector. The larger operations, in particular the multiunit chains and franchise operators from fast food like McDonald's to upscale restaurants like Outback Steakhouses, have benefited most from these advances in technology. Such large organizations have the financial capacity to:

- build up expertise in the implementation of new technology

- develop customized operational systems

- design sophisticated production facilities

- undertake new product research and development with suppliers
- establish comprehensive human resource support systems including training
- select and utilize suitable locations for new operations.

For small restaurant businesses, particularly in underdeveloped countries, competition from such large organizations has presented a considerable challenge. With these advantages large chains can enter new markets in developing countries offering franchises to local operators who then can provide advice so that modifications, necessary for success within the local culture, can be made into menu items.

The nature of catering systems

Foodservice operational systems have frequently been referred to as catering systems. However, there are systems for food production and systems for food service. The guiding principle for any operational system is that of control throughout the operation. For any system there are inputs and outputs. In between, processes are involved in transforming the inputs to outputs and, once this has been achieved, there is feedback. In a restaurant, Johnston (1987) identified three types of processing that take place, *customer processing*, *product processing*, and *information processing*. When a customer enters the restaurant, is seated, orders from the menu and the meal is served, the service staff are involved in *processing the customer*. For production of the menu items, *food is processed*; ingredients are transformed into dishes, which are in turn served to the customer. Furthermore, *information is processed* during the entire operation as ingredients are ordered, received, stored and issued and the menu items sold at pre-determined prices. An important characteristic of processing is the utilization of technology notably in the processing of food in the kitchen and in the collection and analysis of information throughout the operation. Customer processing is more personalized with both staff and customers involved in the service encounter.

Operational design

Application of the principle of control is important, particularly in a competitive environment when costs must be minimized, quality assured and efficiency maintained. Each foodservice operation, therefore, needs a system designed to achieve these objectives. Any operation, which chooses to implement several systems, rather than utilize a single system, increases its own complexity. However, some systems may have to serve several functions and these may be 'multifaceted', or 'dedicated' with only one main function (Pickworth, 1988). A dedicated system might be a single stand-alone café or restaurant providing inside dining only. A multifaceted system may be a restaurant providing inside dining but also with a take-away service or even home delivery, a popular combination with pizza restaurants.

From production line and decoupling to customer participation

Three key approaches have been identified which reduce complexity and enhance control: *production lining, decoupling* and *increased customer participation* (Jones, 1988). In manufacturing industry the *production line* approach has been used for many decades. This principle has been gradually adopted by foodservice operations since the first batch production systems were used in volume catering. It is used in all categories of restaurants. *Decoupling* involves the removal of reliance on customer demand enabling food production to continue uninterrupted by changes in customer demand. This approach introduces a 'time buffer' (Light and Walker, 1990) in between production and service where the processed food is held at a safe temperature before it is regenerated for service. Examples of such systems are cook-chill and sous vide where the food is prepared, processed, packaged (either before or after processing), rapidly chilled and held under refrigeration until required for regeneration and service. *Decoupling* has many advantages. It enables production to be isolated from immediate customer demand; it also enables service to be physically separated from production. This is particularly important when a group of restaurants, like Taco Bell in the USA, utilizes a central production kitchen where the main function of the satellite kitchens at the individual restaurants is principally for regeneration and service rather than large-scale production. The third approach for *increased customer participation* incorporates service activities, which are carried out by the customer, for example in the case of self-service salad bars and buffets, so reducing labour costs while simultaneously increasing service speed.

Process flow

In foodservice operations 'back of house' and 'front of house' operations can be distinguished. In most systems models, however, the service, 'front of house' component, is usually incorporated unless the system is decoupled and the two components of production and service are completely separated in different locations. Systems models may be illustrated in a simple way by using a process flow diagram. The concept of process flow is an essential principle on which all systems depend. Essentially the flow of materials is traced from the point at which the materials enter the operation, through every process stage in the operation to the point when the final process is completed. Figure 2.2 shows models for a traditional à la carte operation and a cook-chill catering system (Jones, 1996b).

For an à la carte operation seven process steps have been identified, while for the cook-chill system an additional three steps have been added; holding, transportation and regeneration (Jones and Huelin, 1990). However, these are simple process flow diagrams and not all processes are shown, for example in cook-chill and sous vide packaging is important, whether the product is sealed in a bag before processing, or vacuum packed after rapid chilling. Furthermore, holding may be introduced in more than one step, for example in cook-chill there may be refrigerated holding in the central production facility before transportation, then holding again at the satellite kitchen under refrigeration before regeneration and service. Jones and Huelin (1990) identified ten generic 'dedicated' systems, which Jones (1994) later categorized into three types:

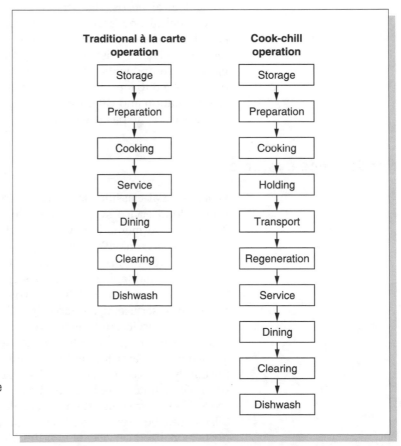

Figure 2.2 Examples of simple systems models of foodservice operations. Adapted from Jones (1996: 13)

- integrated foodservice systems, where food production and service are undertaken in the same operation

- food manufacturing systems, which incorporate 'decoupling' and where food production is separated from service

- food delivery systems, which focus on the service of meals to customers involving either regeneration or assembly of the dishes.

However, none of the aforementioned approaches to restaurant categorization has had the service component examined closely, yet it is this component that is the most visible part of the restaurant operation. Earlier the restaurant product was described as the 'complete meal experience'. This consists of the tangibles, food and beverages, and the intangibles, the service, and restaurant ambience that are closely related to both the food and the service style.

Whether part of an integrated foodservice system, or a food delivery system, the service component features prominently in the achievement of customer satisfaction, i.e. as a major output of the system. While the food and beverage output satisfies the basic physiological needs, the service component satisfies the higher psychological and social needs relating to self-esteem, prestige and status. The restaurant type and concept will strongly influence the service characteristics including the method, speed and interpersonal components of the service encounter. Service systems have evolved to meet the changes in customer demands, advances in information and catering technology, and economic and social changes over the past two decades.

Foodservice systems

While several classifications of catering systems have been proposed, foodservice systems have received little attention (Ball, 2003). Service methods have been addressed in detail by many authors (Lawson, 1987; Kinton, Cesarani and Foskett, 1992; Jones and Newton, 1997; Davis, Lockwood and Stone, 1998) ranging from formal table service, through self-service, quick-service, to take away and home delivery. Towards the formal end of this continuum, service at the table may be plated, semi-plated with some silver service, full silver service or guéridon (when tableside cookery is involved), all attended by 'wait' staff. At the next level, service may be assisted by 'wait' staff for buffets, salad bars, and for family and carvery service. For faster service the personalized service encounter is reduced and counter service for fast food and the self-serve systems such as echelon, free-flow carousel, and blister may be used. The extreme for self-service, where there is no personalized service, is vending. Take-away service involves collection of a packaged meal by the customer either by purchasing within the restaurant at the counter or through a drive thru 'window' service. Finally, at the other end of the continuum there is 'home' delivery when following the ordering of the meal by the customer it is delivered to where they wish to consume it.

The extent to which modern catering systems can be used in any country depends primarily upon the existence of a suitable infrastructure including power and transportation systems. The availability of resources, including ingredients and employees, must also be taken into account and local laws and trade agreements may have a critical impact when the importation of equipment, materials and expertise are involved. The introduction of McDonald's operations in both developed and developing countries is an example of how a modern catering system can be successfully implemented on a global scale.

Market dimensions and conditions

Output/size, value/volume of the sector

The restaurant sector in Western countries contributes significantly to each country's economy. In the USA in 1999, for a population of over 270 million, there were over 844 000 restaurant establishments with recorded sales of over US$354 billion, $227 billion of which accounted for sales by commercial fullservice and limited service restaurants (National Restaurant Association, 1999). In the UK, with a population of nearly 60 million, for over 52 000 restaurants including quick-service establishments (Food Service Intelligence), sales were over £4.58 billion for independent and chain restaurants in 1999. In the UK, there was an increase of 25% in the value (unadjusted real price terms) of the restaurant market between 1994 and 1999 (Mintel, 2000a), while in the USA over the period 1990–1999 the increase was almost 49% (National Restaurant Association, 1999). In countries with smaller populations like Australia, with about 18.5 million in 1999, 12 483 cafés and restaurants generated income of Aus $7.174 billion in 1998–1999 (ABS, 2000a).

Slightly different classifications are used for collecting output data for the restaurant sector in different countries. This may make comparisons confusing. The National Restaurant Association (NRA) in the USA currently uses two segments, fullservice and limited service, while in the UK Mintel (2000a) segments the chain and independent restaurant market into 'ethnic restaurants excluding takeaways and all other ethnic outlets'. In Australia, cafés and restaurants are grouped together. However, despite these different approaches there is scope for comparison as in each case data for independent and chain restaurants are separated from on-site food services, contract caterers and restaurants located in 'lodging places' like hotels.

While the figures for the sector in the USA and the UK have shown strong long-term growth, economic and political conditions can have significant short-term effects. In the UK the restaurant market declined in real price terms in 1995 but recovered with an annual growth rate of over 2% in 1998 and 1999 (Mintel, 2000a). This pattern of decline and growth of the restaurant market in the UK has been linked to the state of the economy, largely because expenditure on food eaten outside the home is discretionary and so when the economy is doing well the restaurant sector does well, but when the economy is struggling the restaurant sector also suffers.

Scale of the sector: small businesses dominant

In most countries small businesses dominate the market, even in the USA. In 1998, over 70% of all 'eating and drinking' places including pubs, taverns, ice cream and other refreshment stands and commercial cafeterias (National Restaurant Association, 1999) employed fewer than 20 people, the market being dominated by independent operators and small restaurant groups (National Restaurant Association, 2001a). In 2000, 46.4% of restaurant businesses in the UK had an annual turnover of below £100 000 and 83.5% generated annual sales of below £250 000 (Business Monitor PA 1003). In Australia, in 1999, 91% of all cafés and restaurant businesses employed fewer than 20 people and accounted for 55% of sector employment and 52% of sector income (ABS, 2000a).

Consumer market

In USA, UK and Australia there has been a trend towards spending more of the food dollar/pound on food eaten outside the home. In the USA in 1999 this exceeded 42% (National Restaurant Association, 2001b) while in Australia it was 26% (ABS, 2000b). According to Mintel (2000c) people in Britain spent £21.4b on eating and drinking in restaurants in 1999 compared with £59b spent on food eaten in the home, i.e. 27% of all food and drink consumed is in restaurants. Factors contributing to this trend include the increase in the consumer's disposable income and busier lifestyles. With longer hours at work, more women in the paid workforce and the consumer's desire for convenience, for value for money and for entertainment away from home there is less time for meal preparation. The result has been an increase in the consumer's food dollar spent in restaurants (Mintel, 2000b; National Restaurant Association, 2000a).

The competitive environment

Restaurateurs operate in a very competitive environment. They are not only in competition with each other but are also in competition with other businesses offering convenient food including hotels, motels, pubs, convenience stores, roadside kiosks, take-away food and home meal replacements from supermarkets.

In recent research conducted by the National Restaurant Association (1999) in the USA and the Centre for Hospitality and Tourism Research (CHTR) at Victoria University in Australia, the issue of competition was identified as just one of the challenges which the restaurant sector will be facing between 2001 and 2010 (Centre for Hospitality and Tourism Research, 2001). The National Restaurant Association (1999) predicted that 'the restaurant industry will experience intense competition' from 2001 to 2010 and, for success, restaurant operations 'will have to provide the highest levels of service and quality food'.

In Australia casual dining is increasing with restaurants and cafés serving a lighter style of food more suited to grazing and snacking. Simultaneously an increase in the number of new entrants to the sector has occurred leading to more intense competition, particularly for casual dining. Much of the competition is price based and, together with rising costs, especially fixed overhead costs, the sector will be forced to emphasize non-price competition and seek ways of controlling costs while still achieving high standards of food and service quality. Furthermore, in Australia, payroll costs are also significant for, unlike in the USA, there is a pay award system which ensures that employees receive adequate payment for work done, so frontline staff are not reliant on tips and sales commissions to boost their basic pay.

In the USA the demographic changes taking place and their effect on the labour force are of greater concern. Labour force growth here is slowing down as the population is ageing. The size of the age groups, 25–34 years and 35–44 years, will actually decrease over the next decade and it is from these age groups that many restaurant employees are recruited (Caplan, 2000). For this reason it is acknowledged that it is difficult to recruit and retain staff. It is recognized, therefore, that there needs to be a focus on training and the creation of improved incentive schemes to retain good staff.

The role of technology in restaurants has also been recognized in the USA, and elsewhere, providing opportunities for greater management efficiency and control of costs. More restaurants will have web sites and consumers will increasingly use the Internet for obtaining information about restaurants and making bookings. In the USA it is expected that, as 'Point of Sale' technology becomes faster and more accurate, efficiency will be improved and costs cut (National Restaurant Association, 1999).

In Australia, with a greater proportion of small businesses, this trend may be a little slower to penetrate the restaurant sector.

With such an increasing intensity of competition, differentiation of restaurant businesses becomes even more important. When businesses cannot compete on price then non-price competition becomes the focus. Service was seen by Caplan (2000) as a means of maintaining 'the competitive edge', while the National Restaurant Association (2001b) is now predicting that, once food and service quality meet consumer demands, the physical setting involving design, décor and atmosphere will be used as a key differentiator, particularly for upscale dining places.

Consumer trends

Consumer trends in the USA, identified by the Yankelovich Monitor (Caplan, 2000), included the return of the focus on the home and family, with eating out providing a chance for breaks from business and the stresses of daily life and for family gatherings. Eating out was seen as convenient and providing new experiences and leisure activity. Furthermore, in the USA and Australia, restaurant consumers are seeking value for money and also are becoming increasingly knowledgeable and discerning about food (National Restaurant Association, 1999; Centre for Hospitality and Tourism Research, 2001).

Eating patterns change as people pass through the family life cycle (BIS Shrapnel, 1998). In households of young 'singles' and where women undertake paid work more convenience and ready-prepared foods are used. More food is eaten 'on the move' or 'at the desk' with popularity of hand-held foods increasing (Sloan, 2001). As a result of irregular work patterns and busy lifestyles, eating at traditional meal times is declining as people eat more snacks at different times in the day (Sloan, 2001). Furthermore, younger households spend more per week than older households on fast food and café meals, with children increasingly influencing family spending on food (BIS Shrapnel, 1998).

In the USA, UK and Australia, the largest group of consumers, the 'baby boomers' born between 1946–1964, is ageing. This group is approaching the 'empty nest' life stage with more disposable income, as their children begin to leave home (National Restaurant Association, 1999; Mintel, 2000a; ABS, 2000b). In the USA, in 1999 there were 77.2 million in this 'baby boomer' group, 28% of the total population. In Australia the 'baby boomer' group was 4.3 million strong in 2000, 24% of the population (ABS, 2000b). This group will be a significant market for the restaurant sector as it ages. For this generation and for the 65 years and over age group there is a greater concern for health and so expectations in terms of nutrition will also increase (Sloan, 1998).

Within the restaurant sector the consumer can choose between a wide range of cuisines. This is especially the case in multicultural societies. In the UK, Mintel (2000a) has segmented the restaurant market into 'ethnic restaurants', with 37% market share, and all 'other non-ethnic outlets' that have 63% market share. Ethnic restaurants offer mostly Asian cuisines, while other non-ethnic restaurants include British, European and American style outlets. Furthermore, despite the bovine spongiform encephalopathy (BSE) crisis in the mid-1990s, traditional British fare is still first choice for consumers in the UK (Mintel, 2000a). In the USA, Sloan (1998), when predicting consumer trends to 2020 and beyond, noted an increasing interest in ethnic cuisines particularly from around the Pacific Rim, the Mediterranean Rim and the Caribbean Basin. In Australia, which has cultural diversity owing to the high rates of immigration over the past two decades, there is a wide range of ethnic restaurants. These restaurants are predominantly Asian (25%), Australian (20%) and Italian (10%) with fewer than 2% with an American theme (Mintel, 2000b). Furthermore, in a recent survey conducted by BIS Shrapnel (1998), the perceptions of growth in specific cuisines for restaurants in Australia was reported as being greatest for Italian cuisine, then 'other Asian', followed by Thai and then Chinese.

Conclusions

The restaurant sector is currently facing a number of significant challenges. The greatest of these is the intensity of competition. While small businesses dominate, they do not attract a proportionate amount of the restaurant sector's total revenue. Multiunit operations, whether chains or franchises, are becoming increasingly significant, particularly in the USA and UK. Rising costs for the sector are leading to greater emphasis on increasing efficiency and on the design of effective operational systems. Economies of scale provide significant advantages for larger operations, although smaller operations can still benefit from advances in technology by the introduction of computerized management systems and use of modern multipurpose equipment.

The growth of casual dining has led to a decline in the number of fine dining restaurants and an increase in quick-service and midscale restaurants. This has been mainly because of the increased pace of life, more women in the paid workforce and people working longer hours. The result is that, over the past two decades, the restaurant sector has changed to accommodate the grazing and snacking consumer who leads a busy life style and is short of time. However, despite this, the consumer is becoming more discerning and, though looking for value for money, expects to receive a quality product. These trends are expected\to continue with little change in the intensity of competition. If there is further slowdown in the economies of the USA and the European Union, the consumer's discretionary spending is likely to decrease and this will have an adverse effect on growth of the restaurant sector.

Ethnic cuisines, particularly those from Asia, have increased in popularity in the UK, but traditional British fare remains very popular. However, the diversity of cultures in the UK and many other countries is expected to continue to influence the range of cuisines offered by their restaurants.

With a challenging future ahead, restaurants will seek better ways of gaining competitive advantage. Differentiation, not only of product and service quality, but also in terms of physical setting and ambience will be important for gaining this advantage. However, even the best marketing intentions must always be underpinned by efficient management and operating systems that are capable of delivering a quality 'complete meal experience'.

Summary

- The term 'restaurant' has been attributed to the French. Originally a restaurant appears to have been a kind of 'soup'!

- A restaurant is an establishment where the public can obtain refreshments or meals, usually for money.

- Restaurants have continually undergone transformations since they first originated.

- Restaurants can be found throughout the world and the total number of restaurants was estimated to be 8.1 million in 1997. These employed 48 million people.

- The structure of the international restaurant sector can be divided according to ownership (independents, chains, franchises and multiunit businesses), concept, market and menu and branded or non-branded restaurants.

- Restaurants can be classified according to menu, service style and price, complexity and innovativeness. The nature of the business, whether independent stand-alone or multichain, should also be considered.

- The 'Expanded Restaurant Typology' proposed by Muller and Woods (1994) has five segments: quick service, midscale, moderate upscale, upscale and business dining.

- Foodservice operational systems, also called catering systems, have been described according to how the complexity of the operation can be reduced, through production lining, de-coupling or increased customer participation (Jones, 1988).

- The concept of process flow enables catering systems to be summarized in terms of essential process steps.

- Three categories of catering system have emerged: integrated foodservice systems, food manufacturing systems and food delivery systems (Jones, 1994).

- In Western countries eating out contributes significantly to each country's economy. In 1999, in the USA, 46% of the food dollar was spent on eating out. In Australia the figure was 26% (ABS, 2000a; National Restaurant Association, 2001a). In the UK 27% of the food pound was spent on eating out in 1999 (Mintel, 2000c).

- The state of a country's economy affects the consumer's discretionary spending which affects the proportion of the food dollar spent on eating out. A weak economy reduces restaurant sector revenue.

- The restaurant sector is dominated by small businesses.

- In Western countries restaurateurs experience intense competition.

- Advances in information and equipment technology have provided restaurateurs with opportunities for greater management efficiency and cost controls.

- When costs rise for the restaurant sector the competitive edge may be gained by product differentiation rather than by price.

- Consumer demographics are changing with the largest age group, the 'baby boomers', as they approach the 'empty nest' stage of the life cycle, having the greatest discretionary spending capacity.

- Ethnic cuisines, particularly those from the 'Mediterranean Rim' and Asia, are increasing in popularity in Western countries.

Review questions

1. What are the origins of the restaurant?
2. What factors make it difficult to determine the size of the restaurant sector of the international hospitality industry?
3. What are the similarities and differences between a McDonald's, a T.G.I. Friday's, a public house and full service restaurants?
4. What are the differences between branded, chain and franchised restaurants?

5. Is there still a place today for fine dining (in upscale restaurants)?
6. To what extent can catering systems be designed to benefit every size of restaurant business?
7. What impact will the Internet and information technology have on the restaurant sector in the future?
8. What role will the 'baby boomer' generation, born 1946–1964, play in the future of the restaurant sector?
9. What factors have led to the trend towards casual dining?
10. How can small restaurant businesses achieve a 'competitive edge'?

References

ABS (2000a) *8655.0 1998-1999 Cafes and Restaurants Industry, Australia*, Australian Bureau of Statistics, Belconnen, ACT.

ABS (2000b) *6535.0 1998-1999 Household Expenditure Survey: Detailed Expenditure Items*, Australian Bureau of Statistics, Belconnen, ACT.

Acheson, D. and Price, S. (1992) Chain reaction. *Business Franchise*. October/November, pp. 25–9.

Acheson, D. and Wicking, N. (1992) Fast food franchising and finance. In Ball, S. (ed.) *Fast Food Operations and Their Management*, Stanley Thornes, Cheltenham, pp. 147–68

Ball, S. D. (1992) Understanding fast-food operations. In Ball, S. (ed.) *Fast Food Operations and Their Management*, Stanley Thornes, Cheltenham, pp. 3–19

Ball, S. (1996) Fast food. In Jones, P. (ed.) *Introduction to Hospitality Operations*, Cassell, London, pp. 172–89

Ball, S. (1999) Whither the small independent take-away? *British Food Journal*. **101**, (9 and 10), 715–723.

Ball, S. (2000) Catering. In Lashley, C. and Morrison, A. (eds) *Franchising Hospitality Services*, Butterworth-Heinemann, Oxford, pp. 145–69

Ball, S. (2003) Food service and dining systems. In Ball, S., Kirk, D., Lockwood, A. and Jones, P. (eds) *Hospitality Operations: A Systems Approach to the Provision of Accommodation, Food and Beverage Services*, Cassell, London (forthcoming).

BIS Shrapnel (1998) *The Australian Foodservice Market*, BIS Shrapnel Pty. Ltd., Sydney.

Buckingham, L. (2000) Economic misery. *Financial Mail*, Sunday, 22 October, pp. 6–7.

Caplan, B. (2000) Dining Out in the 21st Century: A Consumer Perspective. In *Off the Plate*, Restaurant and Catering Australia, Sydney. Proceedings of the 2000 Restaurant and Catering Australia National Conference, Hobart, 8–10 October.

Centre for Hospitality and Tourism Research (2001) *Foodservice 2010*, Victoria University, Melbourne. Research sponsored by the Co-operative Research Centre for Sustainable Tourism and Restaurant and Catering Australia.

Chon, K. and Sparrowe, R. T. (2000) *Welcome to Hospitality an Introduction,* 2nd ed., Delmar Thomson Learning, London.

Davis, B., Lockwood, A. and Stone, S. (1998) *Food and Beverage Management.* Butterworth-Heinemann, Oxford.

Fisher, W. P. (1993) The restaurant and food service industry. In Khan, M., Olsen, M. and Var, T. (eds), *The VNR's Encyclopaedia of Hospitality and Tourism.* Van Nostrand Reinhold, New York.

Frewin, A. (2000) Small chains set to outstrip rival giants, *Caterer and Hotelkeeper,* **13**, January, p. 10.

Goldman, K. (1993) Concept selection for independent restaurants. *Cornell HRA Quarterly,* **34**, (6), 59–72.

Hotel and Catering Research Centre (1999) *The UK Food Service Brands Directory.* The University of Huddersfield, Huddersfield.

International Hotel and Restaurant Association, (1998) *The Restaurant Revolution – Growth, Change and Strategy in the International Food Service Industry 1995–2005.*

Johnston, R. (1987) A framework for developing a quality strategy in a customer processing operation. *International Journal of Quality and Reliability Management,* **4**, (4), 37–46.

Jones, P. (1988) *Food Service Operations.* Cassell, London.

Jones, P. (1988) The impact of trends in service operations on foodservice delivery systems. *International Journal of Operations and Production Management.* **8**, (7), 23–30.

Jones, P. (1994) Catering systems. In Davis, B. and Lockwood, A. (eds*), Food and Beverage Management,* Butterworth-Heinemann, London, pp. 131–144.

Jones, P. (1996a) The hospitality industry. In Jones, P. (ed.) *Introduction to Hospitality Operations,* Cassell, London, pp. 1–17.

Jones, P. (1996b) Restaurants. In Jones, P. (ed.) *Introduction to Hospitality Operations,* Cassell, London, pp. 122–137.

Jones, P. and Huelin, A. (1990) Thinking about catering systems. *International Journal of Operations and Production Management,* **10**, (8), 42–52.

Jones, U. and Newton, S. (1997) *Hospitality and Catering.* Cassell, London.

Kinton, R., Cesarani, V. and Foskett, D. (1992) *The Theory of Catering.* Hodder and Stoughton, London.

Lattin, G. (1997) Restaurants. In *The New Encyclopaedia Britannica Volume 19 Micropaedia,* 15th ed. Encyclopaedia Britannica, London, pp. 1042–1044.

Lawson, F. (1987) *Restaurants, Clubs and Bars, Planning Design and Investment.* The Architectural Press, London.

Light, N. and Walker, A. (1990) *Cook-Chill Catering: Technology and Management.* Elsevier Applied Science, London.

Medlik, S. (1978) *Profile of the Hotel and Catering Industry* 2nd ed. Heinemann, London.

Mintel (2000a) *Restaurant Chains and Independents*. Mintel UK Pty Ltd., London.

Mintel (2000b) *The Australian Foodservice Industry Research Programme 1999/2000*. Mintel Australia Pty. Ltd., Sydney.

Mintel (2000c) *British Lifestyles 2000 – The Wealth of the Nation*. Mintel, London.

Mintel (2001) *Eating Out Review*. Mintel, London.

Muller, C. C. and Woods, R. H. (1994) An expanded restaurant typology. *Cornell HRA Quarterly*, **35**, (3), 27–37.

National Restaurant Association (1999) *Restaurant Industry 2010: The Road Ahead*. National Restaurant Association, Washington.

National Restaurant Association (2000) *2000 Restaurant Industry Forecast*, 2000 [Online] Available: http://www.restaurant.org/research/research/htm (2000, September 8).

National Restaurant Association (2001a) *2001 Restaurant Industry Forecast*, 2001 [Online] Available: http://www.restaurant.org/research/ind_glance.cfm (2001, November 8).

National Restaurant Association (2001b) *2001 Restaurant Spending*, 2001 [Online] Available: http://www.restaurant.org/research/spending.cfm (2001, November 8).

National Restaurant Association (2001c) *2001 Restaurant Industry Forecast*, 2001 [Online] Available: http://www.restaurant.org/research/forecast_settings.cfm (2001, November 8).

O'Connor, J. (2000) What lessons can be learned from the history of dining out? Some influences on current trends in the UK. In Wood, R. C. (ed.) *Strategic Questions in Food and Beverage Management*. Butterworth-Heinemann, Oxford, pp. 225–242.

Pickworth, J. R. (1988) Service delivery systems in the foodservice industry. *International Journal of Hospitality Management*, **7**, (1), 43–62.

Powers, T. F. (1979) *Introduction to Management in the Hospitality Industry*. John Wiley and Sons, New York.

Price, S. (1992) The internationalisation of fast food. In Ball, S. (ed.) *Fast Food Operations and Their Management*. Stanley Thornes, Cheltenham, pp. 188–211.

Restaurants and Institutions (2001) *37th Annual Top 400 Restaurant Concepts*, Cahners, 15 July.

Sloan, A. E. (1998) Food industry forecast consumer trends to 2020 and beyond. *Food Technology*, **52**, (1), 37–44.

Sloan, A. E. (2001) Top ten trends to watch and work on. *Food Technology*, **55**, (4), 38–58.

Spang, R. L. (2000) *The Invention of the Restaurant*. Harvard University Press, London.

Taylor, D. (1977) *Fortune, Fame and Folly*. IPC Business Press, London.

Contract foodservice

K. Michael Haywood and Geoff Wilson

Chapter objectives

This chapter provides information and perspectives on the rapidly evolving sector of contract foodservice. When you have read this chapter you should be able to:

- Identify the key indicators that reveal the size and significance of the contract foodservice sector.

- Discuss the driving forces and critical success factors that are shaping contract foodservice.

- Analyse competitive characteristics of, and contractual arrangements within, the sector.

- Identify key firms and analyse their strategic initiatives.

- Explain the characteristics of, and the changes within, the sectoral markets.

- Critically review major issues and operational trends.

Introduction

Contract foodservice is considered part of the non-commercial or institutional segment of the foodservice sector. The market segments served are healthcare, business and industry, education, military, corrections (prisons) and transportation. The dominant firms that make up this sector are among the largest, most sophisticated and yet the least understood of hospitality businesses. For the most part their business-to-business operations are diverse, geographically dispersed, professionally managed, profitable, yet hidden from public scrutiny. Their penetration, or ability to take over self-managed services, continues to intensify, while simultaneously their product–service mix expands as corporate outsourcing opportunities in such fields as maintenance and cleaning come their way.

Low entry barriers at the entrepreneurial end of the sector have resulted in a plethora of smaller catering firms that concentrate on serving local and regional niche markets. Their ability to compete is usually based on more specialized and personalized services, often to the previously mentioned markets. Mention should be made of the social catering segment for weddings, parties and special events. Contract caterers, for the most part do not get involved with the social catering as these 'one-off' affairs introduce market opportunities for every foodservice operator to capitalize upon, so competition is intense. Many of the smaller contract and social catering firms succumb to the pressures of the business and are either urged to merge or unable to sustain themselves. Compared to the dominant firms they are less sophisticated, more prone to financial hardship, and unable to muster the purchasing power and the depth of programming that are the underlying strengths associated with the major players.

Despite the degree of rivalry, whether on a global, national, regional or local scale, the attractiveness of the sector continues to be strong. The overall sector continues to expand worldwide at approximately a 2–3 % real rate of revenue growth per year. This is due in large part to their inherent competencies. Business and institutional clients recognize that their strategic interests and value creation activities must be focused upon, and dedicated to, their primary missions. For them foodservice is a peripheral activity in which most realize the need for professional management. Similarly, the increasing number of privately catered events attests to the need and desire for professional culinary talent, and the ability to create memorable occasions. So there is little doubt that contract caterers who provide sustenance in a value-laden and cost-effective manner are likely to succeed. Though the provision of nourishment is often perceived as a mundane, routine, talent-less activity, the reality differs. Food preparation and presentation is a creative enterprise in which people working in the sector take pride and accept responsibility for maintaining the well-being of individuals who are in pursuit of work, their health and happiness, their education and entertainment. The systems, procedures and increasing use of technological applications to resolve problems demand an increasing amount of management knowledge and ability.

As the globalization of businesses continues the dominant players are consolidating the sector. Global merger and acquisition strategies are of vital importance to achieve economies of scale and to meet the needs of large client firms who prefer to deal with a single contractor. Even among the catering entrepreneurs, only those who demonstrate innovation and business acumen stay in business and achieve financial success. To appreciate these trends, and to put the contract feeding sector into more complete perspective, this chapter will start with a brief historical context, before proceeding to discussion of the current size and significance of contract catering in different parts of the world.

The forces driving contract catering will then be identified, along with the critical success factors that have to be mastered. This discussion then moves to identification of the emerging characteristics of, and contractural arrangements within, the sector; brief descriptions of key dominant corporations. Knowledge of the major markets served will then be provided, followed by a synopsis of the changing patterns of key issues and operational trends.

Historical overview

Food has always been produced by specialists outside the family. The first serious restaurants were started in China during the Tang dynasty (AD 618–90) (Ackerman, 1990). The great and gross banquets of the Roman era and middle ages were probably catered events (Mennell, 1985). The corresponding spread of restaurants in Europe and North America was a consequence of the agricultural revolution and the desire for mass feeding in urban areas. An international market for foodstuffs developed with changes in transportation, agriculture, marketing, distribution, travel, education, and technological enhancements as mundane as refrigeration. Indeed the prosperity of post-industrial Western societies, particularly in the last few decades, has provided a fertile breeding ground for non-commercial as well as commercial foodservice.

Contract catering was jolted into being during the beginning of the twentieth century and particularly the period following the Second World War. In Great Britain the Emergency Powers (Defence) Factories Canteen Order 1940 and 1943 made canteen facilities compulsory in all factories employing 250 workers or more. Many of the contract catering firms maintained their business after the war, as there was immense economic activity and growth. Though many businesses and institutions initially opted to manage their own foodservice facilities, over time frustrations grew with the technicalities of operating foodservices as plants or industrial complexes grew in size and spread out over a larger territory. High labour costs due to industrial unionized wage rates also encouraged a shift to contract foodservice. Over time the drive for efficiency and cost containment resulted in an out-sourcing of peripheral service activities, and recognition that food-services could be operated more effectively and efficiently by specialized firms.

All the major contract catering firms today can trace their ancestry to small, local establishments that catered to middle- and working-class patrons. They served familiar food as found in customers' homes. For example, the founding firm for the Compass Group began operations in 1941 as Factory Canteens Ltd. Its mandate was to feed munitions workers who were promised one hot meal per day by legislation. This firm evolved into Bateman and Midland Catering, later emerging as Grand Metropolitan Catering Services, and so on. The American roots of Sodexho Marriott started with John Toulson Gardner and Herbert Merchant, who, from humble beginnings, respectively developed a chain of restaurants and chop houses, and a mobile catering business for workers on building sites. ARAMARK was built on a vision by Davre Davidson to put vending machines inside offices and factories – a novel idea at the time. He then merged with William Fishman in 1959 under the name Automatic Retailers of America (ARA) which, in turn, purchased the Slater Company, becoming in the process a national player.

While it is evident that these and other firms have grown through acquisitions, it is their organic growth that is the most interesting and impressive. Contract catering evolved out of the need to feed people wherever they learn, work, play, congregate and recuperate. In essence it was the growing demand for convenience – offering food and beverages consumers want, at the time and place that consumers want them – that drove growth. Catering entrepreneurs were also challenged by potential clients to take food to novel places – oil rigs, remote lumber camps, and prisons. How to get food delivered and prepared in these settings necessitated the design and manufacture of speciality kitchen equipment. As a result of these challenges, the catering industry today has a symbiotic rapport with foodservice equipment manufacturers and kitchen and restaurant designers.

There was also recognition by the industry visionaries that the business-to-business need for convenience differed from the consumer-driven need and necessitated a client-driven mindset. For example, from the history of catering firms we have learned that corporate success is based on how completely they understand the client's rationale for hiring a contract caterer in the first place, and then being able to deliver on the promises made. For instance, in the business and industry category, the productivity of employees is a major priority. Catering firms have learned that the presentation of food, and the ambience in which it is consumed, plays a vital role in keeping people alert and maintaining morale. The convenience factor here is a function of the following: the avoidance of absenteeism due to stress and poor health; the ability to keep employees at work and alert; and the assumption of responsibilities to offer an exciting array of foods that appeal and keep people happy and content. These are becoming difficult tasks as labour forces become increasingly ethnically diverse and respond differently to certain menu items and eating environments.

Size and significance

Contract catering has become an important part of the overall foodservice industry in virtually every industrialized country. Yet its significance is somewhat over-shadowed by a greater public awareness of and discourse about fast food and haute cuisine. Another part of the problem lies with understanding this foodservice segment and the terminology used to describe it. The sector in Great Britain, for example, would prefer to be known as 'foodservice management' to cover the combined feeding people at work in business and industry, and in schools, colleges and universities, hospitals and healthcare, welfare and local authority catering, and other non-profit making outlets. While the term 'contract catering' predominates throughout the world, it is quickly becoming evident that even this term is an inadequate descriptor. On the one hand, quite a number of firms serving non-commercial markets are active in a wide variety of commercial endeavours selling directly to customers in such places as transportation terminals, arts, leisure and entertainment centres, department stores and shopping malls. On the other hand, many of the major firms are simultaneously diversifying their activities and product/service lines. Many business and industrial and institutional clients have decided to outsource a wider range of service support functions – housekeeping, maintenance, security, laundry, asset and property management, retail or convenience shops, social clubs, waste removal, and so on. Rather than remaining contract caterers the major firms are developing new business models that include the provision of these value-added services. As such they are morphing into 'managed service providers'.

Determining the size and growth of contract catering, therefore, is confounded by these evolutionary changes. But there is a more fundamental problem on a global level. Each country defines its contract catering sector differently, and the availability and reliability of data on this industry sector do differ. It is not surprising that the best sources for information on the sector is proprietary. It resides in consultancy firms that charge enormous amounts of money for 'state of the industry' reports, or it rests within the major corporations who employ researchers to assess opportunities and trends worldwide. From the Compass Group, as part of their data gathering activities, we can estimate the size of industry potential for contract catering worldwide for the year 2000 at about £200 billion a year, or US$290 billion. The Compass Group admits that the lion's share of this market globally is still in the hands of self-operators and the company claims to have a 4.0–4.5% share of the market, followed by Sodexho and ARAMARK. Due to recent acquisition and merger activity, however, Sodexho seems to be in the leading position at the moment.

The most thorough and publicly available data on the contract catering sector are provided by the British Hospitality Association, who through its Contract Catering Survey (2001), provides a glimpse into the sector in the UK, France, Germany and the Netherlands. This information, summarized here, is followed by data on the sector in the USA and Canada. Since there is nothing worse than stale statistics the intention in reporting this information is simply to highlight key trends and findings.

The aforementioned UK survey is exemplary because it is thorough and quite complete. It sets the standard for the type of research that could be conducted worldwide. For the operating year 2000, turnover (total billings including food purchases, wages and management fee) was £3.3 billion or $4.8 billion. Turnover (sales revenue) increased 8.5% from the preceding year. Indeed, this growth is exemplified by the 38.5% increase from 1993 when turnover was £2 billion. Wages constituted almost 44% of the turnover figure in 2000, a figure that has been fairly constant over the years. Food represented 36%, management fees 13% (though up 16% in absolute fee income from 1999 due to purchasing efficiencies and higher margins), and other purchases just over 6%. Other findings from the Contract Catering Survey include the following facts:

- Existence of 17 830 contract outlets (50% of the market), down slightly from 1999, 46% representing business and industry, 26% education, 5% healthcare, 2.6% government

- 1.5 billion meals served, up 8% from 1999

- 131 680 full-time equivalent staff, down from 132 307 in 1999. The number of full-time employees fell to 103 424, a drop of 1.3% compared to 1999 and down 10.9% compared with 1998. As in many other industries part-time employment has grown, up 2.8% from the previous year

- Wages rose to £1433 million, up 7% from 1999

- Food purchases rose 7%, mainly because of the increase in the number of meals consumed and more expensive menu items.

For the French market, the Contract Catering Survey (British Hospitality Association, 2001) reports that 30% (80 000) of the foodservice outlets in the non-commercial sector served 2.7 billion meals, and that contract caterers served an estimated 951 million meals from 22 000 outlets. Business and industry accounted for 44% of these outlets and 61% of the meals served.

In Germany, the 50 000 non-commercial outlets served 4.8 billion meals. Contract catering accounts for 4000 of these outlets and 466 million meals. Business and industry represent 32% of these outlets and 67% of the meals. The Netherlands has just over 9000 non-commercial outlets serving 700 million meals of which 119 million are contracted from 2500 outlets.

The market share figures for each country and, therefore, the opportunity for further incursion is contained in Table 3.1.

The same degree of detailed information on North American markets is not available from readily accessible sources. For the USA, the National Restaurant Association (2001) estimates that foodservice contractor managed sales amounted to $24.8 billion, social caterers earned an additional $3.7 billion, and self-operated non-commercial foodservices $32.6 billion in the year 2000. Of course non-commercial or institutional sales are reported at cost, so market penetration is quite low, less than 40%. Nevertheless, contract caterers increased sales year over year by 6.2%, compared to the 2.3% for independently operated non-commercial foodservices. With total foodservice sector revenues around $380 billion contract catering firms produced about 6.5% of this amount.

Canadian foodservice sales reached $38.7 billion (Canadian dollars) in the year 2000 (a 6.6% growth over 1999) according to the Canadian Foodservices and Restaurant Association (2001). Of this amount, non-commercial foodservice, which includes accommodation, institutional, retail and other (vending, sports and private clubs, movie theatres, stadiums and other seasonal or entertainment operations), generated $8.5 billion (Canadian dollars). The social and contract caterers combined brought in $2.6 billion (Canadian dollars) and the institutional foodservice revenue component amounted to $2.4 billion (Canadian dollars). Note that in Canada institutional includes education, transportation, hospital, special care, correctional, military and employee foodservice. It has been estimated that contract caterers hold 19% of the health-

Sector	UK		France		Germany		Netherlands	
	Outlets	Meals (millions)	Outlets	Meals (millions)	Outlets	Meals (millions)	Outlets	Meals (millions)
Business and industry	50	92	63	66	10	11	42	37
Education	17	39	18.5	20	11	13	15	14
Healthcare	5	23	21	22	4	5	4	5
Other	47	76	8	10	4	11	7	15

Source: Foodservice Intelligence Ltd., Feb. 2001; British Hospitality Association, Contract Catering Survey, 2001 (Quest, 2001).

Table 3.1 Share of total market held by contractors (2000)

care market, 85% of business and industry, 57% of education, and 14% of correctional institutions.

Data provided by the NPD Foodservice Information Group (Non-Commercial Foodservice Study) reveal that, in Canada, workplace restaurants and cafeterias account for 44% of the meal occasions and 34% of the dollar share of all non-commercial foodservices, followed by schools at 23% of meal occasions and 18% of the dollar share. Hospitals and medical centres have 13% of the meal occasions, and 18% of the dollar share; leisure represents 14% of the meal occasions and 26% of the dollar share; and travel 3% of meal occasions and 1% of dollar share. In terms of meal parts breakfast and morning snacks account for 31% of the meal occasion, lunch 34 %, supper 7%, and afternoon/evening snacks 27%. The average check (Canadian dollars) in the workplace is $1.64, school $2.07, hospital $2.28, leisure $4.01, and travel $5.81.

In most parts of the world, strong growth in contract catering is reflected in the growth of outlets, meal occasions, and average snack or meal expenditures. The traditional market has been business and industry, though this sector may be softening in certain regions. The main growth areas have been in education, healthcare, and 'public catering', particularly in leisure and recreation venues. Interesting examples of other types of markets in which there are growing opportunities include correctional facilities and the military. Airline catering is a specific transportation market in which contract caterers compete intensely for a share of this business. The International Flight Catering Association (IFCA) and the International Inflight Food Service Association estimate that the total size of this sector for the year 2000 was US$14 billion, of which $10 billion was for the inflight portion: North America $2.6 billion, Latin America $0.4 billion, Europe $2.9 billion, Asia and Pacific $3.2 billion, and the rest of the world $0.9 billion.

Driving forces and critical success factors

Over the past decade the contract catering sector has undergone rapid change based around the nature of the following relationships: caterer-to-customer, caterer-to-client, caterer-to-supplier, and caterer-to-caterer. Starting with the customer in institutional settings, it is commonly perceived that they have been taken for granted – served simple, common food at the lowest possible prices in sterile cafeteria-like settings. How the world has changed! Today this is a business recipe for disaster and is totally unacceptable and unworkable in many settings. First of all, there are no typical customers and, contrary to opinion, they are no longer captive, nor easily manipulated. In every market sector and at every site, customer needs and wants vary. The driving forces attributed to demographic shifts are important, but it is the psychographic, or values and lifestyle, characteristics that are driving acceptance, patronage, expenditure and use. For instance, consumers today are more knowledgeable and discriminating about what they eat. Information on health, diet and exercise has proliferated through the learning channels of education, mass communication, and travel. The trends toward healthy eating, improved and more adventuresome diets have affected contract catering as much as any other food sector.

Harried lifestyles, dual-career or single-parent families, the paucity of time, tight schedules and the daily commute, drive the demand for convenience, however that may be defined – availability of food when and where customers want it; speed of service and delivery; no line-ups, no waiting, and no hassles. In Canada and the USA, where foodservice earns almost half of every dollar spent on food, convenience over quality is strongly in evidence, though in Europe quality might still have the edge. While this requirement shows up in the proliferation of quick-service restaurants and street food vendors, it is also in evidence in non-commercial foodservice outlets. At work more flexible working hours and increasing pressures on time mean that the traditional meal times (particularly lunch) are becoming less significant. Increasingly people are 'grazing', that is, they desire snacks and meals, at all times of the day, and sometimes the evening.

The business-to-business relationship between caterer and client is also being re-shaped. As previously suggested more organizations are coming to the conclusion that their non-core activities should be outsourced. This process typically begins with a company identifying and performing only those value creation activities that form the basis of its competitive advantage. The remaining activities are then reviewed to see whether they can be performed more effectively and efficiently by independent suppliers. This puts considerable pressure on the catering firms actually to prove that this can be done. But this step is only the beginning. With the consolidation and globalization of many industries there is a preference usually to deal with a minimum number of suppliers. Hence the pressure on the leading contract catering firms to expand geographically, and to offer a broader range of non-food services – security, cleaning and laundry, office services, plant operations and maintenance – that increase sales volume and margins. The relationships between caterers (managed service providers) and clients are then structured in accordance with long-term contracts. It should be emphasized, however, that the terms of the contracts are often tied to whether or not the service provider makes an investment. Furthermore, these contractual relationships are managed on the basis of competitive bidding. Obviously, the objective among the catering firms is to become the preferred supplier.

The advantages with outsourcing include the following: a reduction to the client's cost structure and, in most cases transfer of the financial risks associated with operating foodservices on a commercial basis; the ability of both the client and the caterer constantly to improve their ability to differentiate their offerings, and to concentrate value-adding resources to further strengthen their core or distinctive competencies. The only problem is that outsourcing allows clients to become more flexible and responsive to market conditions. Unencumbered by commitments to internal suppliers, a client can switch more easily between providers of non-core value creation activities. Consequently, caterers are now spending considerably more time fostering strong relationships with their actual and prospective clients. The last thing a caterer wants is to respond to a barrage of client requests to improve services. Rather, the perception of providing professional expertise now demands a proactive stance – continually monitoring the prevailing mood and desires of customers and clients and anticipating and implementing needed improvements to menus, services, and dining environments. This calls for extreme vigilance and recognition that client and customer relationship marketing (CRM) are becoming the quintessential tools in managing these relationships.

While the particulars of catering contracts will be discussed further on in this chapter, it is worth pointing out that the changing nature of the caterer–client relationship is resulting in profit and loss contracts becoming more popular as cost-plus contracts decline. A few years ago, cost-plus contracts represented over 50% of all contract catering contracts, but their share has now fallen to only a third of all contracts.

As caterers become larger and more dominant players, the resulting yield is greater power in relationships with suppliers. This is not the case if catering firms remain small and lack the purchasing power to drive down food, beverage and other supply costs. Since excellent supplier relationships are a major factor in helping caterers land and maintain contracts, suppliers are being asked (nudged) to bring more to the table. Supply chain management, therefore, is becoming a critical catalyst in identifying and reining in hidden costs. One of the prime developments that will re-shape this relationship is 'efficient foodservice response' (EFR). In attempts to create a more efficient foodservice supply chain, the goal is to modernize and streamline business practices by eliminating non-value adding activities; improving product flows; improving the timely flow of accurate demand data up the supply chain; integrated product integration processes; re-engineered revenue cycle transaction processing; facilitating the movement of labour intensive food preparation activities out of operations to upstream locations; and adopting information technologies such as bar codes and electronic data interchange (EDI).

Supply chain inefficiencies in the foodservice sector are pronounced in comparison to other consumer goods industries. While technology is the enabler in achieving benefits or value-added, that can be passed on to clients, the impact of these initiatives will go beyond improvements in cost structures and more modernized infrastructures. The contract catering firms would also be positioning themselves for revenue growth in those markets where institutional self-catering would lose its appeal and economic rationale. As these supply chain initiatives work their way through the sector, caterers will have to continue to work with their suppliers in providing new and more innovative meal solutions for today's time- and value-conscious consumers and clients. And, without a doubt, the impact will be changes in business practices, increasing supply chain coordination, and a reversal of the past's inefficient traditional relationships within the sector.

With purchasing leverage becoming the key strategic driver, the push for continued merger and acquisition activity among the major firms will not abate; further sector consolidation is likely. The acquisition of Marriott Management Services by Sodexho in North America is a case in point. In fact, as the key firms get larger, more opportunities to achieve purchasing economies can be realized, simply bypassing distributors and negotiating directly with manufacturers. Some companies are even going further up the food chain and contracting with growers for certain crops, such as coffee. As this trend continues distributors will merely perform a logistics function. It should be noted, however, that distributors are in the process of consolidating as well, thereby improving their geographic coverage and operating efficiencies. Indeed, many are putting a lot of stock in efficient foodservice response (EFR) to bring about needed efficiencies. Because the foodservice sector is so fragmented, distributors will prevail and will become more important partners in the management of the supply chain.

While the demand for contract catering services is expected to grow, there are a number of factors that could serve to limit customer patronage. First of all, many organizations are reviewing their policies regarding meals as fringe benefits, particularly because of the taxable benefit issues. Rules may vary from country to country but there are exceptions based on qualified employee discounts, 'de minimus' fringe benefits, and remote location exclusions, for example. Secondly, employees or customers may decide to avoid the catered facilities, opting to provide their own snacks and meals. This option is quite prevalent in situations where food and beverage costs are viewed as too high or choice and quality of offerings perceived as poor. Thirdly are the trends associated with employment patterns. In many organizations full-time employees are being replaced with part-timers; and then there is the increasing acceptance of home-based employment or tele-commuting.

It should be quite evident that competition among contract catering firms is as intense as in most industries. As the preceding arguments attest, the driving forces within the sector, that are predominantly customer-, client- and supplier-based, result in situations in which there exists exceptional rivalry to land contracts and achieve preferred supplier status. Competition for patronage and share of stomach, however, also emanates from the plethora of commercial establishments that frequently operate within the confines of business, industry, healthcare and educational facilities. Many of these outlets are branded concepts that have won favour with customers. While many contract caterers are co-opting these brands through the formalizing of partnerships agreements, as well as inventing their own brands, the predominant activity in order to retain contracts is investment into leasehold improvements in client facilities, the modernization of eating and dining areas, and efforts to improve the preparation, presentation and merchandising of food. The opportunity for clients to substitute catering with vending machines remains, but usually this type of foodservice is provided as an adjunct.

These and other driving forces represent sequences of events, or forms of behaviour, that are having significant impact on contract catering. Managers are recognizing the need to be aware of these trends in order to track changes in products, services and markets. The critical success factors being employed to capitalize on these trends seem radically different than the usual systems-oriented, cost-driven approaches of the past. Not that these are ineffective or no longer appropriate; they are, but the focus is moving toward a more innovative set of characteristics that characterize entrepreneurs or intrapreneurs – people who can spot patterns and trends, and seize opportunities. These characteristics are:

- Ingenuity – caterers need to be in tune with their customers and clients so that they can think freely and openly, and come up with new concepts, clever approaches to merchandising. This process has been labelled 'coincidental adaptation'

- Flexibility – caterers must have the ability to change their businesses to accommodate new clients and customers

- Niche picking – caterers must have the ability to spot what customers and clients want, and then respond faster, cheaper, and better than the competitors

- New channels – caterers need to notice and exploit new locations, distribution channels, supplier, and partnership relationships.

It could be said that these new critical success factors represent a bit of a paradox. For ages contract caterers have excelled at managing the mundane. Now the fight for competitive advantage requires new skills that force companies into anticipating and planning for the future. There are dual strategies at work. Operating catering businesses and changing them are not sequential but parallel pursuits. Running a successful catering business requires a clear strategy in terms of defining target markets and lavishing attention on those quality, service, cleanliness and value factors which are critical to success. Changing a catering business in anticipation of the future requires a vision of how the future will look and a strategy for how the organization will have to adapt to meet future challenges. Unfortunately, these tasks are typically divided between operations staff and their search for excellence, and senior management and the long-term needs for change. Given how the driving forces are fundamentally changing the contract catering sector, this divide will need to be narrowed as managing for results is ultimately linked to managing for change.

Characteristics and contractual arrangements

Contract catering as a sector within the foodservice industry tends to be dominated by fewer and fewer but larger and larger firms. This phenomenon, as previously explained, is part of the move toward industry consolidation brought about by globalization and the dominance and power of brands. As a consequence barriers to entry seem insurmountable given the market positions and strengths of the incumbents (to be discussed in the next section of this chapter). Entry into the foodservice sector, however, is characterized by low start-up costs, very few institutional barriers, and a generally low level of capital intensity. It is an appealing business for those with entrepreneurial spirit and zeal, and cultural capital. In other words, in operating a foodservice business an owner can make an aesthetic statement about culinary art and the dining experience. Unfortunately, there are limited opportunities for freedom of expression in the field of contract catering. Potential clients are more interested in function than form. Scope for expression is not denied, but it is circumscribed by cost constraints.

As the major players pursue the larger more lucrative accounts, there is room for the more specialized, local and regional firms to personalize their services and to grow their businesses. Brand loyalty can be earned one client at a time, but the ability to grow and expand is severely constrained through an inability to obtain absolute cost advantages and economies of scale. The major players are also able to build greater brand awareness through advertising and marketing, supplier alliances, technological and after-sales support.

Consolidation in the sector does come with its downside. Competitors are interdependent, suggesting that the competitive actions of one company directly affect the profitability and market share of others, and pushing industry profits down. Trying to find that competitive edge is difficult and is leading companies to compete on non-price factors such as food quality, and design. But the effectiveness of this strategy is limited as it is becoming harder to differentiate the sector's offerings.

While the driving forces associated with the power of customers, clients and suppliers were discussed in the previous section, it is worth noting the role of the macro-environment, particularly on demand. The social, cultural and social dimensions have previously been mentioned, but what about the economy. A decade of uninterrupted real growth (up to the year 2001) resulted in tremendous gains in personal disposable income, consumer spending, employment, and low inflation rates. Contract catering along with other foodservice sectors reaped the benefits. With the tragic events of 11 September, 2001, the current movement into recessionary conditions, and declining consumer confidence, contract caterers are feeling the impact. The supermarket, at-home consumption, and 'brown-bagging-it' are providing lower cost alternatives. Nevertheless, eating out is often viewed as an affordable treat, and indeed a necessity on numerous occasions. The downslide is unlikely to be severe. Of course, patients in hospitals, students in school, inmates in prison, workers in remote sites may have little choice regardless of the state of the economy. It is the employment side of the equation, and the business and industry market in particular, that is most vulnerable when it comes to a downturn or upturn in the economy. Contract catering revenues are positively correlated to these movements, though they might lag a downturn depending on the market and the extent of employee layoffs.

As for the entire foodservice industry, contract catering is viewed as a mature industry sector. The effects of this are being seen as the major form of growth is through acquisition and as barriers of entry and profit margins continue to be squeezed. Nevertheless, opportunities for growth do exist in certain market segments, as will be explained in an upcoming section. As contract caterers improve their ability to manage the supply chain, adopt EFR initiatives, and effectively utilize CRM (customer relationship management), market share in the non-commercial side of the sector will be wrestled away from self-managed operations. Over time the value equation will decidedly favour the contract caterer. For these reasons, labelling the sector mature may be premature.

From a global perspective, the sector is not significantly different. The same trends and patterns of behaviour apply, though there are cultural and idiosyncratic differences. Even so the major players are establishing footholds, and in some cases dominant positions, in countries throughout the world. London-based Compass Group made its initial debut in the USA in April 1994 by buying Canteen Corporation for US$450 million. US sales for Canteen at the time totalled US$1.1 billion, and they had 1600 accounts. By the year 2000 Compass Group had expanded to become the world's largest foodservice company with annual foodservice sales in excess of £7.3 billion, and over 250 000 employees working in more than 80 countries. Sodexho, a French contract catering company, acquired Gardner Merchant Services Group in 1995, with 11 745 units worldwide. Then they acquired Marriott Management Services becoming the largest provider of food and facilities management in North America with US$4.7 billion in annual sales. For these and a few other contract catering firms the global opportunities obviously have been rewarding and further globalization of their markets is expected.

This shift to the global markets for the major firms has important implications for competition in the sector. The industry's boundaries go beyond national borders. In fact to become a preferred supplier to the world's leading firms there is no choice but to be a global player. This also means that potential competition can come from abroad. Globalization has also intensified competitive rivalry as the large companies battle for market share in country after country. This rivalry could bring down profit rates, and definitely make it more important for companies to maximize their efficiency, quality, customer responsiveness, and innovative ability. Operating conditions do vary from one country to the next. For example, in Canada (as compared to the USA) consumers do not spend as much on foodservices; catering sites are more geographically spread out; the Quebec market needs to be treated separately because of the cultural and language differences; healthcare is more likely to be publicly funded than privately funded resulting in different cost pressures; and higher rates of unionization place additional pressures on caterers.

To appreciate the true nature of contract caterers it is important to understand the contractual arrangements with clients. First of all, depending on the type of contract, there are a set of agreements and standards to be negotiated. These deal with the provision of meals, operating times, budget allotments for feeding, assigned responsibilities for cleaning, maintenance, equipment replacement, penalty clauses for non-compliance, and so on. Traditionally, there have been two styles of contracts:

- Cost plus management fee. In such an arrangement, the client or institution pays the actual cost of food, supplies, labour and other direct costs plus a management fee. These fees are typically based on a percentage of managed volume. In a cost plus management fee contract, the institution assumes all of the risk but has a higher level of control over the service.

- Profit and loss. In this style of arrangement, the managed services provider collects all revenues and/or invoices for services at a pre-determined rate per person. It covers all operating costs and retains the resulting profits. Some agreements include the payment of a commission or rent back to the client. The ability to pay commission or rent is based on having sufficient volume to cover fixed operating costs and generating sufficient funds after variable costs to earn a reasonable profit with funds left over for commission or rent. In a profit or loss contract, the operator assumes greater risk but also gains the right to upside profits.

In more recent years, contracts have become more sophisticated, reflecting the partnership-style of agreement currently in vogue. The implication is that the client and the contract caterer share risks, rewards and control. They work together – investing in facilities, attracting customers and building demand, sharing the costs, and sharing in the upside profits. Both styles of agreements have evolved to reflect this partnering approach. It should go without saying but, if these arrangements are to work, there must be a 'cultural fit'. In this environment, good business relationships result in client retention.

Key contract catering firms

There are three major worldwide players in the contract catering sector – Compass Group plc, based in the UK, Sodexho, based in France, and ARAMARK, based in the USA. Depending on the country a number of other major players or operators exist. These companies tend to focus on a specific niche sector of the market, or a geographic area. They compete based on their ability to provide more specialized and more personal service, but usually lack the depth of purchasing power and programming of the larger firms. As a consequence these firms are susceptible in two ways: as attractive take-over targets if they have coveted clients, or as a candidate for potential failure. For example, for the year 2000, the Plimsoll analysis of catering firms, revealed that one in every three catering companies was at a high risk of failure (Plimsoll, 2001). The larger firms are more immune from the vagaries and vicissitudes of the market because they have differentiated themselves through branding, unique service delivery models, proprietary programmes, and service partner alliances. Of course, there still remains a large proportion of institutional foodservices that continue to be operated by the institution. To maintain their viability in doing so, some institutions have banded together to form support groups; established purchasing organizations; brought in well-known branded concepts; created their own unique brands; been very innovative in the design of their facilities and in the merchandising of food; and have opened, but then closed, their central commissaries.

To appreciate the prowess of the major firms, a description of the three market leaders and some of their more obvious strategic initiatives follows.

The Compass Group plc

As previously stated the Compass Group has evolved into one of the world's largest foodservice companies with annual 2000 food-service revenues in excess of £7.3 billion. The company has structured itself as a core service provider whose subsidiary companies use their expertise to meet the demands of particular market segments. Eurest services the needs of business and industry, and manages a wide variety of locations from multisite contracts to private dining facilities, as well specialized services for offshore and remote sites and the armed services. Chartwells provides specialized services for students of all ages. It has developed a number of branded concepts to take advantage of the 'Food Courts' frequently found in post-secondary institutions.

Select Service Partner is the largest operator of airport restaurants in Europe. Bateman was created to meet the special needs of an increasingly sophisticated healthcare management industry. The company provides food and hotel services to hospitals and nursing homes. Canteen Vending Services, as its name suggests, provides branded concept foods and healthy alternative fare through an innovative information labelling system. The Compass Group in North America (a US$4 billion subsidiary) operates with the same brands and, in addition, serves concessions and retail through Restaurant Associates and Patina, and Canteen is involved in the corrections market.

The Compass Group is an aggressive, growth-oriented company that has obtained its market leadership through acquisitions and organic growth opportunities in all major markets. A notable feature of this company is its adoption and implementation of a Balanced Scorecard system. Their 'future in practice' is pursued and measured in five core areas: customer and client satisfaction, market leadership, preferred employer, operational excellence, and finally financial performance.

Sodexho Alliance SA

While Sodexho, founded in 1966, is based in France, for comparative purposes, it reported sales of approximately £10.5 billion in 2000. It employs 305 000 people at 22 000 sites in 70 countries. Sodexho Marriott was created in 1998 from the merger of the North American operations of Sodexho Alliance and Marriott Management Services. In 2001 it changed its name to Sodexho, Inc. and is now North America's leading provider of food and management services with annual sales of US$4.7 billion, 111 000 employees at 5000 locations in the USA and Canada.

Among Sodexho's claims to fame is its strong commitment to achieving ISO accreditation throughout the world. It ensures provision of quality services through deployment of customer research programmes such as 'Conviv Styles'. In the business and industry segment it has pioneered 'Relais Gourmand' mobile stands, an Integrated Services Management Information System, and Prestige Sodexho (for important business dining and meeting events).

In the healthcare market it has implemented similar programmes and in the UK has even become an equity partner in three Private Finance Initiative (PFI) hospital projects. For the seniors market Sodexho undertook a major international research project to profile senior citizens, and is active in organizing special events for seniors. Sodexho's involvement in the education market has resulted in other research projects leading to the development of special programmes for students at all levels. Their most notable programme is CrossRoads Cuisines, which has become a benchmark brand. This brand, while extended to school lunch programmes and hospitals, was first introduced in their corporate food services.

Involvement in the corrections market began in France in 1987 with its division SIGES, and this has evolved into multiservice and integrated prison management packages that comprise designing, building and financing. Their division Universal Sodexho provides services to remote sites throughout the world.

ARAMARK

As a privately held company, which recently had an IPO, its reported sales amounted to US$7.8 million with net income of $176.5 million in their fiscal year ended 2001. ARAMARK is a leading international provider of a broad range of outsourced services to business, educational, healthcare and governmental institutions and sports, entertainment and recreational facilities.

Sectoral markets

The non-commercial or institutional foodservice markets with whom catering firms conduct business are described here and key trends and opportunities for contract catering firms are noted.

Healthcare

This category covers institutions that operate in the following categories: hospitals, nursing homes, public and charitable homes for the aged, retirement facilities, homes for the mentally and/or physically challenged, orphanages, and hospices. Foodservices are offered to patients/residents, employees and staff, and visitors and/or the general public. Inroads into the healthcare market by contract caterers have been difficult at times because, in many facilities, particularly those associated with acute care, there is concern that their primary mission or focus on wellness and the recovery of patients could be compromised if foodservice was outsourced. The issue is one of client control over all elements of the healing process. This concern is not as prevalent in long-term care, though nutrition, quality of care and the nurturing of patients are of utmost concern. The debate as to what constitutes core and non-core activities rages on in this market, but the outcome really depends on the philosophies of individual institutions.

Issues of utmost concern in this market are the control of costs, especially labour costs, the application of technology in the preparation and delivery of food, and numerous issues regarding nutrition and the safety of food. To ensure entry into healthcare most contract caterers have established specialized healthcare units that understand the special needs and requirements of clients and customers. The most successful relationships are based on a sharing of values and common objectives, and a partnership whereby the caterer becomes part of the healthcare team. There continue to be great market penetration opportunities for contract caterers.

Business and industry

Foodservice is offered in a wide variety of work places. These include industrial plants, private and public sector (government) offices, research facilities, remote sites such as lumber camps, oil rigs and other mining or resource extraction sites. Line and staff employees, management personnel and visitors are typical customers. In most countries this sector is the most lucrative and sought after and, as was revealed in a previous section of this chapter, accounts for the highest proportion of contract catering revenues and market share. Globalization has spurred international growth and encouraged contract caterers to provide a broader set of non-food service activities that yield higher revenues and margins.

Foodservice volume at plants and factories is driven by employment patterns over time. Meals tend to be heavier and high caloric; average expenditures on a transaction basis tend to be lower. In some unionized plants it has been reported that unions have attempted to provide their own foodservice in order to raise money, thereby creating a challenge for the incumbent catering firm. Remote sites are a major challenge for caterers because of the need for specialized distribution logistics. Meal times are very important in these settings. Breakfasts are very hearty; workers load up their lunch buckets if they have to be out in the field; and the evening meals are traditional high quality offerings. The cost per meal day can be US$25.

In the business dining sector, many businesses have removed their foodservice subsidies, and contract caterers may be in competition with commercially operated branded concepts. This is quite prevalent in North America, particularly for coffee and light snack service. Average transaction expenditures are higher, and menus tend to offer more diverse variety to reflect broader acceptance of ethnic foods. Overall, contract catering firms have sewn up this business and industry market, and there are few significantly large accounts being self-managed.

Education

Foodservice is provided in universities, colleges, private and public schools at all levels. This market consists of students, faculty staff, visitors and the general public. At the elementary and secondary levels in North America, for example, menus and the provision of food are often governed by mandated lunch programmes. The school lunch programmes in the USA specify nutritional requirements. In other jurisdictions, in which the mandates may be loose, contractors are starting to mimic the commercial sector. There is a tendency to offer burger/fries/soft drink combos, and breakfast style sandwiches. The idea is to bundle food and beverage items to build revenues, and the number of transactions, if possible.

College and university accounts represent the cream in this market. Some remain self-catered, but many of the contract catering firms have made significant inroads into this segment by being creative, introducing branded foodservice concepts, and being cost-conscious. Branded concepts and marketplace concepts have become popular.

Corrections

Jails and work camps provide a captive market of inmates, plus a cadre of correctional officers and staff. This is a difficult market to understand, and it is self-catered in most countries. Interestingly, in some areas, management of these facilities is being privatized. These firms either operate foodservices themselves or enter into a strategic alliance with a caterer. ARAMARK in the USA is starting to penetrate the market. Correctional foodservice is cost sensitive and cost per diem is kept low. Obviously an understanding of the operating environment is critical as service offerings should not impinge on the provision and maintenance of security.

Transportation

Foodservice is provided for airlines, railways, ships, ferries, cruise lines, and in their respective terminals. Given the current economic and terrorist events, the transportation industry, and those contract catering firms serving it, have been decimated by the cutbacks in travel, the increased emphasis on safety and security, and the elimination of frills and amenities that add to travel costs. These are challenging times. The firms that operate flight kitchens have been hit hard, though it is important to mention that during the past few years tremendous strides have been made to re-engineer these facilities in such ways as to improve productivity, enhance the distribution processes, and to upgrade the quality and presentation of food.

The military

Military personnel, contractors and guests, whether at bases or in the field, require foodservice support. Throughout the world there has been some willingness to outsource foodservices on static sites or bases that are not core to their missions. The military, however, are aware that they need to be constantly prepared for field operations. Cooks must know how to prepare and serve under the most severe of conditions. Moreover, there is a desire to preserve military jobs, so there may be reluctance for a base commander to give up or share control of this function.

Operational trends and key issues

Throughout this chapter, reference to a number of operational trends has been made. These trends and issues, along with others, are critical to the success of companies operating in the aforementioned contract catering markets and are discussed in this section.

Conversion and consolidation

In certain markets such as healthcare, the majority of institutions continue to operate their own foodservices. Public sector funding pressure and private sector profit pressure is necessitating the delivery of low cost services. This bodes well for managed service providers whose purchasing power and proprietary systems and procedures minimize costs. These companies are looking to convert more 'self-ops' to the outsourced management service they provide. Due to the low margins associated with managed services, however, volume is the key to maximization of profits. Many regional and one-country operators have been purchased by the three large world players in recent years. This trend is expected to continue.

Branding

Brands and the ability to build brand equity have been a strategic thrust in the commercial market for decades. Branding is now finding its way into the contract catering business. The intent is to find ways to differentiate product and service offerings, to raise average spending, and to respond to dining preferences that customers have 'learned' and been introduced to through restaurant chains. Contract caterers utilize a blend of proprietary in-house brands and popular franchise brands to provide balance to the branding trend and the additional costs that come with the operation of a franchise. High volume is required to justify brands, even though caterers are finding creative ways to introduce brands into smaller locations. It should be pointed out that accepted brands ensure the availability of consumer choice, thereby holding a potential clientele as well as attracting new traffic.

Line extension

As has already been identified, the major contract caterers are on the verge of becoming managed service providers and have focused on providing an expanding range of services that clients utilize and may be requesting. This practice yields a variety of benefits including the ability to drive higher margin revenues without obtaining new accounts; the ability to create a more sustainable relationship with clients; and the ability to consolidate client support services over a variety of services, thereby delivering greater value. Becoming a managed service provider requires organizational and cultural changes and a broader set of managerial competencies. There is a learning curve to be mastered; plus there is the possibility of losing focus and/or the ability to excel in the core foodservice activities that initially created the contractual relationship.

Account retention

It is always cheaper to retain an existing client relationship than to build new ones. While developing prospects and building a new client base is a constant and on-going activity, contractors are discovering that they must enhance their competencies in managing existing relationships. Use of customer relationship management (CRM) and other team building strategies is becoming quite common.

Food safety

While the foodservice sector has made significant strides in improving the safety of the food chain, this issue remains front and centre throughout the sector, and is on the minds of both clients and customers. One incident of illness or death due to food-borne contamination is one too many, as a few commercial operators have learned. It destroys demand, profitability, and the most important assets of all – brand and reputation. Contract caterers have gone to great lengths to implement HACCP programmes and other safety initiatives. ISO certification is becoming increasingly important, especially in Europe.

Labour shortages

Despite the growth in the use of technology, foodservice remains labour-intensive. As people have become more educated, affluent, and older, the availability of relatively low-paid personnel for this sector has steadily eroded. The availability of skilled food preparation and management personnel is an even greater challenge. On-the-job training is being taken more seriously; educational institutions are attempting to fill the void; and operators are asking food and food equipment manufacturers to come up with foodservice 'system solutions' rather than just products. Despite these efforts the labour shortage issue is not likely to go away in the foreseeable future. In fact, it will likely become the single most important driving force in terms of increasing the cost of food consumed away from home. It is for this reason that improvements to supply chain management and efficient foodservice response initiatives (EFR) are of critical importance.

Technology

Technological improvements in foodservice are having a positive impact on food service and quality, and have brought some labour savings. In the front-of-the-house there have been improvements in software systems for processing orders and settling transactions. In the back-of-the-house, advances have focused on food preparation and cooking equipment designed to minimize work steps, ensure consistency and promote greater food safety. In the healthcare area, for example, food manufacturers have developed ready to eat/ready to serve meal components in frozen, sous-vide, chilled and shelf-stable formats. A range of popular, speciality diet and texture modifications are available. Computer-driven tray carts have been developed that hold meals in a chilled state until needed. They automatically re-thermalize hot items to eating temperatures at predetermined times, while keeping cold foods cold. If sufficient space is available, re-thermalization can take place in hospital wards. Soiled trays, dishes and utensils are returned to the kitchen in the carts for washing. A wide variety of disposable dishes and liners have been developed to minimize the amount of dishes that require handling and washing.

Key indicators

The institutional foodservice sector has evolved a variety of indicators to measure productivity and performance. The following sample of indicators reveals the link to key success factors in each sector:

Sectors	Key success factor	Key indicator
Healthcare patient/resident	Cost containment	Total managed volume
Correctional	Value	Cost per meal or meal day
Residential education	Management fees or profit	
On-board transportation		
Healthcare staff and visitor	Maximization of capture	Total revenues
Education 'cash' service	Maximization of revenue	Participation rate
Business dining		Average daily sales per capita
Transportation terminal		Profit

The struggle to balance payroll costs and labour shortages with higher revenues in the institutional foodservice sector is still a 'work in progress'. In the USA, a productivity report is prepared based on specific staff counts, payroll and transaction data across all segments. The resulting measures are the average transaction yield for each dollar spent on payroll, and transaction per man-hour.

In concluding this section it must be noted that the well-being of the contract catering sector ultimately revolves around customers. There is a growing demand for healthier eating options, a growing demand for authentic foods, and a growing environmental awareness. Contract caterers that excel at meeting customer and client expectations and implement environmentally sustainable and cost efficient operating practices will continue to prosper and grow.

Conclusion

The business of managing contract foodservice requires astute management. Corporately the challenge is coping with the pressures from clients to become a managed service provider. Should the corporate mandate and competitive strategies be extended, or should foodservice remain the core business? At the business level there exists tremendous pressures to become a low cost provider. Can this be accomplished when there are equally compelling reasons to differentiate services, particularly to market segments with specialized requirements? This is particularly evident at the unit level where there are continuous pressures to alter menus, meal programmes, pricing, and eating environments to correspond with individual client and customer needs.

As stated at the outset of the chapter contract foodservice is far from being a mundane, routine business. In the past few decades it has become the most sophisticated and demanding segment of the foodservice sector. And, as the market continues to mature and competition intensifies, more consolidation is likely to occur. While the major players will extend their global reach, there will remain tremendous opportunities for regional niche players to emerge and flourish. In all cases, however, the true test of corporate longevity and viability will be the ability to deliver memorable meal occasions with consistently high quality food produced in more efficient (lower-cost) ways.

Summary

- Contract foodservice is a non-commercial or institutional segment of the foodservice sector.

- The major markets served are healthcare, business and industry, education, military, corrections, and transportation.

- This sector is dominated by a few large, sophisticated global firms, though there are many smaller, specialized, niche players.

- International clients are showing a preference to contract with global 'managed service providers' who offer a range of value-added services.

- The size of the sector for the year 2000 has been estimated at £200 billion or US$290 billion.

- Average annual real growth rate is in the 2–3% range. This reflects growth in the number of outlets, meal occasions, and average snack or meal expenditures.

- People's lifestyle characteristics are driving foodservice patronage and expenditure patterns.

- As organizations continue to outsource their non-core activities, they demand proof of the ability of foodservice catering firms to create and add value to this function.

- Profit and loss contracts are becoming more popular as cost-plus contracts decline. Clients and caterers are more interested now in sharing risks, rewards and control.

- Customer relationship marketing (CRM) is becoming a tool of choice in managing relationships with clients.

- Supply chain management and use of 'efficient foodservice response systems' and 'electronic data interchange systems' have become critical components in reining in costs.

- The ability to achieve purchasing leverage is a key rationale to continuous merger and acquisition activity.

- To remain successful catering firms are becoming more innovative, flexible and adept at identifying new niche markets, foodservice programmes, services and menus.

- Major sector players differentiate themselves through branding, unique service delivery models, proprietary programmes, and service partner alliances.

Review questions

1. Why does the demand for catered foodservice continue to climb? What factors could cause demand for foodservice offered by contractors to decline?
2. What factors account for the consolidation of this sector of the foodservice sector?
3. What major changes to the contract foodservice operating environment do you predict will have occurred in 20 year's time, and why?
4. If you examine Table 3.1 you will note substantial differences in market share held by contractors from one country to the next. What do you believe may account for these differences? If you worked for one of the major global firms what strategies for increasing market share would you recommend, and why?
5. Examine the on-line annual reports of the major firms in the sector. What differences do you note in regard to their strategies and financial performance? What accounts for these differences?
6. The needs of each sectoral market differ. How would these differences be reflected in bidding documents for the different markets in order to win a foodservice contract?
7. It is difficult to manage what cannot be measured. What are the key success factors and key indicators appropriate to any given market? How could these be incorporated into a 'Balanced Scorecard' to provide a comprehensive set of performance measures for the foodservice contractor?

References

Ackerman, D. (1990) *The Natural History of the Senses*. New York, Random House.

British Hospitality Association (2001) *Contract Catering Survey 2001*, London.

Canadian Restaurant and Foodservices Association (2001) *Foodservice Facts, Market Review and Forecast*. Toronto, Canada.

Jones, P. and Kipps, M. (1995) *Flight Catering*. Longman Scientific and Technical, London.

Mennell, S. (1985) *All Manners of Food: Eating and Taste in England and France from the Middle Ages to the Present.* Basil Blackwell, Oxford.

National Restaurant Association (2001) *Restaurant Industry Food and Drink Sales Projected Through 2001.* Washington, DC.

Plimsoll (2001) *Catering.* Plimsoll Publishing Ltd, London.

Quest, M. (ed.) (2001) *UK Contract Catering Survey, 2001.* British Hospitality Association, London.

Issues

Overview

Part Two of this book is somewhat different to Part One in the sense that it contains a collection of individual chapters focusing on particular operational and strategic issues rather than chapters concentrating on the structure and characteristics pertaining to a given sector of the international hospitality industry. Having read the three chapters in Part One you will now have a sound understanding of the fundamental nature and characteristics of the *Hotels*, *Restaurants* and *Contract Foodservice* sectors. The chapters in this part of the book will enable you to extend your knowledge, understanding and critical analysis of the industry as they require you to think more extensively and deeply about a range of issues facing operators and managers in the industry.

Though each of the chapters focuses upon a specific issue, or set of issues within a particular element of international hospitality endeavour, you should not view these as being discrete and isolated. Of course there are issues that are highly specific to areas such as Diversity management, Finance or Marketing, but equally many of these issues have implications for other areas of international hospitality operations. The point here is that, although you may wish to concentrate on a specific aspect of these operations for a particular need in your studies, you should also seek to consider the relationship/s between the particular and the general. The real world does not operate within nice convenient boxes and neither should your thinking! Look for similarities, differences and inter-relationships and do not simply accept the views of the authors uncritically. This will develop your thinking beyond the mundane and enable you to stand out from the crowd. To gauge the importance of this I suggest you read Judie Gannon's chapter where the future requirements for unit general managers are articulated.

In the final chapter of the book I identify some recurrent or over-arching themes from the chapters in Part Two, in conjunction with those from Part One. However, here I will give you a flavour of the Part Two chapters to whet your appetite! In Chapter 4 Roy Wood provides a very interesting and insightful review of the current state of play in Diversity management (DM). This is a relatively new area of academic enquiry and managerial concern within hospitality and, as a consequence, little has been written on

DM within this context, especially in the international arena. As you will see Roy takes an organizational/human resource management perspective to DM and raises a number of searching questions and issues of relevance to academics and managers seeking to grapple with the conceptual and practical problems of DM.

What he does not do, and could not in the space afforded to him, is explore DM in the context of service delivery and the customer base. Apart from various publications concentrating on cross-cultural issues in relation to international operations there is, surprisingly, relatively little of substance written, at least explicitly, on this aspect of DM. I say surprisingly because the very nature of international operations embodies considerable diversity within the markets and customer base/s served by international hospitality operators. Of course we have the standardization versus customization literature and cross-cultural studies, but the issues associated with managing diversity in the markets served by companies, their customer bases and the organization–customer interface are relatively poorly served in general, and in the hospitality context in particular.

In Chapter 5 Peter O'Connor and Gabriele Piccoli provide a much-needed analysis of the current situation in Information Technology (IT) application within the international hospitality industry. They take us from the historical legacy of 'solution importation' through to the strategic importance of IT in the contemporary international hospitality organization. Identifying along the way the shift in emphasis from an internal focus on cost control and task efficiency to the relationship between IT and the entire value chain. Not only is there a great deal of food for thought in relation to the application of IT in this chapter but Peter and Gabriele also clearly indicate the pervasive and central role that IT is increasingly playing within all aspects of the hospitality business and the revolutionary effects it is having on prevailing business models and thinking.

In Chapter 6 Michael Riley makes a remarkable job of exploring the dilemmas facing hospitality managers and companies. Not only does he identify the universality of these dilemmas in general, he then proceeds to distil their essence into a framework centred on the issues of uncertainty and complexity in relation to the external environments faced by hospitality companies, the vagaries of subjective and unpredictable customer evaluations of the product/service offer, and the coordination/control problems endemic to hospitality operations, particularly those of international hotels. Through this discussion he raises many issues and questions concerning the inbuilt conflicts international hospitality managers face when trying to reconcile numerous business imperatives, both at unit and organizational levels.

In Chapter 7 Adee Athiyaman and Frank Go focus on the Strategic Choices facing international hospitality operators. As a background to this they provide an excellent summary of the current strategic landscape facing international hospitality companies and then proceed to discuss the concentration versus diversification choices facing such companies. Adee and Frank then focus on the strategic choice implications of competitor identification and analysis and relate this to the value chain and product life cycle. This is a very interesting analysis that contains some novel conceptual frameworks and highlights the influences of competitors, market entry timing and the product life cycle on a company's choice of strategic posture.

The marketing aspects of international hospitality operations are discussed by Alex Gibson in Chapter 8. Alex provides us with some very interesting and useful insights into a number of contemporary marketing issues and problems facing the international operator. In addition to covering many familiar issues, such as branding, standardization versus customization (global versus local), environmental scanning and marketing alliances, he also points to the marketing issues contingent upon the divergent developmental status and degrees of competitive intensity existing in different destination regions. Furthermore, issues emanating from relatively new forms of marketing, i.e. permission and relationship, the associated changes in distribution channel thinking and practice, and the drivers behind these, are also discussed by Alex.

A slightly different chapter to the others in this Part is Chapter 9, International Hospitality Managers, written by Judie Gannon. This is different in the sense that it is not primarily concerned with a particular functional area of international hospitality operations but the changing nature of the unit general manager's (UGM's) role and the implications of this for the type of skills and competencies needed to operate effectively in this role. Judie identifies the changing nature of the requirements for the international hospitality UGM via the journey she takes us on from the past, through the present, to the future. Along the way she cogently discusses a range of issues, that are both driving, and are contingent upon, this changing managerial landscape. Among these are issues associated with the relative importance of technical (hard) and interpersonal (soft) skills, operational competence derived from extensive prior experience versus higher order strategic and social/cultural skills, career paths and mobility, and expatriate failure. The conclusion she reaches is that the future international hospitality manager will need to be a very different type of individual than was the case in the past, or even is today!

Finally, Paul Beal's chapter on Finance is an excellent review and parsimonious summary of the key financial management issues facing the international hospitality business. This is a very accessible chapter for the non-financial mind as Paul takes us through a range of issues, such as branding, consolidation, cost control, revenue generation and asset leverage, financial reporting and transparency, the financial structures associated with different forms of ownership/operation and the future promise of information technology, in a very readable style. For those who usually baulk at reading anything associated with finance/accounting I would highly recommend Paul's chapter as this is really written for the non-financial specialist and complements many of the other chapters in this part of the book very well indeed. Many, if not all, of the issues discussed in the chapters on strategy, marketing, IT and operational dilemmas have a financial dimension. By reading Paul's chapter in conjunction with any, or all of these you will significantly increase your awareness and understanding of the bottom-line significance of the issues discussed in these chapters.

Diversity management

Roy C. Wood

Chapter objectives

When you have read this chapter, you will be able to:

- Define the concept of 'diversity management'.

- Discuss how the concept of diversity management is applied in the organizational and human resource context.

- Evaluate current debates about, and critiques of, the concept of diversity management.

- Assess the relevance of the concept of diversity for international hospitality organizations.

- Critically discuss issues relating to the future potential of the concept of diversity management.

Introduction

Since the mid-1980s there has been growing interest in the concept of diversity and, relatedly, 'diversity management'. With its origins mainly in the USA, the term 'diversity management' in an organizational context refers to a set of evolving philosophies and practices concerned with the utilization of the variety of human characteristics, orientations and dispositions in satisfaction of ethical precepts and the pursuit of business goals. Ethically, diversity management practices recognize both individual and systematic social and psychological differences between people. Thus, any individual is a unique person, with a unique psychological and social persona, but will also belong to clearly identifiable social groups by virtue of sharing characteristics with others – male/female; heterosexual/homosexual; black/white; working class/middle class and so on. In terms of business goals, a major purpose of diversity management is, through guaranteeing the dignity of people in the workplace through ethical treatment of individual and social differences, to utilize these differences to enhance organizational performance. Indeed, a central theme of the diversity management literature is that the celebration of diversity frees organizations from artificial constraints in a manner that can be built upon to yield positive bottom line results.

This chapter will explore some of the key themes in the diversity management literature as it pertains to organizations, and as a feature of human resource management practice. Attention will be paid to both the advocacy and critique of diversity management at a conceptual level, as well as applications of diversity management in the context of hospitality organizations.

Diversity: the organizational and human resource management framework

Although there is a fairly extensive literature on diversity and diversity management (among the most accessible are Bartz *et al.*, 1990; Thomas and Ely, 1996; Liff, 1997; 1999), it is Kandola and Fullerton (1998) who provide one of the enduringly significant reviews of diversity management in organizations. Although highly programmatic and prescriptive in their approach, these authors provide a fair review of the research evidence on diversity management in a human resources framework drawing on both UK and US material. A brief summary of their approach is therefore a shortcut to familiarization with the main issues.

Kandola and Fullerton (1998) begin by noting that several definitions of diversity are in circulation but all of these have three things in common, namely:

- individual differences and human diversity if managed effectively should 'add value' to the organization

- the term 'diversity' includes all ways in which people differ, even if these differences are not immediately visible

- in achieving diversity, the primary focus of attention is organizational culture and environment.

Kandola and Fullerton's (1998: 8) own definition of diversity is worth quoting:

> The basic concept of managing diversity accepts that the workforce consists of a diverse population of people. The diversity consists of visible and non-visible differences which will include factors such as sex, age, background, race, disability, personality and work style. It is founded on the premise that harnessing these differences will create a productive environment in which everybody feels valued, where their talents are being fully utilized and in which organizational goals are met.

This definition is contrasted to what the authors call 'melting pot' theories of organizational culture that emphasize the assimilation of minorities as the optimum strategy for achieving organizational harmony, and to conventional concepts of 'equal opportunities'. Diversity management, Kandola and Fullerton (1998: 9–12) argue, is much more than simple equal opportunities, differing in the following ways:

- managing diversity is not simply about discrimination, but ensuring that all individuals maximize their potential and contribution to the organization

- equal opportunities approaches tend to focus on a narrow range of groups, specifically women, ethnic minorities and disabled persons, whereas diversity approaches embrace a broad range of people

- equal opportunities is normally seen as falling within the remit of human resource management practitioners, whereas (successful) diversity management requires the concern of all individual members of an organization regardless of status

- effective diversity management differs from equal opportunity strategies in its focus on competencies, rather than group approaches which tend to rely on affirmative action approaches.

Even the most naïve reading of Kandola and Fullerton's core arguments leads one to think immediately in terms of the old 'motherhood and apple pie' cliché. Their definition of diversity is based on the explicit premise that effective diversity management places the organization and the individuals that make it up in a 'win-win' situation. Diversity management makes good business sense, but it also contributes to the general human good. It makes good business sense because, advocates of diversity management argue, of substantial demographic change. In the USA and Western Europe in particular, they argue, there are increasing numbers of women and ethnic minorities entering the workforce and there is an ageing population. If such a heterogeneous workforce is to be managed effectively, it is argued, organizations must devise flexible ways of accommodating the needs, motivations and desires of different people to the benefit of all. This is a somewhat tenuous argument to which the cynic might justifiably respond that organizations need do no such things for so long as they are in a buyer's market with regard to labour and continue to hold the upper hand in specifying terms and conditions of employment. Yet, it is these changes in demography that many commentators in this field see as being the principal source of justification for adopting diversity management practices.

It can usefully be added that the emergence of diversity management, especially in the USA, owes much to the acceptance and growing legitimacy of social pluralism in American society, a trend encouraged by various civil rights movements since the 1960s, including, for example, the black rights and gay liberation movements (Kaiser, 1998; Carr-Ruffino, 1999).

The relative novelty of the concept 'diversity management' must logically limit expectations as to the extent to which organizations have thus far adopted a diversity philosophy and associated policies. Certainly, Kandola and Fullerton (1988) present evidence from an extensive survey to suggest that diversity management is far from the apex of many organizations' agenda and, where diversity initiatives have been pursued, they have been often limited in their design and impact. They undertook a survey of 2500 organizations from 30 industrial sectors across the British Isles (i.e. including Eire) to which they had an 18% (445) response rate. Some 57% of these were private sector organizations, and 41% from the public sector. More than half (55%) of the organizations employed more than 500 people. The survey sought to identify the range and extent of diversity management practices. The five most and least frequently used initiatives are shown in Tables 4.1 and 4.2 respectively.

The generally negative evidence from Kandola and Fullerton's survey is reinforced by their scrupulously fastidious examination of the benefits of diversity management proposed by the concept's advocates. They classify these benefits under three headings: proven benefits; debatable benefits and indirect benefits. Thus they argue that proven (from research evidence) benefits include access to talent (making it easier to recruit scarce labour and reducing costs associated with excessive labour turnover and absenteeism); and enhancing organizational flexibility. Debatable benefits include those relating to teams (promoting team creativity; improving team problem solving; and ensuring more effective team decision making); customers (including enhanced customer service and increasing sales to minority groups); and improving the quality of systems, products and services. For these debatable benefits, the research evidence is at best ambivalent in respect of the application of diversity management techniques. Finally, there are indirect benefits which are those believed to be achieved when proven and debatable benefits have been attained. Once again,

Initiative	Percentage of organizations having
Formal induction process for all new recruits	91.4
Criteria for selection and advancement that are open to all	90.0
Having an equal opportunities policy	85.1
Emphasizing equal opportunities as an organizational value	76.5
Eliminating age criterion from selection decisions	74.3

Table 4.1 The top 5 most frequently conducted 'diversity management' practices in organizations uncovered by Kandola and Fullerton's 1996 survey

Initiative	Percentage of organizations having
Providing diversity training for staff	7.5
Assessing managers on diversity management as part of their appraisal	7.5
Assessing all employees on their adherence to the values	8.0
Conducting diversity training for all managers	9.6
Assessing managers on equal opportunities as part of their appraisal	10.4

Table 4.2 The top 5 least frequently conducted 'diversity management' practices in organizations uncovered by Kandola and Fullerton's 1996 survey

therefore, these are conditional in nature and more an article of faith than hard fact. Indirect benefits include satisfying work environments; improved morale and job satisfaction; improved relations between different groups of employees; greater productivity; and a better public image and greater competitiveness for the organization.

In summary, Kandola and Fullerton's advocacy of diversity management is tempered by a good deal of empirical data suggesting that, in the British Isles at least, organizations are far from incorporating diversity practices into their human resource strategies. There are a number of possible explanations as to why this might be the case.

First, though posited as an organization-wide philosophy, it is most likely that interest in diversity management will develop through the human resource function in organizations. Though human resource management (HRM) as a philosophy valorizes the idea of people as an organization's most valuable asset, research evidence is suggestive that in reality, much HRM practice is far more pragmatic and less sophisticated than this (Goldsmith *et al.*, 1997; Wood, 1997). Thus, the organizational climate is likely to be an inhibitor to the adoption of diversity management strategies. Diversity management, as with any relatively new concept, requires a champion or champions and is thus likely to be a management initiative based on some explicit expression of employment philosophy. Exhibit 1 provides just such an example, initiated by organizational leaders of the Scottish Executive (the effective government of Scotland comprising ministers, parliament and civil service).

Exhibit 1. Extract from 'Diversity in the Scottish Executive: strategy for change' Report of the Scottish Executive's Diversity Working Group – Summary

The Scottish Executive is committed to working with Scottish Ministers to improve the well-being of Scotland and its people. Within the Executive, the Equal Opportunities Unit is leading the work to ensure the Executive becomes and remains an exemplar employer in terms of its equal opportunities policies. The Equality Unit has developed an Equality Strategy with the aim of mainstreaming equality throughout the policy making process. The EOU and the EU work closely together to deliver Ministers' objectives.

The Executive's long-term objective is to value and manage diversity. The Diversity Working Group was set up to assist the Executive in drawing up a 5-year Diversity Strategy and Action Plan to provide a framework for this work. The Group included representatives from personnel, policy makers and managers within the Executive, the Trades Union side, the staff disability network, the Commission for Racial Equality, the Equal Opportunities' Commission and a private sector employer. A list of members is attached. The Strategy sets out a number of specific action points aimed at increasing the diversity of staff. The focus in the early years is on increasing at all levels in the organization, the numbers in the main under represented groups – women, people from ethnic minorities and people with disabilities.

The Scottish Executive is committed to ensuring that all staff are treated equally irrespective of their sex, marital status, age, race, ethnic origin, sexual orientation, disability or religion. Its objective is to be amongst the leaders in equal opportunities practices in Scotland. It aims to be an organization that is effective, broadly representative of the communities it serves, values the contribution of all its people and is committed to equality of opportunity.

The Report sets out the five main drivers to our diversity policy:

- It is right. All the Executive's staff are entitled to be treated with respect. Their selection and their subsequent prospects must be determined on merit.

- Policy. Ministers are committed to putting the promotion of equality at the heart of policy making and to making government work for the people of Scotland. The Executive must lead by example and demonstrate that it follows best practice. A credible equal opportunities policy is essential to 21st century government.

- Civil Service Reform. The Executive, as an employer, is committed to achieving demanding targets for the representation of women, ethnic minorities and people with disabilities.

- The law. The Executive is required by law not to discriminate on the grounds of sex, marital status, disability and race.

- The business case. In a competitive labour market discrimination or under-representation of significant groups will inhibit the Executive's ability to attract and retain available talent. The Executive needs diversity of experience and outlook to be more representative of the communities it serves and ensure more responsive policy development.

Source: www.scotland.gov.uk/publications/recent.

Secondly, and more interesting, is the extent to which the various individuals and parties that make up organizations may or may not view diversity as an issue. That something is not regarded as important is hardly conducive to the implementation of policies centring on that 'something'. More than this, there is a danger that many might see recognition of diversity and the introduction of diversity management policies as *divisive* in an apparently harmonious organization. This is an issue of the 'if it ain't broke, don't fix it' kind. The problem with such a view is, of course, that a perception that all is well may not correspond to reality, and the perceptions of people in organizations are not necessarily to be entirely trusted.

A final, and not unrelated factor that could contribute to understanding the limited extent to which diversity management has been taken up in organizations is resistance to notions of 'political correctness'. There has arguably been a backlash against the phenomenon of political correctness that acts most upon language to avoid traditional biases in usage (Dunant, 1994). The notion of diversity management might be seen as a further attempt to over-regulate language and concepts relating to relatively unproblematic issues. Indeed, this is in essence what is at the heart of those few systematic criticisms of diversity management in the public domain, to which consideration now turns.

Some criticisms of diversity management

Diversity management has attracted the usual share of 'common-sense' criticism about its tendency to political correctness and a reasonable amount of largely internal academic debate about the merits of the concept.

Mainly in the first category is Furnham (1998: 67) who asserts that in America, 'A country that once celebrated the melting pot concept, where assorted immigrants become good Americans, now encourages native-born Americans to become cultural foreigners'. He adds that 'Having spent time and money on recruitment and selection to ensure a clear, distinct, homogeneous corporate culture, the human resource people are now trumpeting diversity of heterogeneity' (Furnham, 1998: 68). Furnham (1998: 67–70) goes on to outline seven reasons why diversity training can fail. These are as follows:

- Trainers are often selected from 'outgroups', i.e. those from 'minority' backgrounds on the mistaken (in Furnham's view) assumption that their own triumph over adversity and 'victimhood' will inspire those being trained. Furnham suggests that there are cases where 'insiders' carry more authority with trainees and are better able to relate to, and overcome, their fears and prejudices.

- Often, diversity training targets specific groups perceived as especially inimical to the implementation of diversity policies, e.g. white males, thus promulgating the very types of prejudice that diversity management training is intended to overcome.

- Diversity training sometimes aspires to be 'value free' which it is not. Furnham claims that the message of tolerance of diversity and individual differences is a kind of fuzzy relativism when, at the same time, it implicitly assumes that behaviours associated with certain groups, notably Anglocentric masculine behaviours are in some way morally wrong (Furnham appears to have something of a complex about white male behaviour in this regard, a point returned to below).

- Much diversity training can be guilt-driven, focusing on real or past injustices to the extent of developing sensible policies for addressing existing and likely future problems of organizational cohesion. Guilt-driven training can serve to repress those values that diversity training seeks to eliminate, driving them 'underground' rather than obviating and eliminating them.

- Furnham (1998: 70) claims, without much supporting evidence, that training focusing mainly on cross-cultural issues (this itself suggests Furnham has only partially understood the nature of diversity management which he defines rather strangely in this context as meaning 'understanding and communicating with work colleagues') is likely to be less successful than when such issues are incorporated into 'real training courses' focusing on leadership, appraisal or team building.

- Diversity training often emphasizes deployment of 'politically correct' language that shifts attention away from organizational injustices to emphasis on relatively meaningless word games, although it is understood that language and naming problems can be important to many people at work.

- Diversity training is often predicated on unverifiable notions of what organizational futures might look like, rather than dealing with critical contemporary issues and problems in the workplace.

In some respects it is tempting to see Furnham's analysis as an antidote to the saccharin content of much of the diversity management literature. However, it seems that he is pursuing a not-so-hidden agenda. Evidence in support of many of his propositions is notable by its absence and there is a tendency to invite acceptance of his views on a 'truth by authority' basis that is unattractive. He also seems to operate with a partial definition of diversity that focuses only on multiculturalism while implying that a preoccupation of diversity management training is male, white Anglo-Saxon attitudes. Not only does this miss the point about the all-encompassing ambitions of the exponents of diversity management, a much more worrying feature of the phenomenon, but it panders to stereotypes abandoned long ago by all except those subscribing to vulgar feminist theories of male oppression.

In the second category, as Maxwell, McDougall and Blair (2000) note, there are a number of debates and tensions between scholars of diversity management. These centre on the differences, if any, between equal opportunities and diversity management approaches, subsuming concerns about the appropriate role in organizations of the shared collective needs of groups as opposed to individuals and the means by which any 'bottom line' benefits of diversity management might be measured. According to Maxwell *et al.* (2000) some such writers believe these differences to be minimal; others that the approaches are interdependent; and yet others who see equal opportunities approaches as points on a scale towards the achievement of equality in organizations. In their review, Maxwell *et al.* (2000) point to the source of these tensions as arguments over the extent to which equal opportunities approaches in organizations are driven by external forces such as the need for legislative compliance and more generalized concerns for social justice. In contrast, advocates of diversity management approaches have as their fulcrum the desire to maximize individual human potential in pursuit of a better bottom line. In fact this latter goal is nearly always subordinate in the advocacy of diversity management approaches, giving the appearance more of a persuasive tool for suspicious non-believers than a prime directive.

One of the most persuasive exponents of a 'compromise' position between equal opportunities and diversity management approaches is Liff (1999). She notes that whatever perspective is taken on the equal opportunities/managing diversity relationship, there exists a danger of underestimating the wider significance of the latter term in the extent to which it reminds us that employees are not a homogeneous group. At the risk of overly crude simplification of Liff's analysis, the point at issue between equal opportunities/managing diversity approaches centres on how to re-inject the individual into predominantly social (i.e. group oriented) analysis of workplace relations. Even Liff, however, cannot resist rather casual rejection of the grander claims of managing diversity approaches in organizations, arguing that if managing diversity is understood as merely one equality strategy among many, then this:

> ... highlights the need to rethink structures, cultures and policies so that they are more compatible with the characteristics and needs of different employees and contrasts with the maintenance of a form of organization which benefits the dominant group but has some add-on procedures designed to help out-groups to fit in. As such, it means that equality strategies cannot rely simply on procedural change ... but must also engage in cultural change (Liff, 1999: 67).

Liff seemingly endorses the view that diversity management is an extension of equal opportunities approaches but, in so doing, identifies a key weakness of the former as process based. Managing diversity approaches in organizations are, in this view, important because they serve to remind managers of the limitations of process approaches, namely to treat the workforce as homogeneous. Liff's analysis has other important aspects, especially when placed against those critics of diversity management like Furnham (1998) considered earlier. If, at the risk of caricature, we look upon Furnham's views as emanating from an essentially conservative or rightist viewpoint, then Liff, rather more forensically perhaps, focuses on the liberal intellectual dilemma of how to integrate acceptance of individual human difference(s) and variation(s) into accounts of evidently social (i.e. group based) phenomena (in this case in terms of (in)equalities of opportunity and outcome in the workplace).

Liff (1999, see also 1997) tackles this issue with great vigour. She uses the term 'dissolving differences' to describe an organizational ideal type whereby some individual differences, for example in personality and tastes, are as important or more important than social group based differences, for example, gender and ethnicity. In contrast, the 'valuing differences' approach represents more the equal opportunities position in that it focuses on social group membership as a basis of tackling inequality. In the end, Liff cannot help but come down broadly in favour of the latter, viewing managing diversity approaches as untried. She marshals some interesting (if limited) evidence in support of this position, suggesting that the 'valuing differences' approach is grounded in reality, i.e. in what organizations are actually doing.

Liff's idea that some individual differences in taste and personality highlights the iterative problem with definitions of diversity, i.e. at what point do we stop recognizing difference as diversity? Unfortunately, she and other writers do little to address these questions and Liff's ultimate position is as disappointing as Furnham's, though for different reasons. Both writers arguably offer some reflection on the extent to which individuals and individual differences have been 'written out' of sociological analysis, Furnham proffering a relatively unsophisticated view of the balance between such differences and social group membership. One problem for Liff's analysis and position is, of course, that traditional equal opportunities to some degree rely on the visibility of disadvantaged groups, visibility in two senses, namely:

(a) definable group characteristics (gender, age, ethnicity); and
(b) definable disadvantage as established by evidence.

Thus, we know from research that women and ethnic minorities are disadvantaged in the workforce in terms of career, pay, promotion and other factors. But what, for example, of gays and lesbians in the workforce? Gays and lesbians are not always visible, indeed adopting invisibility as a strategy is one way in which homosexuals cope with organizational life and avoid the disapprobation of those who possess animus against homosexuals. An individual preference for discretion might be built on top of this, even in an organization with explicit equal opportunities policies for gay and lesbian employees (e.g. pension and other rights for partners equal in status to those for married heterosexual partners). However, there may be a reluctance to take up such benefits because of an individual's personal predisposition against disclosure of their sexual orientation. One might argue that equal opportunities focus primarily on protection, encouragement and development, whereas a managing diversity approach in organizations entails a root and branch removal of barriers based on a generic benchmarking of individual 'rights' to equality in society.

It would be easy to dismiss the tension between equal opportunities and diversity management approaches as typical of academic self-indulgence. The objectives of equal opportunities and diversity management approaches do not seem so widely different. Yet it is a debate that in many ways strikes at the very heart of the philosophy of social science, concerned as it is with the treatment and, by implication, the relative status and importance of individuals and groups. In this sense, if we accept that the objectives of diversity management are intrinsically laudable, we have to reach, and deal with, individuals who must expose themselves to possible social disapprobation if we are to be successful in implementing diversity management. This in turn makes us consider whether diversity management *is* intrinsically good and it throws us back on questions of ideology. At a more practical level, it is hardly surprising that equal opportunities approaches find favour among those of a socially liberal outlook. Persuading governments to initiate and endorse social change lends authority, however spurious, to such change. Government can always be invoked (or blamed!) for the need for organizations to achieve compliance with new procedures. This might be a slower and higher risk process in the equality arena, but it is one that at least rests on the consensual authority that government is presumed to command.

Diversity management in hospitality services

Relatively little has been written on diversity management in the hospitality industry, especially the international hospitality industry. As this is a book about the international hospitality industry, the inclusion of the present chapter may seem a little bizarre. However, there are a number of legitimate responses. First, while there is limited primary research of consequence in the public domain relating directly to diversity management there is, quantitatively, a growing academic literature on the importance of 'culture' in international hospitality operations. In addition to academic studies, there are semi-regular journalistic forays into equal opportunities issues in hospitality. In the UK this has tended to be in response to government initiatives, most recently the phased introduction of the UK Disability Discrimination Act 1996 (e.g. Hashml, 1999) or to broader equal opportunity questions, e.g. relating to racism (see Clark, 2000).

Secondly, there is a genuine conceptual conundrum to be addressed. By definition, to talk of a diverse workforce is to talk of a diverse population. Internationalism, or globalism is thus implicit to any mention of 'diversity'. One can no more talk of the international dimensions of diversity than one can talk of 'tough love'; to do so is to cultivate an oxymoron. This observation dovetails neatly with another concerning the 'culture' literature alluded to above. In the context of the international hospitality industry this research has mainly focused on such 'problems' as:

● cross-cultural awareness (e.g. Mallinson and Weiler, 2000)

● cultural understanding and misunderstanding between various ethnic groups in defined workforces (e.g. Gilbert and Tsao, 2000)

- managing relationships between corporate and national cultures (e.g. Mwaura, Sutton and Roberts, 1998)

- the difficulties faced by expatriate managers in the hospitality industry (e.g. Feng and Pearson, 1999).

Many writers on diversity management, including as we saw above, Liff (1999), see organizational culture change on a large scale as a necessary element for the success of diversity management. The term 'culture' here is used in an internal and external sense. In the research noted above, worthy though it is, culture tends to be perceived in terms of a narrower concern with the impacts of external host culture influences on the internal (usually Western) culture of the international hotel or hospitality organization. There is some irony here as the international hotel, or its non-indigenous staff, is in reality the external culture operating in the internal culture of the society in which it is based. What we see with this research is a perfect example of Taylor and Edgar's (1999) 'managerial problematic' at work, with research defined in terms of a 'tyranny of relevance' (in this case for managerial problem solving) instead of for its intrinsic value. In this case, 'culture' is normally a metaphor for perceived, potential or actual conflict between sets of values – and there are no prizes for guessing that in the majority of cases, these values are Western ones.

Concluding remarks

To simplify the above, we can say two things. First, we can follow the pessimistic lead of Maxwell *et al.* (2000) who are sceptical about the human resource track record of the UK hospitality industry and its likely commitment to diversity in employment practice. They are right to be pessimistic in the light of the consensus of research literature (Wood, 1997; Lucas and Wood, 2000). To say that there is some doubt as to whether in the UK hospitality industry, employment practices can at the present time support 'diversity management', is to court accusations of understatement. This pessimism can be carried over into consideration of the international research on 'culture' in hospitality organizations. A preoccupation with 'managing' cultural differences according to whatever agenda does not suggest potential for embracing diversity management.

Secondly, it is easy to be blinded by the worthiness of the concept of diversity management to the extent that we grant a concrete status to something that is in effect so ill defined, nebulous and confused that sensible discussion of its potential is practically impossible. As we have seen, highly programmatic approaches to defining diversity management simply throw up more and more iterative challenges to such definitions. While for some social scientists it is unfashionable to advocate positivistic research approaches based on precise definitions of concepts and their elaboration through the application of theory, hypotheses and rigorous investigation, diversity management as a concept, because of its tenuous qualities, might usefully benefit from being subject to these processes. Conceptually, diversity management is atheoretical, its epistemological status defined only in relation to an ideology of 'goodness' and in opposition to, or as a development of, equal opportunities. Until some effort is made to circumscribe what it is we talk about when we talk of diversity management, the relatively sterile debates reviewed in this chapter are likely to continue.

Summary

- Diversity management is a relatively recent concept that embraces the idea that forms of individual difference should be celebrated as a resource on which organizations can draw to improve 'bottom line' performance.

- Diversity management is conceived as differing from equal opportunities approaches in organizations by its emphasis on the full range of human diversity and a focus on individuals rather than 'out groups'.

- Empirical research suggests that the concept of 'diversity management' has yet to catch on to the extent of being an integral part of organizational human resource management philosophies and policies.

- There is considerable academic debate about the relative merits of equal opportunities and managing diversity approaches centring on the idealistic nature of the latter and its attainability in the 'real world' of organizations.

- There are also unresolved ideological and epistemological issues attendant on the concept of diversity management. These relate in particular to the exact role of individual differences in human diversity and the extent to which these may influence useful working definitions of the concept.

- In the international hospitality context, comparatively little research has been undertaken into diversity management. Instead, there is a considerable output on 'cultural' issues in international management that tends to place emphasis on controlling factors to overcome cultural 'problems' rather than capitalizing on the diversity represented by such situations to evolve alternative modes of managerial strategy.

- The concept of diversity management has a doubtful future unless it can be better clarified in the context of appropriate theoretical and investigative structures.

Review questions

1. How are diversity management approaches in human resource management meant to differ from assimilation and equal opportunities approaches?
2. Is the concept of diversity management too idealistic to be widely accepted and implemented in organizations?
3. What are the implications of the statement 'Fat people are an oppressed minority' for defining the possible range of individual characteristics that constitute 'diversity'?
4. How might the impact of diversity measurement on organizational performance be measured?
5. Why might the implementation of diversity management in organizations be viewed by some social groups as threatening rather than liberating?
6. If the concept of diversity management simply reminds us that the workforce is not homogeneous, is such a concept of any real value?
7. Do 'cultural' approaches to international hospitality management focus on attempting to reconcile rather than embrace cultural differences?
8. Can diversity be managed?

References

Bartz, D. E., Hillman, L. W., Lehrer, S. and Mayhugh, G. M. (1990) A model for managing workforce diversity, *Management Education and Development*, **21**, (5), 321–326.

Carr-Ruffino, N. (1999) *Diversity Success Strategies*. Butterworth-Heinemann, Woburn, MA.

Clark, S. (2000) Race – the final frontier, *Caterer and Hotelkeeper*, 5 October, pp. 26–28.

Dunant, S. (ed.) (1994) *The War of the Words: the Political Correctness Debate*, Virago, London.

Feng, F. and Pearson, T. E. (1999) Hotel expatriate managers in China: selection criteria, important skills and knowledge, repatriation concerns and causes of failure, *International Journal of Hospitality Management*, **18**, (3), 309–321.

Furnham, A. (1998) *The Psychology of Managerial Incompetence: A Sceptic's Dictionary of Modern Organizational Issues*. Whurr Publishers Ltd, London.

Gilbert, D. and Tsao, J. (2000) Exploring Chinese cultural influences and hospitality marketing relationships, *International Journal of Contemporary Hospitality Management*, **12**, (1), 45–53.

Goldsmith, A. L., Nickson, D. P., Sloan, D. H. and Wood, R. C. (1997) *Human Resource Management for Hospitality Services*. International Thomson Business Press, London.

Hashml, A. (1999) The access powers, *Caterer and Hotelkeeper*, 15 July, pp. 29–30.

Kaiser, C. (1998) *The Gay Metropolis 1940–1960*. Weidenfeld and Nicolson, London.

Kandola, R. and Fullerton, J. (1998) *Diversity in Action: Managing the Mosaic*, 2nd ed. Institute of Personnel and Development, London.

Liff, S. (1997) Two routes to managing diversity: individual differences or social group characteristics, *Employee Relations*, **19**, (1), 11–26.

Liff, S. (1999) Diversity and equal opportunities: room for a constructive compromise? *Human Resource Management Journal*, **9**, (1), 65–75.

Lucas, R. E. and Wood, R. C. (2000) Work and employment practices. In Brotherton, B. (ed.) *An Introduction to the UK Hospitality Industry*. Butterworth-Heinemann, Oxford pp. 93–120.

Mallinson, H. and Weiler, B. (2000) Cross-cultural awareness of hospitality staff: an evaluation of a pilot training program, *Australian Journal of Hospitality Management*, **7**, (1), 35–44.

Maxwell, G., McDougall, M. and Blair, S. (2000) Managing diversity in the hotel sector: the emergence of a service quality opportunity, *Managing Service Quality*, **10**, (6), 367–373.

Mwaura, G., Sutton, J. and Roberts, D. (1998) Corporate and national culture – an irreconcilable dilemma for the hospitality manager, *International Journal of Hospitality Management*, **10**, (6), 212–220.

Taylor, S. and Edgar, D. (1999) Lacuna or lost cause? Some reflections on hospitality management research. In Brotherton, B. (ed.) *The Handbook of Contemporary Hospitality Management Research*, John Wiley, Chichester, pp. 19–38.

Thomas, D. A. and Ely, R. J. (1996) Making differences matter: a new paradigm for managing diversity, *Harvard Business Review*, **74**, (5), 79–90.

Wood, R. C. (1997) *Working in Hotels and Catering*, 2nd ed. Thomson Learning, London.

Further reading

Two essential texts, both cited in this chapter, the first important for a US perspective, the second a UK view, are as follows:

Carr-Ruffino, N. (1999) *Diversity Success Strategies*. Butterworth-Heinemann, Woburn, MA.

Kandola, R. and Fullerton, J. (1998) *Diversity in Action: Managing the Mosaic*, 2nd ed. Institute of Personnel and Development, London.

For economy and clarity the following review of diversity management is indispensable:

Maxwell, G., McDougall, M. and Blair, S. (2000) Managing diversity in the hotel sector: the emergence of a service quality opportunity, *Managing Service Quality*, **10**, (6), 367–373.

The impact of information technology

Peter O'Connor and Gabriele Piccoli

Chapter objectives

When you have read this chapter you will be able to:

- Identify the effects of developments in information technology on hospitality management and operations.

- Analyse current key issues associated with information technology and explore their implications for the hospitality industry.

- Evaluate key challenges limiting the use of technology within the international hospitality sector.

Introduction

The use of information technology in the hospitality industry has grown tremendously over the past 20 years. This journey has not always been smooth, but it has become clear that information technology is now a critical competitive weapon in the industry. This chapter examines how the use of information technology in hospitality has developed, highlights the current role that information technology plays within international hospitality companies, and examines current trends and issues while also attempting to speculate on the role that this technology will play in the industry in the early part of the 21st century.

Information technology in hospitality

Information technology was first used in the hospitality industry in the 1950s, when multinational hotel chains began experimenting with the developing field of computer science. As in most other industries, the majority of the initial applications focused on accounting and automating repetitive and time-consuming tasks. Software was 'borrowed' from other industries on the assumption that it could be 'easily' adapted for use by hospitality companies. However, such conversions were usually only partially successful, and a large number of changes to business processes and procedures were often needed to accommodate the requirements of the computerized system. Moreover, the expense and technicality involved in both developing and running systems made the use of computerization economical only for the largest companies (O'Connor, 1999).

Despite these problems, the hospitality industry at large has pioneered many information system innovations. Airline reservation systems, for example, were completing electronic commerce transactions long before the commercialization of the Internet and the dot-com bubble of the late nineties. In the early 1970s, the Hotel St Jacque in Paris introduced software that automated reservations, check-in, guest billing and various aspects of management control. Punched cards were issued to guests, allowing charges to be instantly posted directly onto their 'electronic' bill. Also the telephones and mini-bars in each room were linked to the system, automatically posting charges directly onto the relevant guest folio.

While the improved control introduced by computerized systems justified implementations from a cost perspective, computer systems were still perceived as being overly technical and difficult to use. This was due in part to the manner in which the systems were created – by accountants working in conjunction with the developers – and to the fact that they had to be ultimately used by front-line employees. Overly focused on the control of operations, and lacking usability, early systems were resented by end-users generally not involved in the design and development activities. In addition, the fragmentation of the software industry also compounded the problem introducing incompatible systems that could not be easily integrated. These factors combined to make the use of IT with the hospitality industry complex, expensive, and frustrating. Systems were seen as being badly designed, overly technical and inflexible and rather than simplifying hospitality operations and management, they were perceived to make life more difficult. Considerable resistance to the use of technology built up as a result and was reinforced by the conservative nature of the industry, its widespread fragmentation, the absence of dominant vendors and by a lack of IT understanding on the part of many managers (Whitaker, 1987).

Despite such early difficulties, falling hardware prices, the development of the personal computer and graphic user interfaces, and the explosive growth of the Internet have made computerized systems practically ubiquitous throughout all sectors of the industry today. Moreover, as computers have become progressively easier to use and embedded in society, problems stemming from usability have been partially subdued even though the typical hospitality computing environment can be quite complex (see Figure 5.1).

Over time, individual systems have developed to act as the information hubs of the hospitality organization. Within restaurants and food service, the EPOS (electronic point of sales system) performs this role, while within hotels and cruise ships, it is the property management system (PMS) that has developed into the key application. Better integration means that such systems now perform a key coordination and control function, acting as the central system around which all the others revolve and interact.

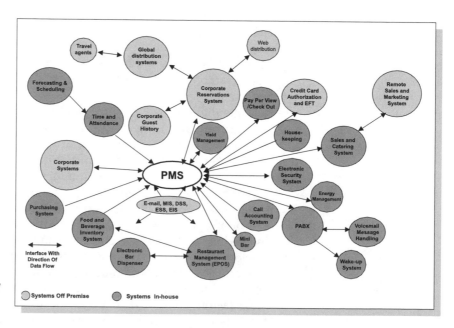

Figure 5.1 Hospitality computer systems

Future outlook: reaching outside the hospitality organization

Much promise lies in approaching IT holistically, both internally and reaching outside the organization. For hospitality companies, this changing focus calls for a shift from internal control towards a more 'strategic' approach to information systems design and utilization, by reaching externally both forwards and backwards in their value chain to communicate better with customers through electronic distribution, and with suppliers though e-procurement and supply chain management.

Distribution

Go and Pine (1995: 307) define a channel of distribution as one that provides 'sufficient information to the right people at the right time and in the right place to allow a purchase decision to be made, and provides a mechanism where the consumer can purchase the required product'. Effective distribution is especially important in the airline, hotel and cruise sectors, as such products are extremely perishable. Revenue from an unsold room or cabin is lost forever, and thus selling each product at an optimum price is critical. Both hotels and cruise companies have traditionally used a variety of distribution channels to help maximize sales (see Table 5.1). However, channels involving intermediaries are relatively expensive, and increasing emphasis is being placed on using electronic channels, as they have the potential to reduce costs without sacrificing geographical or market reach.

Composition of advanced reservations	1995	1996	1997	1998	1999
Direct inquiry	38.3	36.9	35.1	34.0	33.5
Own reservations system	18.9	14.5	14.0	14.7	14.2
Independent reservations system	6.0	5.2	5.3	4.3	5.1
Travel agents	15.7	18.1	19.8	20.7	20.4
Tour operator	12.7	16.5	18.1	16.4	15.9
Hotel representatives	8.4 (other)	5.7	4.3	6.5	5.9
Transportation company		2.3	2.0	1.6	2.2
Web site/Internet		0.8	1.4	1.8	2.8

Source: compiled by the authors from Horwath & Horwath Consulting (1996, 1997, 1998, 1999, 2000).

Table 5.1 Composition of advanced reservations

Electronic distribution systems have many advantages over their traditional, labour intensive, counterparts. They have few capacity limitations, offer infinitely more geographical reach, have a low marginal cost and are able to incorporate dynamic data such as room inventory/rates. Furthermore, while traditional channels have to be used in pairs – as both an advertising medium (e.g. brochures or guidebooks) and an interactive medium (e.g. a telesales agent or a travel agent) to complete the transaction – electronic systems can potentially fulfil both roles and allow travellers to make reservations in a fraction of the time, cost and inconvenience associated with traditional methods (O'Connor, 2001a). These benefits have changed the way in which travel goods and services are sold ... forever!

Electronic distribution of the hospitality product has traditionally centred on the travel agent focused Global Distribution Systems (GDS). Originally conceived as internal inventory control systems by the airlines, the GDS subsequently broadened their product scope to include most hospitality products and provide direct access to the system for travel agents. GDS now allow agents to see real time availability/pricing information and to make instant bookings – valuable benefits for the travel agent. Processing reservations manually is a time consuming, labour intensive and costly process. In contrast, processing reservations using a GDS is cheaper and more efficient. Airline deregulation accelerated the travel agents' adoption of technology as computerized systems became, to a large extent, essential to untangle the increased number of flight and fare options. GDS today are used by approximately 95% of travel agencies worldwide, and many of the major agency chains will no longer make a booking for a client unless it can be processed electronically (HEDNA, 1997). Thus, representation on a GDS is essential for any hospitality company wishing to sell its products through the travel agent market.

However, the GDS are not without their limitations. They service a small (although influential) user base – in effect just the travel agent community. Although consumers can now access GDS directly over the Internet, their structure and methods of operation still focus on the needs of travel agents, resulting in complex procedures, cryptic codes and unintelligible data. A further problem is the lack of flexibility in terms of the data displayed to the user. While this is less of a problem in the USA – where hospitality chains predominate – most hospitality products tend to be heterogeneous, complex and unique (and in many cases it is these characteristics that make them attractive in the first place). As the GDS were designed to distribute the simpler and more homogeneous airline product, their databases cannot cope with the depth and diversity of data needed effectively to market diverse hospitality products. Changing the structure of these databases is a nearly impossible task, given their size, complexity and the fact that they rely on technology that is over 20 years old. In response to this lack of flexibility, many hospitality companies developed their own Central Reservations Systems (CRS) with a more appropriate database structure, and subsequently linked them electronically to the GDS.

To enable connectivity among GDS and CRS, technical and costly interfaces had to be developed. In most cases several were needed as each GDS services different geographical markets – something that quickly became too expensive for individual hospitality management companies. To minimize costs, the major hotel companies cooperated to create a 'universal switch' – a 'multiway' translator – connecting the subscribing CRS to the numerous GDS platforms. As a result, each company only needed a single interface to give access to all of the major GDS systems. Despite this saving, the capital cost of developing and maintaining a reservations system is still substantial. For this reason, many companies currently out-source their electronic distribution (HEDNA, 1997).

More recently, representation companies have emerged to represent smaller non-chain affiliated hotels and provide them with CRS capabilities. The use of Destination Management Systems (DMS) could also be regarded as a similar strategy. DMS concentrate on distributing a wide variety of different tourism products focused primarily on the leisure customer, are generally government sponsored and pay particular attention to distributing smaller and independent tourism suppliers. However, with the exception of some European countries, the impact of DMS has been minimal, as most have failed to evolve into full commercial systems.

Until the early 1990s, electronic channels of distribution were as described above – a cosy status quo where systems cooperated rather than competed with each other. Relationships were effectively linear and participants had a mutually beneficial role to play. From the perspective of the hospitality operator, use of electronic distribution was effective but expensive. Between 1993 and 1997, commissions and other reservation costs associated with these systems increased by approximately 117% (Waller, 1999). This cost increase, coupled with advances in information technology, convinced many of the need to find alternative ways to distribute their product. At the same time, one of the most revolutionary technological infrastructures of all time – the Internet – was becoming available to the public and commercial enterprises. The development of the World Wide Web (the Web) – one of the services of the Internet – provided the opportunity for suppliers to reach customers directly. In contrast to earlier electronic channels, the Web allows for a much richer product selection experience, putting a full colour, interactive brochure directly into the hands of potential customers at a relatively low cost. Furthermore, the Internet offers two-way communications, allowing transactions to be carried out directly with the customer. Thus, intermediaries, such as travel agents, can potentially be eliminated, reducing the cost of distribution.

Most hospitality companies have begun experimenting with Web distribution and it has had a profound effect on the way products are being marketed, distributed, sold and fulfilled. In addition to cooperating with each other as they did in the past, most distribution channel participants have started to compete by creating their own Web sites with information provision and booking facilities. In essence, the level of mutual dependence between participants in the hotel electronic distribution arena has decreased and each intermediary now has the potential to distribute directly to the end consumer. For example, the majority of the hotel chains have taken advantage of the opportunities presented by the Web. A 1999 survey of the top fifty hotel companies revealed that over 90% of chains had a company Web site, with nearly 80% of these providing reservation facilities to allow direct booking (O'Connor and Horan, 1999). Chain sites appear to be highly effective, generating the majority of Internet bookings. The resulting cost reductions are estimated to be substantial, with cumulative gross savings for the 2000 to 2003 period forecast to reach US$1.3 billion, or 1.7% of total industry profits in 2000 (Ader *et al.*, 2000).

Paradoxically, in addition to greater competition, there is also more cooperation. Most sites need to offer multiple products (air, hotel, car, etc.) from multiple vendors. As a result, they need detailed content and reservation facilities for multiple products, which they can only get by cooperating with other intermediaries. In effect, the arrival of the Web has upset the distribution apple cart and prompted major change in the hotel distribution arena. Direct selling has become more common as both business and leisure travellers increasingly make their own travel arrangements using various Web-based services. This makes it essential for hospitality companies to list their products electronically.

E-procurement and supply change management

Another area that has attracted much attention, due to its potential for creating efficiency gains, is that of procurement. Here the focus is on IT that enables external integration with partners in the value chain, rather than narrowly focusing on automating internal operations. Traditionally the hospitality sector has had an inefficient purchasing process. Multiple units, fragmented supply chains and inefficient business processes all adversely affected the purchasing process by creating inefficiencies and increasing costs. In general, unit-level staff managed procurement, and there was a high frequency of low value orders to multiple suppliers, which resulted in high administrative costs. Even where contracts existed for specific products, the unpredictability of hospitality operations meant that 'maverick' purchases from unapproved vendors were, and still are, common, further increasing costs.

Using technology to facilitate the purchasing process overcomes many of these problems while potentially creating some others. By digitizing the processes involved in purchasing, great efficiencies can be achieved when sourcing, specifying, ordering, tracking delivery of, and paying for, purchases. In effect e-procurement involves electronically managing the entire purchasing process from product identification through requisition to payment. One of the minimal but immediately apparent effects of using e-procurement is that process improvements mean that the labour and other administrative costs associated with purchasing are reduced. The use of a computerized system also makes vendor comparison easier, results in tightened adherence to approved products and vendors, helps to ensure quality standards are met and minimize off-contract purchasing. Good systems also help users to identify appropriate suppliers and facilitate the aggregation of small purchases from multiple units. This allows smaller organizations to benefit from economies of scale that previously could only be enjoyed by the larger international companies.

In most cases, the Internet facilitates e-procurement. As a ubiquitous communications medium, it makes it easy to bring buyers and sellers together into what have become known as 'marketspaces'. While initial e-procurement solutions focused on giving customers access to vendors electronically, this type of approach was expensive and time-consuming to implement. Digital marketplaces bring multiple buyers and sellers together to exchange goods and services, and three distinct models currently exist. First, *vertical marketplaces* support transactions specific to a particular industry by aggregating buyers and sellers to reduce transaction costs. Secondly, *horizontal marketplaces*, on the other hand, serve a wide range of disparate industries and provide a vehicle for many types of buyers and sellers to advertise, share content, bid on products, participate in auctions and manage their supply chains. Hybrid models are also emerging. For example VerticalNet's e-hospitality.com acts as an exchange for food service, hospitality and grocery industry members and provides access to food and beverage suppliers. The advantage for buyers in this scenario is they can potentially access more sellers and therefore have more bargaining power. The third model is that of the *in-company marketplace* – a system developed within a franchise or management contract company and used as a way to attract and retain members. Using such technology, the larger chains are now in a position to leverage their size, experience, knowledge and purchasing power to re-engineer the relationship with suppliers and generate considerable benefits for their members.

As procurement processes are moved online, cost savings are forecast to become substantial. Savings from more efficient supply chain management are currently estimated to be at $3.5 billion to

$4 billion in the USA alone, and $7 billion globally. Hospitality procurement of more than $20 billion domestically and $10 billion internationally is forecast to be online in the next 12–18 months (Travel & Tourism Intelligence, 2001). However, as with the adoption of all technology solutions, the industry as a whole has been slow to adopt fully-fledged solutions to date. In addition to the resistance to technology problems outlined earlier, other reasons for the lack of adoption include an unwillingness to abandon existing large investments in legacy systems, concerns about privacy and security, as well as reliability issues associated with the Internet, particularly outside the USA and Western Europe.

Challenges

As can be seen from the above discussion, the industry's use of technology has moved beyond one of merely controlling operations towards a more strategic role. However, a variety of challenges still remain if the industry is to maximize the benefits it can potentially gain. The greatest lies in the effective use of the data collected during day-to-day operations. As more and more tasks are supported and enabled by IT, vast amounts of valuable data are routinely collected by systems such as the PMS and EPOS, but the power of these data is largely ignored. In an era where hospitality products are increasingly being regarded as commodities, opportunities lie in the ability to differentiate by providing personalized service (Olsen, 1995).

Customer relationship management (CRM), a strategic orientation consisting of offering individual service to guests based on their relationship with the company, is widely regarded as the managerial tool to achieve this kind of differentiation. While CRM is not synonymous with IT, technology is the fundamental enabler of CRM. As with electronic commerce, hospitality enterprises have been pioneers in the use of CRM. Almost since the beginnings of the industry, luxury hotels have maintained comprehensive records of the preferences and spending habits of their most frequent guests. Known as guest history systems, such information systems were originally maintained on manually updated paper index cards and used to provide the exceptional personalized service for which such hotels were famous (Main and O'Connor, 1998). The staff at these hotels 'remembered' each valued guest's idiosyncrasies, automatically personalized their service accordingly and thus made each customer feel special.

Developments in technology have dramatically altered what can be done in terms of data collection, storage and processing and therefore IT has significantly broadened the potential magnitude of CRM initiatives in a number of respects. First of all, the growth in the use of hospitality computerized systems means that most of the guest's transactions are now being recorded in electronic format. Developments in communications mean that such data can be collected and consolidated, allowing a central database to be updated automatically as guest transactions occur. Furthermore, the dramatic reduction in the cost of data storage that has occurred over the past three decades (from £1 per character in the 1960s to less than one penny per million characters today) has made it both feasible and economical to store more comprehensive data. As a result, instead of just storing the guest's name, contact details and basic information on their aggregate spending to date, there is an increasing trend towards 'full-folio' storage, where details of each individual transaction are added to the central data warehouse for subsequent analysis. This potentially allows an accurate, in-depth picture to be built up of each guest's likes and dislikes, which could subsequently be used to provide a more personalized service. Moreover, this can be done across multiple units, increasing the consistency of service and the value of the brand.

Building a data warehouse, particularly on a chain wide basis, allows a company to get to know its customers at different levels. First, as with the manual systems, it allows the company to focus on its most frequent guests and serve them better. For example, for a particular guest the hotel can tell where they typically stay, on what day of the week they typically arrive and depart, how far in advance they book, how often they cancel, what time they typically check in and check out, when and what they like to eat, if they make use of leisure facilities or the business centre, where they call on the telephone, and potentially even what channels they watch on television and what temperature they like their room to be! At a basic level, these data can be used to provide a more personalized service and make the guest feel that they are recognized and valued for their repeat business to the company. Such recognition is acknowledged as a key factor in gaining customer loyalty and, since it is widely believed that it costs substantially less to retain existing customers than to acquire new ones, this in itself may justify the investment necessary.

However, the database can also be analysed for patterns, both at the individual customer and aggregate levels – a process often referred to as data mining (IBM, 2001). For the individual customers, this should result in more closely customized offers that perhaps actually interest them instead of the usual mass-market junk mail. Taking such a one-to-one marketing approach is acknowledged to bring benefits in terms of lower costs and increased customer loyalty. Hospitality companies such as Starwood, Bass and Hilton are leading examples of the successful use of such database marketing techniques. Each uses analysis of their corporate database to improve the targeting of marketing and sales efforts, resulting in increased response rates and a reduction in the costs of direct marketing (O'Connor, 2001b).

While using customer data in this way brings short-term benefits, it is when the data are analysed in aggregate form that the greatest potential benefits can be seen. CRM is based on knowing your customer – on an individual basis and in the macro sense. As the corporate wide database now potentially contains comprehensive, detailed, longitudinal data about each customer's interactions with each property, a much more accurate picture of typical customer behaviour than was previously possible can be established. Companies that use CRM are now able better to assess the overall value of each individual customer segment as well as their propensity to respond to various offers. They can use powerful pattern matching software to trawl through the vast sea of data and identify previously unseen trends and relationships. This allows accurate profiles of the behaviour of each segment to be compiled and monitored. The information within the database, combined with externally sourced demographic, socioeconomic and psychographic data, can be interactively 'sliced and diced' in a multitude of ways to allow management to build up detailed pictures of each subgroup of customers.

Yet this is still not the challenge in the true sense. Database marketing and CRM are not synonymous – the latter requires a major change in philosophy throughout the entire organization. The successful use of CRM revolves around placing the customer at the centre of the organization. To do this, the organization must capture exhaustive data about existing and potential customers, profile them accurately, identify their needs and expectations and generate actionable customer knowledge that can be used at each point of contact. Simply having a database of customer information does not, in and of itself, imply a CRM approach. The information in that database must be used – something that we in the hospitality industry are not good at doing. In effect, the company must consistently treat different customers, and types of customers, differently. Maintaining a customer database allows a company to identify its mainstream customers and to quantify this segment's spending patterns, preferences and other behaviour.

Adopting a CRM approach means targeting the company's products towards these needs and squeezing such customers for every penny they can yield. Similarly, analysing the database should identify the company's best customers – those individuals or corporations that contribute significantly more to the company's success. These need to be treated with loving care and nurtured to ensure that company continues to meet or even exceed their expectations. And lastly the database allows the identification of the least profitable customers, and little effort should be made to encourage business from this segment.

The beauty of a CRM approach lies in its ability to help a company manage this portfolio of customer types – ensuring that its best customers receive more personalized service while the company benefits from higher revenues, lower costs and increased customer loyalty. Unfortunately, the hospitality sector has to date largely failed to exploit the valuable data stored in its systems – data that are routinely discarded as organizations fail to recognize their value.

Another major challenge is the effective exploitation of the Web as an enabling technology. As discussed earlier, the Web has, in many ways, become central to hospitality management and operations. While developments in both distribution and procurements have been to a large extent driven by the growing power of the Web, the potential still exists for more dramatic developments – the development of the digital hospitality organization. According to Roger S. Cline, Head of Hospitality Consulting with Arthur Andersen, 'The successful hospitality management companies of the future will be those that are able to reinvent themselves continuously, incorporating e-business capability into the length and breadth of their operations' (Cline, 1999:6).

Initial steps are being taken to achieve this. Many hospitality software applications are being developed using an Application Service Provider (ASP) approach. ASP technology uses the Internet to deliver the functionality of a software package to an end user, while at the same time storing the program and its associated databases on a central server at a remote location. The application 'runs' in a Web browser on the user's computer, but in reality this is just the user interface – the data input screens and reports that allow the user to interact with the application – that is being displayed.

The advantages of such an approach are many. Investment in hardware is minimized because as long as the computer runs a Web browser, the application will work! Software costs are reduced as most ASPs use innovative pricing mechanisms, characterized by either payment based on a fixed monthly fee or a pay-as-you-use structure. Updates and maintenance are also simplified – just change the application on the central server and every location is instantly and automatically updated. Particularly for companies in multiple geographical locations, ASP greatly simplifies the management of the IT resource. However, while substantial, these effects do not reflect the more strategic benefit of using an ASP. Once the ASP approach has been chosen, all aspects of operations and management start to become digitized. This means that the Web becomes integrated into the company's methods of operation thereby promoting a different attitude towards technology use than has traditionally been observed. All the information needed to manage can be made available electronically. This, in effect, turns the Web into a digital nervous system for the hospitality organization allowing it to react quickly and efficiently to all or any stimuli (Gates and Hemmingway, 2000). It is perhaps for this reason that hospitality companies such as Accor and Cendant are investing heavily in developing ASP-based applications to help manage their organizations. Both are consolidating functions as diverse as their PMS, accounting, reservations and client databases into a single integrated ASP-based application, leveraging the power of digital systems to create a more effective and reactive organization.

Conclusion

The above discussion has highlighted how technology now plays a central role in hospitality management and how this role will increase rather than decrease in importance in the future. This has a number of important effects and implications for players within the industry. In particular, it is likely that the increased emphasis on technology will hasten the pace of consolidation and also result in an increase in the number of restricted strategic alliances between hospitality companies.

One of the longest standing deterrents to the use of technology in the hospitality industry has traditionally been cost. Investing in a computer system required a significant outlay of scarce capital on an asset that was often obsolete as soon as you bought it and whose return on investment was difficult to demonstrate. Moreover, given the structure of the hospitality industry, there is usually tension between owners and managers as to what capital expenses are reasonable given the difficulties of estimating the benefits of IT. Despite cost-reducing developments such as ASP, implementing technology-based systems still requires considerable capital resources. In particular this places smaller chains and independent operators at a disadvantage, as they normally have less access to capital than their publicly traded counterparts. Furthermore, smaller operators are less likely to have the necessary expertise among their staff to select, implement and run technology-based solutions. Chain operators are already the better performing segment of the hospitality sector, and the widespread adoption of advanced operational, distribution and e-procurement systems is likely to further increase these differences. The only way for independent operators to take advantage of such systems is to join management or franchise chains, or alternatively to band together in industry wide consortia to develop such systems for themselves. As the technology solutions will increasingly be ASP based it is clear that the balance of power will be with the chains rather than the owners of hospitality operations. Technology has in effect decreased the bargaining power of owners as leaving or even switching brands would mean abandoning organization critical systems such as the PMS, reservations system, e-procurement system and the client database. However, given the pace of technological change, it is unlikely that even the international chains can continue to work in isolation.

Although often installed to improve management control, technology based systems now have the potential to generate competitive advantage by facilitating interaction with customers (e-distribution) and suppliers (e-procurement), transforming their scope into one of strategic importance. The use of multiple, simultaneous channels of distribution has become the norm. Emphasis is being placed on direct electronic routes as a result of their perceived ability to reduce costs. However, considerable capital is required to develop and maintain multiple electronic routes to the customer.

Automation of the procurement process similarly offers costs savings potential and potentially generates economies of scale. However, once again, considerable investment is required to develop and implement such systems. Increased integration means that many hospitality organizations possess a valuable bank of customer data that can be exploited to personalize customer service. On the other hand, the potential of CRM has largely failed to be recognized by the majority of the international hospitality management companies.

Two barriers still limit the use of technology-based systems by hospitality companies. A lack of understanding of the strategic role of IT limits the scope of what computerization is used for within the industry, while the issue of cost also prevents many companies from implementing appropriate technology based systems. Despite the cost reductions resulting from technological advances such as ASP, implementing technology-based systems is still expensive. As a result, multinational chains, with their easier access to capital, have an advantage, and further industry consolidation is likely as technology becomes essential for survival.

Summary

- Technology-based systems now have the potential to generate competitive advantage by facilitating interaction with customers (e-Distribution) and suppliers (e-Procurement), transforming their scope into one of strategic importance.

- The use of multiple, simultaneous channels of distribution has become the norm. Emphasis is being placed on direct electronic routes as a result of their perceived ability to reduce costs. However, considerable capital is required to develop and maintain multiple electronic routes to the customer.

- Automation of the procurement process similarly offers cost savings potential and potentially generates economies of scale but considerable investment is required to develop and implement such systems.

- Increased integration means that many hospitality organizations possess a valuable bank of customer data that can be exploited to personalize customer service. However, to date the potential of CRM has largely failed to be recognized by the majority of the international hospitality management companies.

- Two barriers still limit the use of technology-based systems by hospitality companies. A lack of understanding of the strategic role of IT limits the scope of what computerization is used for within the industry, while the issue of cost also prevents many companies from implementing appropriate technology-based systems.

- Despite the cost reductions resulting from technological advances such as ASP, implementing technology-based systems is still expensive. As a result, multinational chains, with their easier access to capital, have an advantage, and further industry consolidation is likely as technology becomes essential for survival.

Review questions

1. Hospitality computer systems now have the potential to be fully integrated, to collect and analyse comprehensive customer data and to personalize the guest experience. Based on your experiences as both a customer and an employee, are hospitality organizations succeeding in exploiting this opportunity?
2. While many hotel companies use frequent guest programmes to reward their most loyal customers, the restaurant and food service sectors have to date largely ignored such developments. Why do you feel this to be the case?
3. The advantages of using multiple simultaneous channels of distribution were stressed in the text. Does such a strategy have disadvantages? What is stopping more organizations from more fully exploiting this opportunity?
4. E-procurement is being hyped as one of the key hospitality technology developments of the future. What are the barriers to its widespread adoption by international hospitality organizations?
5. The major international hospitality management companies are implementing most of the developments discussed in this chapter. What strategy/s can the smaller, independent operator pursue to survive?

References

Ader, J., Lafleur, R. *et al.* (2000) *Global Lodging Almanac (2000 Edition)*, Bear, Stearns & Co. Inc., New York.

Cline, R. (1999) Brand marketing in the hospitality industry – art or Science, *HSMAI Gazette*, **1**, 6–7, 14.

Gates, B. and Hemmingway, C. (2000) *Business @ the Speed of Thought: Succeeding in the Digital Economy*, Warner Books, New York.

Go, F. and Pine, R. (1995) *Globalization Strategy in the Hotel Industry*. Routledge, New York.

HEDNA (1997) *Onward Distribution of Hotel Information via the Global Distribution Systems*. Partners in Marketing, London.

Horwath & Horwath Consulting (1996) *Worldwide Hotel Industry Study*. Horwath & Horwath Consulting, London.

IBM (2001) *A Blueprint for Customer Relationship Management in the Travel Industry*. IBM Travel and Transportation, New York.

Main, H. and O'Connor, P. (1998) The use of smart card technology to develop a community based affinity/loyalty scheme for SMES in tourism and hospitality. In Buhalis, D., Tjoa, A. M. and Jafari, J. (eds), *Information and Communications Technologies in Tourism*, Springer-Verlag, New York, pp. 7–15.

O'Connor, P. (1999) *Electronic Information Distribution in Tourism and Hospitality*, CABI, London.

O'Connor, P. (2001a) *The Changing Face of Hotel Electronic Distribution*, Travel & Tourism Analyst (Economic Intelligence Unit), No. 5, pp. 61–78.

O'Connor, P. (2001b) Customer relationship management – it's all about oranges, lemons and peaches! *IT Solutions (Supplement to Hotel and Restaurant Magazine)*, April, pp. 41–42.

O'Connor, P. and Horan, P. (1999) An analysis of web reservations facilities in the top 50 international hotel chains, *International Journal of Hospitality Information Technology*, **1**, (1), 77–87.

Olsen, M. (1995) Into the new millennium. A White Paper on the Global Hospitality Industry: Executive Summary, Paris, International Hotel and Restaurant Association.

Travel & Tourism Intelligence (2001) The international hotel industry – corporate strategies and global opportunities, *Travel & Tourism Intelligence*, p. 155.

Waller, F. (1999) The distribution revolution, *Hotels*, March, p. 103.

Whitaker, M. (1987) Overcoming the barriers to successful implementation of information technology in the UK hotel industry, *International Journal of Hospitality Management*, **6**, (4), 229–235.

Further reading

Chaffey, D. (2002) *E-Business and E-Commerce Management*, Prentice-Hall, New York.

Gamble, P., Stone, M. and Woodcock, N. (1999) *Up Close and Personal – Customer Relationship Marketing @ Work*, Kogan Page, London.

O'Connor, P. (2000) *Using Computers in Hospitality*, 2nd ed., Continuum, London.

Operational dilemmas

Michael Riley

Chapter objectives

When you have read this chapter you will be able to:

- Identify the problems that lie behind the process of decision-making at both the unit and corporate operational management levels.

- Explain the essential properties of a choice dilemma.

- Discuss sources of uncertainty in hospitality operations.

- Analyse in-built economic and technological conflicts.

- Evaluate the range of solutions that confront decision-makers.

Introduction

There are two sets of problems under examination here, first and most importantly, are those associated with running a hospitality unit – the everyday issues of hospitality management. Secondly, taking a wider perspective, there are the problems of running an international hospitality operation. The most appropriate starting point is in the operation itself.

In looking at the dilemmas that face operational management, it is difficult to avoid two conclusions. Namely, that the problems of running an operation are fairly universal and, more significantly, they appear to be the same in units of different sizes. This is not a counsel of 'nothing new' or one of 'managers do not solve problems' – on the contrary, there are new approaches and managers do solve their problems. However, managers only solve the problems that stem from inherent fundamental dilemmas – in a world of continuous change many things remain constant. The aim here is to outline the choices management faces by analysing these dilemmas. The notion of a dilemma always implies, and often combines, three particular properties: choice – which path to go down? with, uncertainty – what are the paths and where do they lead? and, to make it harder for the decision-maker, possible conflict between the alternatives – the essence of a dilemma!

It follows therefore that in understanding dilemmas we must seek out key decisions and then identify the sources and level of uncertainty, the range of alternative solutions possible and the in-built conflicts that attach themselves to the problems. At one level the generic sources of uncertainty are obvious – the marketplace, competition and the human dimension. Some of the alternative solutions are equally conspicuous – to make or buy-in, to seek new markets or to stay loyal to the existing customers, to use full-time or part-time staff. Similarly, it is relatively easy to see the sources of conflict within decisions – economic imperatives, of which profitability is central, versus sustainable quality. In production terms, there is, for example, the speed versus quality balance to be struck. This broad sweep analysis is important for perspective but, in operational terms, what really matters is the detail. However, in looking at the detail it is equally important to remember the three properties that are invariably at work – uncertainty, competing alternatives and built-in conflicts.

Operational issues

Management in hospitality lives in a world dominated by two primary sources of uncertainty – variable demand and the consumer's subjective evaluation of its products and services. It is from these twin pillars that many operational dilemmas ensue. A good place to start therefore might be with the consequences of uncertain demand. Given that hospitality-operating units have a fixed capacity, and that the products are perishable, the goal of maximizing occupancy is problematic. There are two components to this problem – the level of demand and its fluctuating nature.

Attractiveness and the level of demand

The economics of all hospitality units are based on throughput for which the key concept is the breakeven point. Achieving this overrides almost everything. Given a degree of cost control the solutions lie mainly within the realm of marketing, but marketing can only work from the product or service itself and here a number of dilemmas lie. There are three issues – how wide to pitch the appeal of the product, how much choice to offer and how to maximize the average spend. The decision to go for a wide range of market segments implies the product has properties that will appeal to different consumers. For example, within the same range of disposable income might lie retired, middle-aged, youth, business, tourist – local, national and international markets. This may be good for business, especially if they all seek the same satisfaction from the product, but this may not be so in which case management have to work to make the same product satisfy different sets of expectations. If the latter is the case, the solution is to know which attributes of the product appeal to which markets – the dilemma is that there is a limit to how far a product can be altered to have multiple appeals to a differentiated market. Creating an image, which has multiple appeal and a reality that satisfies it, is the point where operations and marketing meet. The alternative is for the product to be positioned in a way that it appeals to a specific market or small range of markets. In this case it is more crucial for marketing to know what attributes would appeal to that market and then for operational management to design the product and service to meet that demand. What lies behind both cases is the argument that the less uncertainty there is for the customer, the more likely they are to consume.

The second issue relates directly to this problem of controlling uncertainty for customers. How much choice do we give customers? The initial dilemma being is wide choice attractive? If wide choice is deemed to be an attractive attribute, then another dilemma follows. Wide choice leaves open the opportunity for products and service to be provided *but not consumed*. For example, a large range of dishes on a menu may entice the customers to dine but if they choose narrowly then the avoidance of waste becomes an economic issue and a managerial objective. In these circumstances, the ideal solution would be for everything to be cooked to order. The problem is that the very attractions of cuisine work against cooking to order – some dishes require long cooking times. The solutions lie in the technology of food production, storage and regeneration. The alternative to wide choice is specialization – offering to produce a small variety at a controlled level of quality. This would be more productive but may reduce the size of the market.

In a sense the width of choice dilemma is about appeal versus productivity. One concept, which straddles both these ideas, is that of branding, whereby although the choices on offer can be wide or narrow, specifying the choices within the overall concept of the brand reduces some of the uncertainty for the customer. It does not remove the issue of range of choice versus productivity, but takes it in the identity of the product and by so doing handles the attractiveness issue separately from the production issues. An example would be helpful here. Compare a restaurant that has a

large range of French dishes on the menu with a hamburger bar –
they are different markets and the latter will be more productive
than the former. Compare these extremes with a branded bistro
chain that offers choice but not as much as the French restaurant. It
increases its attractiveness by offering not just a range of dishes
but also the reassurance of quality control through standardization. Similarly, an American restaurant concept might expand
choice beyond the hamburger but still maintain productivity
and attractiveness. In both cases, reducing uncertainty is seen as
a form of attractiveness (Riley, 2000b).

Fluctuating demand

At the macro level it is easy to see a pattern of seasonality in
demand but, for operational purposes, the key issues lie in the
handling of short-term fluctuations in demand. In the context of
accommodation, the key decision is how many rooms are there left
to sell that day. The guiding stars are the 'house count' for that
night, advanced reservations and scheduled checkouts for that
day. It is a decision based on some information and its consequences are the degree of alacrity with which sales strategies are
pursued. However, uncertainty intervenes in the form of:

- How many of the advance reservations for that day will
  actually show up?

- How many 'chance' customers will turn up without
  reservations

- How many customers who said they would check out that day
  decide not to do so?

The only solid fact is the number of rooms occupied.
Management's solution to this problem is to take the three
unknown and the known variable and model them into an equation that uses historical data to form the basis of a 'rolling forecast'.
Large organizations will computerize the equation and use sophisticated data analysis but, in essence, it is the same for small units.

If, to the problem of maximizing occupancy is added the issue
of maximizing revenue then the equation expands. One way of
filling rooms is to alter the price. This has led to a sophisticated
form of pricing (or discounting) known as yield management. In
this scheme of things prices are altered at a rate that reflects the
state of demand and rooms vacant ratio (Raeside and Windle,
2000). This is a formalized way of expressing the inherent dilemma
of filling the house versus maximizing revenue. Selling cheap
might fill the house but reduces revenue and profits. The arrival
of an unexpected coach party only willing to pay at a large discount for numbers may give the duty manager a headache.

Pricing is one of many competition mechanisms and it is competition that lies at the heart of uncertainty. The key questions are – who is the competition? And, how do we compete? Market information is never perfect but the best information we have is, on the one hand, on the performance of units in our market category (similarly positioned) and, on the other, whatever we can glean from our own customers. There are two basic dilemmas here, first, do we compete on price and therefore logically on discount in line with competitors or on other dimensions? If it is on qualitative dimensions, should we be negative about the competition or simply emphasize the merits of our unit? Marketing always speaks of 'differentiating the product' even within the same market – but how? Surely, a room is a room, breakfast is just breakfast – this is where the ingenuity and creativity of management comes to the fore. Many managers speak of competing on service and that raises the issue of, what is good service?

The supply side of operations too has concerns about fluctuating demand. In order to maintain profitability the unit needs to adjust supply in line with demand. The hardest part of this dilemma surrounds labour costs. If demand is fluctuating then a degree of labour supply flexibility will be required. The solutions are well-documented – numerical, earnings and functional flexibility. Numerical flexibility means constantly altering the numbers employed, which creates an unstable element within the workforce. Only functional flexibility (moving people between jobs to suit demand) offers the chance to maintain continuity in employment (Riley and Lockwood, 1997). The problem of multiskilling is that people need an occupational identity – it is part of their motivation. Moves towards functional flexibility always have to confront this perfectly understandable desire. This is reinforced by uniforms and the strong hand of tradition. The problem is compounded by the indirect relationship between technology and the demand for labour. As in all forms of management, there is a process of seeking efficiency through labour substitution. For the most part this involves either the direct substitution of the outputs of labour through buying-in those outputs or by the replacement of skills by machines. An example of the former would be buying in bakery goods instead of employing a baker and an example of the latter would be a cash machine that calculates customer's change thus reducing the need for mental arithmetic (Riley, 2000b; and of the consequences of de-skilling; Riley, 1981).

Advocates of quality suggest that employment continuity is a key element. The dilemma here is profitability versus continuity of service in circumstances where the demand for labour varies. Resolution of this dilemma seems impossible. Its containment is a driving force of human resource management (HRM). HRM advocates argue that, in hospitality, the permanent and the temporary, the skilled and the unskilled, the high tech and low tech all have to live together and that this very diversity does not need the added complication of workforce instability. The dilemma for HRM is whether to manage the whole workforce as if it were skilled and permanent or as unskilled and temporary. Economics goes for the latter while quality advocates the former (Riley, 2000).

The whole versus the parts

Most hospitality units offer more than one product or service but even where there is only one product there is often a multiplicity of processes within. Three issues are of concern in the relationship between the whole and its parts. First, is the customer's experience a holistic or a differentiated one? Secondly, in relation to economics, how should each part be managed when they make different contributions to profits, revenues and costs? Thirdly, in operational terms, what are the inherent conflicts between the separate processes that comprise the whole?

Subjective evaluation

If the thrust of most market research is to ascertain what attributes are attractive to what category of customer then the post-purchase approaches are concerned with satisfaction and how quality is perceived. There is still a great deal to learn about satisfaction and quality in hospitality, but one of the themes to emerge is that whatever impressions particular attributes make there is always an overall element involved. In other words, the overall image and the overall impression count. Whether the latter are related to experiences is still a matter of research (Ekinci and Riley, 1998; 1999). People often express satisfaction with things they did not use! 'The hotel was really nice, it had a wonderful pool. Did you use it? No'. This is not as nonsensical as it might seem. However, the problem this creates for management is that they must ensure the guest has an equal chance of having a good experience in all parts of the unit. This is a seriously difficult standard setting and coordination problem.

A more pragmatic issue is the treatment of sections on the basis that they make different contributions to the whole. Should all parts of the business be profitable? Even if the answer is yes there are further issues about priorities. Food and beverage does not make as much profit as selling rooms and this has led historically to an emphasis on rooms management. However, food and beverage makes a different contribution involving, among other things, profits, cash flow, image enhancement and direct connections into the local rather than the transient market (Riley, 2000a). Riley and Davis (1992) point out that these contributions come into their own during a recession. Hospitality, like other industries, engages in out-sourcing: the contracting out of specific services or provision of goods. The dilemma is one of lower cost versus lack of control. Where management believe they can control quality by specification and where the service does not contribute sufficiently to profits then the option to choose a 'market solution' rather than handling it 'in house' may be preferred. The theoretical basis of this practice lies in transactional cost theory (Barney and Westerly, 1999). The dilemma for management is how far the work of a contractor can be coordinated within the holistic concept of the unit.

Although the hospitality business is usually referred to as a 'service industry' many of its units contain both service, distribution and production functions. As all processes have priorities this sometimes leads to what are known as technological or work process conflicts. For example, in a hotel, reception want the rooms ready now, whereas housekeeping wants them clean – it is a speed versus quality dilemma. Similarly, as good service is never slow the waiter wants the food now and the chef want it to be just right – these are in-built conflicts, which often have to be managed.

One approach to efficiency that cuts across all these issues is that of seeing the organization in terms of processes – systems that serve the goals of efficiency and customer service. It is about flows of customers and materials, and their timing. It is about conceptualizing products and services and delivering them in ways that are efficient in terms of resources and inviting to customers. There are two dilemmas here. First, that such systems design must begin with a conceptualization of the service or product, which has the confidence of the market. To start designing a process from a concept surrounded by uncertainty is to make the whole organization uncertain as to its own efficiency – the basic dilemma of process engineering. It is right for management to assert their designs on the product rather than be simply reactive to the market, but there are risks. The second dilemma is that system design places all its emphasis on the service to the customer and makes resource provision subservient to that. This carries the tendency to favour out-sourcing and de-skilling because the wider implications of change are excluded from the vision.

The immediacy of decisions

Most forms of analysis of managerial work always combine the seriousness of the decisions being made, in terms of consequences of error, against the time pressure under which those decisions are made. In the hospitality industry there is a sense of immediacy brought about by contingent demand and perishable sales. Whether it is deciding how hard to push today's unsold rooms or ordering tomorrow's fresh ingredients against an uncertain expectation of demand, the pressure comes from the short time span. What is more, these contingent decisions are continuous. If, to this flow, we add the huge range of areas of decision-making and the fact that calculations will invariably be necessary, then the dilemmas of decision-making in hospitality become clear – it is a constant, complex and basically tactical process. Gore and Riley (2000) suggest that this constant pressure to make decisions leads to managers reducing that complexity to a few simple dimensions that become part of their managerial style.

The human dimension

The customer is always right

Perhaps the most common reason given for wanting to work in hospitality is the desire to deal with people. But people can be difficult! The customer is always right is a perennial of course – he or she is right even when they are wrong! Management is not about objective truth in the same sense of science but it must be concerned with the root causes of problems and of successful remedy. But, at the same time, it is also equally concerned with the subjective view of those involved. A complaining customer may in truth be wrong but has to be taken seriously. Hospitality management is possibly just a busy case of the general law of managing people – treat the cause and the symptoms simultaneously. How the customer and the member of staff perceive a situation is the manager's reality! It is precisely because the relationship with customers is a matter of expectations and perceptions on both the consumer and the provider sides, a case of inter-subjectivity, that managers are concerned to influence customer perception through information. There is a clear role in the future for information technology to make the 'deal' – what you get for your money – clear. The problem is how much information do you give? This is a problem shared with internal merchandising. If you overload the customer he/she becomes indifferent, note, not dissatisfied but worse, couldn't care less. Given the need for internal marketing, the development of the tactical use of information is a future challenge for management.

Are they a group or a set of individuals?

One of the most difficult tasks of management is to discern whether they are managing a group or a set of individuals. The textbooks are full of the distinction but, in everyday life, it is hard because most tasks have overtones of group and individual aspects. A lot of jobs and tasks in hospitality look individual but the context is firmly that of the group. Idiosyncratic characteristics like pooling tips add support to the 'groupness' of what is a set of individual tasks. The dilemmas flowing from this include: should people be selected primarily for their skills or for being able to fit in with the team? How do we evaluate individual merit within group performance? And, how is merit to be balanced against loyal service in terms of rewards? These questions are at the very heart of hospitality management because the group dimensions of the task are of overwhelming importance. If the experience of the customer is felt in a holistic way then ensuring quality throughout the possible range of consumed services and products is an enormous task of coordination.

The hospitality industry is not immune to the age-old problem of initiative versus control. Management needs to control how workers do their jobs but workers want a degree of autonomy in work. Getting the balance of trust and control is what managing people is about. What creates a special problem in the hospitality industry is, first, that workers tend to look for autonomy as a compensation mechanism for relatively low pay and, secondly, they are attracted to the industry because of the scope and lack of control it offers in comparison to manufacturing industry (Riley, Ladkin and Szivas, 2002). One consequence of this is that the focus of loyalty tends to be the industry as a whole rather than the specific unit. The dilemma this creates is one concerned with how to motivate and if incentives are actually aligned with the satisfaction workers seek. One of the attractions of hospitality management is that some of the problems, and most of the solutions, require dealing with people. This raises the issue of how managers and workers work together. Traditionally, the basis of this relationship has been the amount of shared knowledge and skill. Hospitality education has always fostered this quality with the consequence that managers understand workers' jobs. If management becomes more business orientated and less technically inclined then the basis of the relationship changes.

International dilemmas

The dilemmas at the corporate level, in the context of managing an international company, are principally the problems of exchange rates, distance and the national differences. Distance in the sense that management is, to an extent, remote from the operation and has to manage by information and differences in that, operations exist in national and local cultures.

The literature on the impact of multinationals and global human resource management raises issues of potential conflict whereby global strategy and corporate culture are ranged against local labour laws, national culture and custom and practice. There are no generic solutions – the argument goes. Therefore everything that matters happens at the local level. In fact, the message from practitioners is rather different and few companies have difficulty in thinking globally and managing locally. Company policies rarely go against the principles ensconced in local labour laws. If it means you have to pay above a minimum wage here and not there; recognize unions in one place and not in another then so be it (Riley, 1992). Multinationals are often, in the field of human resource management, sources of good practice in the local market and can even influence labour laws through the political process (International Labour Office, 1981).

Problems do occur, however, when corporate strategies try to override and ignore local practices (Baldacchino, 1997). Global goals and values can only be maintained if the means, i.e. the policies, are adapted to local circumstances without losing their global significance. For example, a policy that makes training compulsory may vary the content because of local differences in knowledge, but not the fact that it must take place. It is not unreasonable to expect some 'friction' between local practices and company policies, but then that is a problem for local managers.

One of the common strategies for integrating a multinational company into a foreign country is to use a limited number of expatriate managers to train local managers. However, this is a strategy often constrained by local political forces if not by law – there are limits and national governments usually expect to see a conspicuous cohort of indigenous managers. Thus, a balance has to be struck. The problem is exasperated by the issue of having to import skills because of imported taste. If guests' demand home cooking or international cuisine when abroad, then the cooks have to be imported before the locals can acquire the skills. One recurring problem is balancing salary levels between indigenous and imported skilled labour. A healthy extension of the problem of imported labour is the development of international careers. Cross-national mobility has the effect of ameliorating the problems of different cultures. A more pragmatic problem is that of the pay levels of multinational companies and their effect on the local market. Large overseas employers usually have a serious influence on the state of competition in the labour market. Even without being the labour price leader the mere fact that they can offer more opportunity gives them market leverage. Too much advantage could lead to the deskilling of the other units in the tourist destination and reduce its overall quality and attractiveness. Setting the level in order to recruit the best but not to disturb seriously the local market is a matter of judgement. It is made difficult because of the employment of expatriates, who expect remuneration in line with their home country, to work alongside locals.

As organizational culture is based on organizational values it does not tend to contravene local laws but it can come up against local custom and practice because of its dependence on selecting people to fit into the culture. Fortunately, hospitality is a human concept that transcends national borders but problems occur, however, when hospitality is translated into 'service'. Interpretations of 'service' are culturally derived and have strong political meaning. Needing tourists for economic reasons and not wanting a 'nation of busboys' is a political dilemma that sits on the shoulders of the hospitality industry. Service and servility are always at the forefront of political and economic development. Most hotel companies have service as part of their mission, but the problem of making it uniformly high is one of making organizational values override cultural differences in the interpretation of service. The influence of acceptance by local managers and incentives is crucial here.

National culture also has a determining influence on attitudes to work and therefore to productivity. It is undoubtedly true that labour does vary in its output to a degree that differences in training cannot explain. Individualist and collectivist societies confer different meanings on words like effort and productivity that have behavioural consequences (Hofstede, 1980; Hoecklin, 1995). This is not a problem for local managers but it is one for corporate managers because they have to set performance targets and budgets. Hard-to-explain differences in productivity make it difficult to achieve equivalence in making comparisons between performance measures in units (International Labour Office, 1989). An acceptable target in one country may be unreasonable and unrealistic in another. Yet management by information is a necessity at the corporate level. The growth of information technology makes it easier to communicate measurement and to measure more things but it does automatically make measurement more accurate. Knowing local conditions and constraints is necessary for plans to be realistic.

The notion of management by remote control through targets has implications for organizational structure. Measurement is, by definition, a formal process but this gives rise to the question of just how formal or bureaucratic can hospitality organizations be? Does more information mean rigid structures and rules. Simms *et al.* (1988) showed that hotels, despite having a fairly rigid structure operate in fairly informal ways. The dilemma for corporate management is that if they go on demanding more performance measures they may cause the organizational structure to be more formal and less flexible. The rush to control and standardize may constrain the service ethos with its implicit demand for reasonable flexibility. This is a dilemma for all service industries newly armed with information technology.

Exchange rate differences are hugely important to marketing and pricing and consequently to profits (Go and Pine, 1995). Varying exchange rates mean that profits will fluctuate. Not only will profits vary over time, but the profit made on any one day may become a different sum when the time comes to transport it to the home country of the company. Furthermore, although in the industrialized world capital is free to cross boundaries without currency restrictions, this is not necessarily true of the developing world. If an air-conditioning system or expensive decor fabric have to be imported to build a new hotel this eats into the currency reserves of the country – such capital expenditure becomes part of the multinational/client state economic equation. Similarly, imported food for guests cuts back the contribution of tourism to the local country. These are issues that exist when the multinational is seeking to enter a new country.

To steal, or not to steal?

Hospitality management is not an island, it cannot escape the influence of modern trends in generic management. Perhaps the most significant change in the last decade has been the rise of corporate governance with its emphasis on maximizing shareholder returns. This has led the way for specialization – focusing on doing one thing well and towards outsourcing non-core activities. Hospitality companies are growing in size and the main ones are global companies. As companies grow, senior management become managers of the 'business' rather than managers of a production and service process; they become separated from what they are managing with eyes on the balance sheet and the share price. In these circumstances communication becomes mainly a matter of targets and data. In reality what this means is that unit managers are often working under strategies devised by people unconnected with the operations.

Following modern management trends means adopting new techniques and approaches. These ideas tend to emanate from manufacturing or from information science (Hum, 1997). The dilemma lies in whether or not they worked where they were first tried out and, if they did, are they applicable to hospitality? Quality control ideas gleaned from manufacturing, where specification of standards is not subjective, lose power when translated into a field where evaluation is subjective. Similarly, the twin towers of commitment and empowerment, which on the surface seem tailor-made for services, are built, in the hospitality field, on the shifting ground of fluctuating demand for labour. What are directly transferable from generic management are those personal managerial competencies that enhance any manager's ability to organize in any context (Ladkin and Riley, 1996).

Conclusions

One obvious conclusion is that, at the operational level decisions are essentially tactical and aimed at solving problems that are perennial. However, two changes are beginning to take effect in the industry, namely, the increase in business education and increasing applications of information technology to sources of uncertainty. Guests have more information and what is more, they are less dependent upon staff for that information. This may lead to different expectations. A second obvious conclusion is that we still do not really know what attracts customers to specific establishments nor what makes them satisfied. In both cases the search is still on.

If hospitality operations management is full of decisions under time pressure there is at least a context that is supportive to this type of decision-making. Despite the rigours of competition, there is a common culture within hospitality, which is derived from common skills, mutual problems and shared knowledge (Wood, 1997; Cameron, 2001).

The dilemma of international hospitality falls into two areas. First, how 'native' does a multinational need or want to go? Employing only local people and using only local products certainly contributes to the country's economy, but is it realistic? By contrast, too much imported labour and materials and the value of tourism to the local community diminishes and the companies involved lose credibility in the political community. Secondly, how formal does a multinational want to be? The key question here is, does the increasing ability to control mean that control should be extended and, if it is, will it damage the notion of hospitality itself?

Summary

Beneath the surface of hospitality management lies a set of contradictions and therefore choices – it is this element of choice that provides the dilemmas.

- Speed of service versus quality of service.

- Increasing formal control versus maintaining ethos of relaxed hospitality.

- Maximizing revenue versus maximizing occupancy.

- Offering diversity of products and services versus higher productivity.

- Narrow focused appeal versus wide appeal.

- Maintain a holistic image versus subcontract.

- Continuity of staff versus need to match labour supply to demand.

- Customization versus standardization.

- Imported skills versus indigenous labour.

- Corporate culture versus national and local culture.

- Organizational culture versus occupational culture.
- To produce versus to subcontract.
- To manage staff as a group versus as individuals.

Even when the choices are not mutually exclusive the matter of emphasis is itself, a dilemma.

Review questions

1. What determines the final occupancy of a hotel on any one night?
2. What is the basis of the historical data needed to forecast?
3. What factors must be considered before a manager offers a room at a discounted price?
4. Can the attributes of a hospitality establishment be made to appeal to a variety of markets?
5. What are the advantages of branding?
6. How can labour supply be adjusted to match variable demand?
7. Should every service in a hotel be made to be profitable?
8. What are the disadvantages of out-sourcing?
9. People can be managed as a group and as individuals simultaneously – do you agree?
10. What is the role of information in:
    (a) internal selling and marketing?
    (b) creating expectation in the mind of the customer?

References

Baldacchino, G. (1997) *Global Tourism Informal Labour Relations: The small-scale syndrome at work.* Mansell, London.

Barney, J. B. and Hesterly, W. (1999) Organizational economics: understanding the relationship between organizations and economic analysis. In Clegg, S. R. and Hardy, C. (eds) *Understanding Organizations: Theory and Method*, Sage, London, pp. 109–141.

Cameron, D. (2001) Chefs and occupational culture in a hotel chain: a grid-group analysis, *Tourism and Hospitality Research*, **3**, (2) 103–114.

Ekinci, Y. and Riley, M. (1998) A critique of the issues and theoretical assumptions in service quality measurement in the lodging industry; time to move the goalposts? *International Journal of Hospitality Management*, **17**, (4) 349–362.

Ekinci, Y. and Riley, M. (1999) Measuring hotel quality: back to basics, *International Journal of Contemporary Hospitality Management*, **11**, (6), 287–293.

Go, F. M. and Pine, R. (1995) *Globalisation Strategy in the Hotel Industry*. Routledge, London.

Gore, J. and Riley, M. (2000) A study of the perception of the labour market by human resource managers in the UK hotel industry: a cognitive approach, *Tourism and Hospitality Research*, **2**, (3), 232–241.

Hoecklin, L. (1995) *Managing Cultural Differences; Strategies for Competitive Advantage*. EIU Addison Wesley, London.

Hofstede, G. (1980) *Cultures and Consequences: International Differences in Work Related Values*. Sage, Beverly Hills CA.

Hum, S. H. (1997) Strategic hotel operations; some lessons from strategic manufacturing, *International Journal of Contemporary Hospitality Management*, **9**, (4/6), 176–180.

International Labour Office (ILO) (1981) *Employment effects of multinational enterprises in developing countries*. ILO, Geneva.

International Labour Office (ILO) (1989) Sectoral Activities Programme – Hotel Catering and Tourism Committee Report 111: Productivity and Training in the Hotel Catering and Tourism Sector, Geneva.

Ladkin, A. and Riley, M. (1996) Mobility and structure in the career paths of UK hotel managers: a labour market hybrid of the bureaucratic model? *Tourism Management*, **17**, (6), 443–452.

Raeside, R. and Windle, D. (2000) Quantitative aspects of yield management. In Ingold, A., McMahon-Beattie, W. and Yeoman, I. (eds), *Yield Management*, Cassell, London, pp. 45–66.

Riley, M. (1981) Declining hotel standards and the skill trap, *International Journal of Tourism Management*, **2**, (2), 95–104.

Riley, M. and Davis, E. (1992) Development and innovation; the case of food and beverage management in hotels. In Cooper, C. (ed.) *Progress in Tourism, Recreation and Hospitality Management*, vol. 4, Belhaven Press, London, pp. 201–208.

Riley, M. (1992) Labour utilization and collective agreements: an international comparison, *International Journal of Contemporary Hospitality Management*, **4**, (4), 21–23.

Riley, M. and Lockwood, A. (1997) Strategies and measurement for workforce flexibility; an application of functional flexibility in a service firm, *International Journal of Operations and Production Management*, **17**, (4), 414–421.

Riley, M. (2000) *Managing People* 2nd ed. Butterworth-Heinemann, Oxford.

Riley, M. (2000a) Can hotel restaurants ever be profitable? Short- and long-term perspectives. In Wood, R. C. (ed.) *Strategic Questions in Food and Beverage Management*. Butterworth-Heinemann, Oxford, pp. 112–118.

Riley, M. (2000b) How can we better understand operational productivity in food and beverage management? A resource substitution framework. In Wood, R. C. (ed.) *Strategic Questions in Food and Beverage Management*. Butterworth-Heinemann, Oxford, pp. 119–128.

Riley, M., Ladkin, A. and Szivas, E. (2002) *Tourism Employment: Planning and Analysis*. Channel View, Clevedon, UK.

Simms, J., Hales, C. and Riley, M. (1988) Examination of the concept of internal labour markets in UK hotels, *International Journal of Tourism Management*, **9**, (3), 3–12.

Wood, R. C. (1997) *Working in Hotels and Catering*, 2nd ed. International Thomson Business Press, London.

Further reading

Carmouche, R. and Kelly, N. (1995) *Behavioural Studies in Hospitality Management*. Chapman and Hall, London.

Riley, M., Ladkin, A. and Szivas, E. (2002) *Tourism Employment: Planning and Analysis*. Channel View, Clevedon, UK.

Phillips, P. A. and Moutinho, L. (1998) *Strategic Planning Systems in Hospitality and Tourism*, CABI Publishing, Oxford.

Phillips, P. A. and Moutinho, L. (2000) The Marketing Planning Index: a tool for measuring strategic marketing effectiveness. In Moutinho L. (ed.) The hospitality sector in *Strategic Management in Tourism*, CABI Publishing, Oxford, pp. 283–292.

Riley, M. (2000) *Managing People*, 2nd ed. Butterworth-Heinemann, Oxford.

Schmenner, R. W. (1995) *Service Operations Management*. Prentice-Hall, Englewood Cliffs, New Jersey.

Wood, R. C. (1997) *Working in Hotels and Catering* 2nd ed. International Thomson Business Press, London.

Wood, R. C. (ed.) (2000) *Strategic Questions in Food and Beverage Management*. Butterworth-Heinemann, Oxford.

Strategic choices in the international hospitality industry

Adee Athiyaman and Frank Go

Chapter objectives

When you have read this chapter you will be able to:

- Discuss key trends and influences on strategic decision-making in the international hospitality industry.

- Critically evaluate the changing patterns and dynamics of competition within the international hospitality industry.

- Critically review the basis, or bases, for determining the nature of competitors.

- Analyse the relationships between the product life cycle and competitive structures/strategies.

- Discuss the effects of asymmetry in relation to the formulation of competitive strategies.

Introduction

The international hospitality industry is characterized by an industry structure composed of a relatively small number of large multinationals and a large number of locally operated small and medium-sized enterprises. In recent years the international hospitality industry has been affected by the effects of globalization (Go and Pine, 1995), the information technology revolution, the fragmentation of consumer demand and the emergence of economic integration of suppliers within networks. Developments such as intensified competition, globalization and the introduction of new technological developments imply a complex business landscape and an increasing degree of blurring organizational boundaries. Simultaneously, the changing competitive environment, including emerging strategies, decentralized decision-making and knowledge flows in self-organizing units, forces hospitality managers, both in large and small firms, to re-examine their decision-making capacity. Many hospitality managers in today's global knowledge environment are engaged in organizational experiments without the guidance of a fundamental framework (Athiyaman and Robertson, 1995). However, they are expected to sustain competitive advantage and improve the bottom line.

In the knowledge economy, hospitality managers will have to balance exploration and exploitation. Within such a dynamic market environment, strategic decision-makers are continuously trading off between alternative modes of coordinating production and exchange, including the trade off for organizing the transactions and their related costs that support these activities. As a consequence Go and Moutinho (2000) identified the following emerging trends that are relevant for the international hospitality industry:

- The asset evolution phenomenon, whereby hospitality firms liquidate where possible their assets to meet shareholders' expectations for continued bottom-line growth

- The impact of information and communication technology challenging firms to turn properties into flexible hotel operations

- The proliferation of branding leading to consumer confusion and the need for clear positioning

- The labour issue: due to the dearth of supply will imply more demanding staff and the need for professional hospitality managers who are educated and can think and capitalize on opportunities by adapting an organization to changing economic realities

- The continued impact of government regulations on the international hospitality industry, despite liberalization as a consequence of pollution and industry capacity control concerns. In capitalist society there is some freedom of choice and forces at work to reduce transaction costs and eliminate inefficient forms of production. Other relevant issues have been detailed in Go and Pine (1995)

- The market functions on the basis of competition that establishes rules and guides strategic decision-making. The literature on strategy recognizes that a firm's intended strategy may differ from its realized strategy due to misjudgements about competitors' actions and/or reactions (Mintzberg, 1978; Davis and Devinney, 1997). Thus competitor identification is a prerequisite to strategy formulation. The importance of competitor analysis to strategy formulation has resulted in a number of researchers attempting to identify competitors at the firm level (see, for example, McGee and Thomas, 1986; Smith *et al.*, 1997). Since this type of research often lacks *a priori* theory to guide empirical analysis, Barney and Hoskisson (1990) have labelled research on competitor identification as 'data mining'. In essence this strategic process is concerned with bridging the 'uncertainty' gap with knowledge, learning theory and decision science.

In this chapter we will focus on relevant strategic issues, such as the effects of globalization, changing demographics and lifestyles and rising environmental concerns that, among others, affect the strategic posturing of the existing and potential hospitality competitors and pinpoint the changing patterns of competition. Then we will advance a framework designed to make the 'right' strategic choices within the context of an integrated 'value-chain' analysis approach that seeks to emphasize the impact of the economic 'game rules' that direct the behaviour and performance of hospitality firms. The chapter concludes with an analysis of competition at the firm level, particularly competitor identification and competitive asymmetries and techniques to cope with change, risk and uncertainty, and the threat of competitive entry into a product market and strategic choices within the various stages of the product life cycle.

Changing patterns of competition

International hospitality firms that established their *modus operandi* mainly in the 1960s and 1970s were forced in the 1980s and 1990s to adapt to global realities and new challenges. For instance, major operators placed considerable pressure on Forte, UK (previously Trust House Forte) to abandon its preference for freehold hotel property ownership, which caused the firm to expand at a slow pace (Go and Pine, 1995: 42). During the 1990s most international hospitality firms opted for either a strategy of concentration or a strategy of diversification. The majority of international hospitality firms have chosen either a strategy of concentration or one to obtain scale economies derived from a uniform product in a single market, using a single dominant technology. Most small and medium-sized hospitality firms will be forced to opt for either a strategy of concentration, for instance by joining a franchisor or consortium or a diversification strategy. We shall address the diversification issue later on.

The forms of concentrated growth are strategic alliances, franchising, management contracts, joint ventures and acquisition. Each of these business formats reflects the unique nature of the hospitality industry's almost pure competitive status. Strategic alliances are common in the international hospitality industry. Many, if not most international hospitality firms have one or more strategic partnership with another hotel chain and increasingly with synergistically related organizations such as car rental organizations, airlines and life insurance companies. Franchising is one of the most common and preferred forms of expansion for international hospitality firms. It is linked to the proliferation of branding that is evident in the international hospitality industry. The franchise method can be either applied to licensing a single franchisee or a master licence that gives the franchisee the right to open an agreed number of units within a particular geographic area. Choice Hotels International introduced product differentiation on a grand scale into the international hospitality industry in 1981 and it pioneered the application of branding in the US hotel industry, including Sleep Inns, Comfort Inns and Suites, Quality Inns and Suites and Clarion Hotels, Resorts and Suites, and has become one of the leading franchisors of hotels and motels (Go and Pine, 1995: 42).

Management contracts have also become an increasingly popular means of hotel operation. Through a legal agreement, the management contract, it enables the owner to employ an operator to assume full responsibility for the professional management of the property. Four Seasons Hotels, Hyatt International and InterContinental are examples of successful hotel management contract companies. Typically the joint venture strategy of expansion in the international hospitality industry has taken the form of a large real estate developer joining forces with a hospitality operator. They decide to join primarily for marketing purposes. The joint venture of World International and Wharf Holdings may serve as an example. Finally, the number of acquisitions continues to rise. Such activity is driven by the need to achieve scale economies. Examples of hospitality related acquisitions are Ladbroke's takeover of Hilton International, Grand Metropolitan's takeover of Pillsbury and its Burger King subsidiary.

The diversification issues

What does this concentration trend imply for small and medium-sized enterprises (SMEs)? Will standardization lead to uniformity in the international hospitality industry? We doubt it for several reasons. First, the globe is, and likely to remain a culturally diverse planet. Recently this has been rather forcefully demonstrated by fundamentalists' attacks on the Twin Towers in New York. Also the mounting pressure by anti-globalist demonstrators should cause international hospitality industry managers to reflect on the new realities in the world.

McDonaldization may continue its march to conquer the world market, but the 'Slow Food' movement, that emerged in Italy in 1986 in reaction to the opening of a McDonald's outlet in Rome, is yet another signal of resistance to global branding. Since then it has expanded across Europe and represents a strategic scenario that builds on the 'sustainability' paradigm. The 'Slow Food' movement clearly has placed the diversity issue and the cultural identity of the host community centre stage. In such a context hospitality management should transform toward capitalizing on cultural diversity, for instance by linking the cultural identity of the host community as expressed by locally grown food and beverage, through an integrated chain of hospitality competencies to customers, both local and global, in order to create optimal value for both host and guest.

Second, the evolution towards sustainable development, especially in second and third tier urban and rural areas, will require hospitality managers to broaden their marketing concept (Kotler and Levy, 1969) to include the interest of the host community. It implies the 'application of service marketing in a strategic marketing context implemented with a social marketing conscience and viewed in a global context' (Go and Haywood, 1990: 136) and may, in the future, cause the international hospitality industry to design and develop hospitality facilities that fit the fabric of the host community.

Third, the rise of mass individualization offers SMEs a great opportunity to add value through differentiated production and marketing. In general, small business hospitality operators have little, if any awareness of global standards. However, hospitality has the potential to serve as a change agent due to its function of connecting host and guest. Within the regional culinary heritage concept, selected restaurants and hotels are connecting regional food processing companies and farms to deliver high quality products and sustain local pride in craftsmanship. If they are to succeed, such hospitality initiatives must embrace globalization, yet treat it with a local focus. Specifically, it requires translating pride of heritage in a unique hospitality identity that is anchored in trust and fine-grained relationships and clearly communicated with the aid of information and communication technology and inter-firm alliances (Go and Appelman, 2001).

In summary, competitive scenarios in international hospitality management differ in nature. Given the fierce competitive hospitality landscape, managers should invest in an approach and means that will contribute to enhancing organizational capability.

Alternatively, they may risk losing market share. While concentration appears to rule today's business environment, it may not be inferred that a standardization strategy is a panacea. At the beginning of the 21st century it appears that one of the central issues for the international hospitality industry is to embrace globalization, yet treat it with a localized focus (Go et al., 1996). Within such paradoxical context hospitality operators, both large and small, have to make strategic choices. However, due to a lack of space here, we shall restrict our analysis to competition at the firm level.

Competition at the firm level

First, we start with a *lexical* definition. A lexical definition is nothing more than a basic definition of the concept (Fredericks and Miller, 1987). Accordingly, competitors for firm 'x' could be defined as, 'all other firms functioning in the industry(s) in which "x" operates'. Note that this definition groups firms on the basis of attributes such as products offered – the *supply-based* approach.

The lexical definition could be operationalized using industrial classification systems such as the Standard Industrial Classification (SIC) or the KOMPASS classification (www.kompass.com). For instance, KOMPASS classifies hotels and motels in Sydney, Australia under the four digit industrial or product classification code '69-10' (see KOMPASS AUSTRALIA, 29th ed., 2000, pp. 1266–1270). The list includes 32 hotels and motels within the Sydney region. While it is plausible that hotels such as the Holiday Inn, and Hyatt Regency are competitors – both are four-star establishments located within the Sydney central business district – it could be erroneous to conclude that Holiday Inn, for example, is competing with all the other hotels in the Sydney region. In fact, research into managerial perceptions about competitors suggests that there are less than nine competitors for any one business (see Clark and Montgomery, 1999).

Guthrie (1960) suggests that we learn to be disturbed by many stimuli. Put another way, we learn to require or need many things. For example, consider the disturber 'thirst'. Thirst could be satisfied in many ways: by drinking water, beer, soft drink, etc. A company producing mineral water could be thought of as competing with all other thirst quenchers or, more narrowly, with other *natural* alternatives such as plain drinking water. The definition of competition that one adopts in this situation would be based on consumers' judgement or perception about interdependencies among products. Put simply, if it were found that buyers perceive mineral water and plain drinking water as alternatives, but not mineral water and beer, then competition is said to exist among mineral water and plain drinking water. This approach is *demand-based* since it relies on the consumer to identify competitors.

Consider the following conceptualization of competition that brings together both the supply-based approach, and the demand-based approach to defining competition (Figure 7.1). It suggests that competition should be understood using the concept of the business system or value chain. In other words, a firm competes in every step or stage of its activities, from product design to product utilization by the final customer (McGee and Thomas, 1986). Put another way, firms with similar upstream activities (e.g. production processes or resource similarity), and similar downstream activities (e.g. target markets or market commonality) are said to be in competition with one another (Chen, 1996; Cooper and Inoue, 1996).

This conceptualization of competition suggests that it can be inferred from the characteristics of competing firms. To illustrate, assume that you are identifying competitors for a large hospitality firm. Further, assume that you have the following indicators of upstream and downstream activities for all large firms in the region shown in Table 7.1.

The next step in the analysis is to compute a linear combination of upstream and downstream variables for each of the firms. Specifically, $z_{upstream} = w_1$R&D intensity $+ w_2$capital intensity $+ w_3$asset utilization, and $z_{downstream} = v_1$advertising intensity $+ v_2$sales volume $+ v_3$inventory turnover. Note that the ws and the vs are the 'weights' or importance of variables in the equations. These weights are often derived using statistical procedures such as principal component analysis, but they can also be estimated using managerial judgement. It is presumed here that the principal component analysis of the upstream and downstream variables will result in two factors: one factor for each set of variables. Moving on, the next step in the analysis is to find the distance between the linear combinations for each of the firms. The distance measure could be the common Euclidean distance: for example, $[(u_{pstream (FOCAL FIRM)} - u_{pstream (competitor 'i')})^2 + (d_{ownstream (FOCAL FIRM)} - d_{ownstream (competitor 'i')})^{2[sbc]}]^{1/2}$. The results of this computation: i.e. computing the distance between the focal firm and each of the other firms on $u_{pstream}$ and $d_{ownstream}$ could be plotted on a two dimensional map as shown in Figure 7.2.

What is the main implication of such observation? Firms closer to the focal firm would be its direct or most influential competitors, i.e. the focal firm should expect that such rivals are likely to

Figure 7.1 Competition

Upstream	Downstream
R&D intensity (e.g. expenditure on new product development), capital intensity, and asset utilization	Advertising intensity, sales volume, and inventory turnover (e.g. occupancy rate for hotels)

Table 7.1 Upstream and downstream activities

engage in competitive behaviour that would be characterized by price cutting and/or sales promotions (Smith *et al.*, 1997; Hauser and Shugan, 1983; Urban *et al.*, 1984). But the question remains; how do we decide which firms are to be considered as direct or the most relevant competitors for the focal firm? Here, further quantitative and/or qualitative analyses could help provide an answer.

As mentioned earlier, the first step is to compute the Euclidean distance between the focal firm and each of the other firms on upstream and downstream variables. The results of this computation could be subjected to a statistical cluster analysis and the resulting cluster solution can be viewed as direct competitors for the focal firm. As regards qualitative analysis, discussions with industry experts could help (Mascarenhas and Aaker, 1989). Specifically, industry experts, including executives with the focal firm, could be asked to decide on the most relevant or direct competitors. While this procedure seems to make the whole exercise of mapping competitors irrelevant: if industry experts are to decide the direct competitors, why not ask them directly who their competitors are, the procedure would help the analyst go beyond the industry(s) in which the firm presently competes to identify potential competitors. In other words, firms closer to the focal firm in either upstream or downstream activities, functioning in related

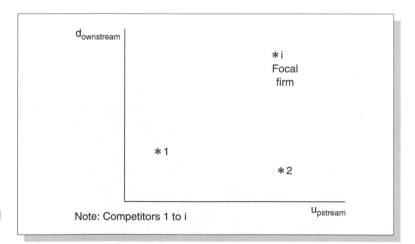

Figure 7.2 The focal firm and competitor's distance

and/or unrelated industries, could be identified and assessed for potential competitive threats.

Understanding potential competition

Earlier, the method that we used to define competition at the firm level took into account the activities that are necessary to deliver a product or service to the market: the upstream and downstream activities. In this section the focus is on understanding threats from potential competitors. Using market entry timing as the criterion concept, plausible threats (and opportunities) to the focal firm from similar upstream or downstream competitors are assessed.

We start by defining the criterion concept: market entry timing. Market entry timing is the order of entry of firms into a product market. In measurement terminology, the *natural variable* is presumed to have *properties* that can be ordered sequentially, as the first entrant or the pioneer, second entrant, third entrant, and so on. Most strategy researchers tend to agree that there is a positive relationship between order-of-entry and market share; i.e. the first to enter the market will have the largest share, the second entrant will have the second largest market share, and so on (Kalyanram and Urban, 1992; Bowman and Gatignon, 1996). We posit that two factors underlie order-of-entry into a product market: firm – a supply-side factor – and consumer – a demand-side factor. We start by discussing firm factors.

Management theorists often classify organizations into discrete and collective categories for detailed analysis (Philip, 1992). One such classification groups organizations into 'boundary spanning', and 'production units' (Daft, 1995). Boundary spanners are responsible for exchange with the environment, e.g. the marketing function. Production units focus on the production or manufacturing of product/service outputs.

Thinking in terms of the hospitality industry, a firm with production or manufacturing skills would tend to be an early entrant into a new product market. This is because the product is relatively easy to improve upon. On the other hand, a firm with marketing skills will be a late entrant into a product market since late entry would require focusing on niche segments (Robinson, Fornell and Sullivan, 1992). Thus, in new markets, possession of manufacturing skills is negatively related to order of entry, and in existing markets, possession of marketing skills is positively related to order of entry.

Another firm-specific characteristic, which is related to possession of both manufacturing and marketing skills, is the size of the firm. The theory is that large firms would like to learn from the pioneer's mistakes and then move in as an early entrant to capture a substantial market share. In other words, large firms may be a potential threat only in growing or mature markets. Expressed in terms of a functional relationship, firm size is negatively related to order of entrant.

Finally, Kalyanraman and Urban (1992) suggest a formula that can be used to assess the relationship between market share and order of entry: $1/(\text{order of entry})^{1/2}$. The focal firm can use this formula to compute probable market share for any new entry.

However, consumer learning is also an important influence on market entry timing. Specifically, if product attributes are objective, i.e. easy to evaluate, then success in the product-market will depend on educating the customers about the brand. In other words, all firms will aggressively advertise and promote their brands. In this case, consumer learning may have little or no influence on order of entry. However, there is research evidence that learning about brands decreases with order of entry (Bowman and Gatignon, 1996). Indeed, their research shows that order of entry tends to decrease the market response to quality and promotion (see their Table 3, p. 238).

On the other hand, if product attributes are difficult to evaluate, then the pioneer will have the competitive advantage. There are at least two explanations for pioneer advantage. The first explanation is that when consumers successfully use the pioneer's brand, they will know with certainty that it works and thus will form a preference for it over the other follower brands (Schmalensee, 1982; Robinson and Fornell, 1985; Golder and Tellis, 1993). Another explanation highlights that consumers may learn to *equate* the pioneer's product with the ideal product (Carpenter and Nakamoto, 1989).

Yet another consumer factor that favours the early entrant over later entrants is the 'network effects', i.e. the influence of triers or adopters of the product on non-users or potential purchasers of the product (Eliashberg and Robertson, 1988). Since innovators tend to be opinion leaders (Sheth, Mittal and Newman, 2000), it is likely that the first entrant or the pioneer would benefit more from these network effects.

Switching costs is another consumer concept that has been associated with market entry timing. Switching costs are one-time costs incurred by the consumer for adopting the new product or converting to the new product (Eliashberg and Robertson, 1988). Note that switching costs would include the purchase price of the product and the related costs of changing the consumption system. Logically, if the switching costs are high, and if the diffusion rate is rapid, then one would expect the pioneer to gain the most. It is also plausible to pose a rival explanation. High switching costs or purchase price of the product may induce most consumers to delay their purchase. This delay could favour later entrants if they had entered the market with a differentiated and/or a low price product (Kalyanram and Urban, 1992).

In summary, we posit that competitive entry into a product-market will be positively related to firm size, firm marketing skills, and negatively related to manufacturing skills, and R&D capability. Also, the attraction of a product-market will differ from one consumer-learning situation to another. For example, if consumers learn to equate the pioneer's product with the ideal product, then pioneer will have the competitive advantage. If the product is easy to evaluate, then success in the product-market will depend on educating the customers about the brand. In this situation, firms with marketing expertise will enter and aggressively advertise and promote their brands.

Dynamics and symmetry of competition

Earlier, we defined competition at the firm level using 'upstream' and 'downstream' variables. Furthermore, it was shown that competitive entry into a product-market is influenced by firm-specific characteristics such as manufacturing skills and consumer learning within the product category. Based on the above, it is possible to infer the likely competitive structure that would evolve as the product progresses through its life-cycle stages. This analysis will reveal strategies for competing within different life-cycle stages.

Competitive structure over the product life cycle

As you may recall from your earlier studies, the classical product life cycle suggests that products move from the introductory phase, through to growth, maturity, and decline stages (Levitt, 1965). During the introductory phase of the life cycle, it is highly likely that the production technology is still evolving. In this scenario, the competition will mostly be confined to product innovation and development: an upstream activity. In line with Robinson, Fornell and Sullivan (1992), only few firms with R&D skills will be present in the industry (product category). The firms' marketing activities will be directed at inducing both primary or category demand, and primary sales: the latter is also labelled secondary demand (Hanssens, Parsons and Schultz, 1990). Other generic marketing approaches would include high pricing to recover some of the excessive costs of launching and selective distribution (Peter and Donnelly, 1988). During this introductory phase, it is possible that consumers' preference becomes shaped by one of the first entrants (see the consumer preference formation discussed in the earlier section, also see Carpenter and Nakamoto (1989)). In other words, since the attributes of the product may be difficult to evaluate by most, if not all consumers, the pioneer's product or one of the first entrants' product, will become the industry standard (see Figure 7.3).

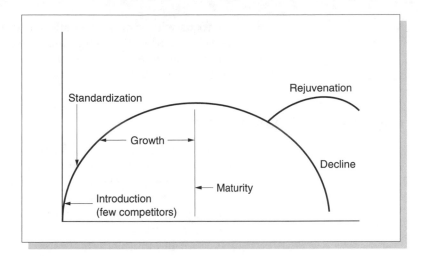

Figure 7.3 The product life cycle

The evolution of a brand as the industry standard will result in firms directing their attention to the production or manufacturing process. The emphasis will be on low delivered cost. Note that this argument is in line with Cooper and Nakanishi's (1989) observation that competition reduces competitive offerings to standardized products with respect to important attributes. Also, in this scenario, it is logical to expect firms with manufacturing skills to enter the market (Robinson, Fornell and Sullivan, 1992). In general, the competition, or more properly the competitive focus, will shift towards upstream activities. Marketing efforts will primarily be directed at inducing primary sales and advertising elasticity will be the highest (Hanssens, Parsons and Schultz, 1990). The distribution of the product will be intensive. This is the growth stage of the product (Figure 7.3).

During the maturity stage of the product life cycle, it is highly likely that firms with marketing skills will be entering the market. This is because of the need for the late entrants to serve a 'niche' market (Robinson, Fornell and Sullivan, 1992). On the other hand, it is also likely that at least some of the early competitors will exit or be driven out of the market (see Golder and Tellis, 1993 for some evidence in this direction). This is the stage when marketing activities, will be at their peak. Specifically, consumer sales and promotion expenditures will be heavy to encourage brand switching, but advertising will be moderate since most buyers will be aware of product/brand characteristics. Another reason for the low levels of advertising is the low advertising elasticity; Hanssens, Parsons and Schultz (1990) argue that advertising elasticity will be the lowest during the maturity stage of the product life cycle. Note that in this phase, new entry will often be through acquisitions (Robinson, Fornell and Sullivan, 1992).

Finally, during the decline stage of the product, competition will be among few firms with a rapid shakeout of weak members.

The focus will be on rejuvenation: product innovation. Generally speaking, during this stage, the firm's marketing efforts will be minimal (Peter and Donnelly, 1988). Figure 7.3 shows the product life cycle. Figure 7.4 is a pictorial summary of the discussion.

Asymmetry in competitive effects

Asymmetry in competitive effects is said to exist if a change in a brand's marketing effort affects each competitive brand differently. According to Hanssens, Parsons and Schultz (1990), asymmetry can arise in durables because of the saturation effect, i.e. the pool of potential customers decreases as sales are made. In addition, asymmetry in durables could arise because of switching costs and word-of-mouth effects (Erdem, 1996). Similarly, in frequently purchased goods including non-durables, consumer behaviour can be used to explain the persistence of asymmetries in market structure. Specifically, a consumer might prefer a brand because her preferences may be reinforced by usage, inertia or learning-combined risk aversion (Erdem, 1996).

Earlier, it was mentioned that during the introductory phase the focus would be on product innovation. Contemporary marketing theories suggest that this phase would be characterized by mini-

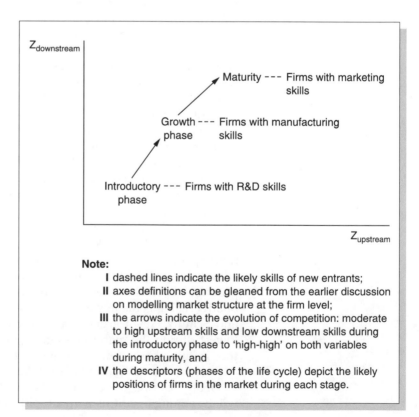

Figure 7.4 A pictorial representation of the evolution of competitive structure

mal competition: 'none of importance' according to Peter and Donnelly (1988). One reason for this minimal competition could be that firms may lack sufficient information systems to detect changes in a competitor's marketing mix such as price and advertisements (Carpenter *et al.*, 1988). Also, competitive reactions may be less severe since each firm or operator will be attempting to expand the market rather than attacking competitors' relative positions (Dekimpe and Hanssens, 1995).

Generally, marketing theory suggests that the elasticity of managerial decision varies, e.g. price and advertising increase over the growth and maturity stages and decrease during the decline stage. However, empirical evidence for the theory is sparse (Hanssens *et al.*, 1990). Dekimpe and Hanssens' (1995) research indicates that during the growth phase, a firm's advertising will have a carry-over effect lasting as long as 12 months or more. Although their research did not consider the varying impact of a firm's marketing efforts on competitors, it could be said that advertising would benefit the early entrants more than the late entrants as it gives innovators an incentive to try the product after which imitation effects take over creating higher sales.

Much research on asymmetry in marketing efforts has been conducted with mature products (Carpenter *et al.*, 1988; Branenberg and Wathieu, 1996; Erdem, 1996). Generally, the research shows price, advertising and/or promotion asymmetries in non-durables. For example, Branenberg and Wathieu (1996) demonstrate that in order for price promotions to be effective, competing brands should have a larger quality gap than the price gap. Similarly, Erdem (1996) highlights the need for perceived dissimilarity among brands to exist for free sample offers to be effective. However, these asymmetries appear to be temporary. In other words, as observed by Dekimpe and Hanssens (1995), in mature markets in which primary demand is absent, the relative position of the players is only temporarily affected by their marketing activities.

Conclusions

The strategic posture of firms depends on understanding existing and potential competition. This chapter brings together the literature on competitor identification, market entry timing, and asymmetries in competition under a single strategy development framework. Briefly, we identify competitors using the value chain framework. Next, we explore threats from potential competitors using the 'market entry timing' concept. We argue that firms with research and development skills will be pioneers, firms with manufacturing skills will be first entrants, and firms with marketing skills will be late entrants into a product-market. Finally, using the classical product life-cycle concept, we posit that asymmetries in competitive action will exist during different phases of the life cycle.

Summary

- Competitor identification is a prerequisite to strategy formulation.

- Competitors for firm 'x' could be defined as, 'all other firms functioning in the industry(s) in which "x" operates' (the *supply-based* approach).

- The *demand-based* approach to studying competition relies on the consumer to identify competitors.

- Our conceptualization of competition brings together both the supply-based approach, and the demand-based approach to defining competition.

- We contend that firms with similar upstream activities (e.g. production processes or resource similarity), and similar downstream activities (e.g. target markets or market commonality) are said to be in competition with one another.

- Firms closer to the focal firm on upstream, and downstream variables would be its direct or most influential competitors.

- The procedure that we describe for 'mapping' competitors would help the analyst go beyond the industry(s) in which the firm presently competes to identify potential competitors.

- Using market entry timing as the criterion concept, plausible threats (and opportunities) to the focal firm from similar upstream or downstream competitors can be assessed.

- We posit that two factors underlie order-of-entry into a product market: firm – a supply-side factor – and consumer – a demand-side factor.

- Competitive entry into a product-market will be positively related to firm size, firm marketing skills, and negatively related to manufacturing skills, and R&D capability.

- Also, the attraction of a product-market will differ from one consumer-learning situation to another. For instance, if the product is easy to evaluate, then success in the product-market will depend on educating the customers about the brand. In this situation, firms with marketing expertise will enter and aggressively advertise and promote their brands.

- The classical product life cycle suggests that products move from introductory phase, through to growth, maturity, and decline stages.

- During the introductory phase of the life cycle, it is highly likely that the production technology is still evolving. In this scenario, the competition will mostly be confined to product innovation and development: an upstream activity. Also, since the attributes of the product may be difficult to evaluate by most, if not all consumers, the pioneer's product or one of the first entrants product, will become the industry standard.

- The evolution of a brand as the industry standard will result in firms directing their attention to the production or manufacturing process. The emphasis will be on low delivered cost. This is the growth stage of the product.

- During the maturity stage of the product life cycle, it is highly likely that firms with marketing skills will be entering the market.

- Finally, during the decline stage of the product, competition will be among few firms with a rapid shakeout of weak members. The focus will be on rejuvenation: product innovation.

- Generally, marketing theory suggests that elasticity of managerial decision variables, e.g. price and advertisement, increase over the growth and maturity stages and decrease during the decline stage.

Review questions

1. What positive contributions has the emergence of multinationals made to the international hospitality industry?
2. What are the strategic implications of globalization in the international hospitality industry both at the global and local levels?
3. Why do hospitality firms need to make strategic choices and formulate, implement and control strategy?
4. What you believe to be the purpose of competitor analysis, and what challenges does it pose for the manager?
5. How do the approaches to expansion adopted by Forte hotels and Choice Hotels International differ, or not?
6. What value does the value chain or business system approach to defining competition have?
7. Why do you think mapping competitors using upstream and downstream activities provides more relevant information for managers?
8. What is meant by 'market entry timing', and how can such a concept be used to assess potential competitive threats?
9. What are the determinants of market entry timing?

10. What relevance does the product life-cycle concept have for understanding strategic choice in an industry?
11. If consumer learning in a product market is characterized as 'inertia', how then would you describe the competitive structure of the industry?
12. What is meant by 'asymmetry' in competitive effects and what are its implications?

References

Athiyaman, A. and Robertson, R.W. (1995) Strategic planning in large tourism firms: an empirical analysis. *Tourism Management*, **16**, (3),199–205.

Barney, J. B. and Hoskisson, R. E. (1990) Strategic groups: untested assertions and research proposals, *Managerial and Decision Economics*, **11**, 187–198.

Bronnenberg, B. J. and Wathieu, L. (1996) Asymmetric promotion effects and brand positioning, *Marketing Science*, **15**, (4), 379–395.

Bowman, D. and Gatigon, H. (1996) Order of entry as a moderator of the effect of the marketing mix on a market share, *Marketing Science*, **15**, (3), 222–242.

Carpenter, G. S., Cooper, L. G., Hanssens, D. M. and Midgley, D. (1988) Modelling asymmetric competition, *Marketing Science*, **7**, (4), 393–412.

Carpenter, G. S. and Nakamoto, K. (1989) Consumer preference formation and pioneering advantage, *Journal of Marketing Research*, **26**, (3), 285–298.

Chen, M. (1996) Competitor analysis and inter-firm rivalry: toward a theoretical integration. *Academy of Management Review*, **21**, (1), 100–134.

Clark, B. H. and Montgomery, D. B. (1999) Managerial identification of competitors. *Journal of Marketing*, **63**, 67–83.

Cooper, L. and Inoue, A. (1996) Building market structures from consumer preferences, *Journal of Marketing Research*, **33**, (3), 293–306.

Cooper, L. G. and Nakanishi, M. (1989) *Market-Share Analysis*. Kluwer Academic Publishers, Boston.

Daft, R. T. (1995) *Organization Theory and Decision*. West Publishing, New York.

Davis, J. and Devinney, T. (1997) *The Essence of Corporate Strategy: Theory for Modern Decision Making*. Allen & Unwin, Sydney.

DeKimpe, M. and Hanssens, D. (1995) Empirical generalizations about market evolution and stationarity, *Marketing Science*, **14**, (3), G109–G121.

Eliashberg, J. and Robertson, T. (1988) New product pre-announcing behavior: a market signalling study, *Journal of Marketing Research*, **25**, (3), 282–292.

Erdem, T. (1996) A dynamic analysis of market structure based on panel data, *Marketing Science*, **15**, (4), 359–378.

Fredericks, M. and Miller, S. I. (1987) The use of conceptual analysis for teaching sociology courses. *Teaching Sociology*, **15**, (10), 392–398.

Go, F. and Appelman, J. (2001) Achieving global competitiveness in SMEs by building trust in inter-firm alliances. In Wahab, S. and Cooper, C. (eds), *Tourism in the Age of Globalisation*. Routledge, London, pp. 183–197.

Go, F., Choi, T. and Chan, C. (1996) Four Seasons-Regent: Building a global presence in the luxury market, *Cornell Hotel and Restaurant Administration Quarterly*, **37**, (4), 58–65.

Go, F. and Moutinho, L. (2000) International tourism management. In Moutinho, L. (ed.), *Strategic Management in Tourism*. CABI, Oxford, pp. 315–335.

Go, F. and Pine, R. (1995) *Globalization strategy in the Hotel Industry*. Routledge, London.

Go, F. and Haywood, K. M. (1990) Marketing of the service process: state of the art in tourism, recreation and hospitality industries. In Cooper, C. (ed), *Progress in Tourism, Recreation and Hospitality Management* Vol. 2, Belhaven Press, London, pp. 129–150.

Golder, P. N. and Tellis, G. (1993) Pioneer advantage: marketing logic or legend? *Journal of Marketing Research*, **30**, (2), 158–170.

Guthrie, E. R. (1960) *The Psychology of Learning*. Peter Smith, Gloucester.

Hanssens, D. M., Parsons, L. J. and Schultz, R. L. (1990) *Market Response Models: Econometric and Time Series Analysis*. Kluwer Academic Publishers, Boston.

Hauser, J. R. and Shugan, S. (1983) Defensive marketing strategies, *Marketing Science*, **2**, (4), 319–360.

Kalyanaram, G. and Urban, G. (1992) Dynamic effects of the order of entry on market share, trial penetration, and repeat purchases for frequently purchased consumer goods, *Marketing Science*, **11**, (3), 235–250.

Kotler, P. and Levy, S. (1969) Broadening the concept of marketing, *Journal of Marketing*, **33**, (January), 10–15.

Levitt, T. (1965) Exploit the product life cycle. *Harvard Business Review*, **43**, 81–94.

Mascarenhas, B. and Aaker, D. (1989) Mobility barriers and strategic groups, *Strategic Management Journal*, **10**, 475–485.

McGee, J. and Thomas, H. (1986) Strategic groups: theory research and taxonomy, *Strategic Management Journal*, **7**, 141–160.

Mintzberg, H. (1978) Patterns in strategy formation, *Management Science*, **24**, (9), 934–948.

Peter, J. P. and Donnelly, J. H. Jr (1988) *A Preface to Marketing Management*. Business Publications Inc., Plano, Texas.

Philip, R. (1992) The organizational taxonomy: definition and design, *Academy of Management Review*, **17**, (4), 758–781.

Robinson, W. and Fornell, C. (1985) Sources of market pioneer advantages in consumer goods industries, *Journal of Marketing Research*, **22**, (3), 305–317.

Robinson, W., Fornell, C. and Sullivan, M. (1992) Are market pioneers intrinsically stronger than later entrants? *Strategic Management Journal*, **13**, 609–624.

Schmalensee, R. (1982) Product differentiation advantages of pioneering brands, *American Economic Review*, **72** (June), 349–365.

Sheth, J. N. Mittal, B. and Newman, B. I. (2000) *Customer Behavior: Consumer Behavior and Beyond* The Dryden Press, Fort Worth, Texas.

Smith, K., Grimm, C., Wally, S. and Young, G. (1997) Strategic groups and rivalrous firm behavior: towards a reconciliation, *Strategic Management Journal*, **18**, 149–157.

Urban, G. L., Johnson, P. L. and Hauser, J. (1984) Testing competitive market structures, *Marketing Science*, **3**, (2), 83–112.

Further reading

Clark, B. H. and Montgomery, D. B. (1999) Managerial identification of competitors. *Journal of Marketing*, **63**, 67–83.

Cooper, L. G. and Nakanishi, M. (1989) *Market-Share Analysis*. Kluwer Academic Publishers, Boston.

Davis, J. and Devinney, T. (1997) *The Essence of Corporate Strategy: Theory for Modern Decision Making*. Allen & Unwin, Sydney.

Mintzberg, H. and Quinn, J. B. (1991) *The Strategy Process: Concepts, Contexts, Cases* 2nd ed. Prentice Hall, Englewood Cliffs, NJ.

Urban, G. L. and Star, S. H. (1991) *Advanced Marketing Strategy*. Prentice Hall, Englewood Cliffs, NJ.

CHAPTER 8

Marketing options

Alex Gibson

Chapter objectives

When you have read this chapter you will be able to:

- Describe the international environment scanning process.

- Describe the strategic international marketing planning process.

- Evaluate a number of specific challenges and drivers to international marketing activities.

- Discuss a number of key business and marketing strategy issues for international hospitality marketers.

- Analyse the marketing mix considerations in international marketing.

- Discuss the circumstances favouring customization or standardization in international marketing activities.

Introduction to global marketing management

The hospitality industry is becoming increasingly internationalized. Indeed, we can say it is globalized, where a common global experience is taking place. This is prompted by both supply and demand factors. On the supply side there has been an explosion in tourist destination, product distribution and marketing choices. Destinations that once seemed exotic are now served by mass-market package tour operators. In the hospitality product we have seen the international expansion of budget hotels at one end of the quality spectrum and boutique hotels at the other. In developed markets, both types of product have seen acceptance not just from international visitors, but also from the domestic markets. The demand side of the global expansion is equally important. The rise in incomes in developing and the former Soviet bloc countries has led to international hospitality chains seeking to develop a presence in such markets for both domestic and international travellers.

The international business traveller can be seen as a relatively homogeneous animal. They can be observed looking frazzled at airport terminals laden down with such icons as mobile phone, Palmtop organizer and laptop. Throughout the developed world such travellers are increasingly exposed to common information sources such as CNN, Time and Businessweek. They desire from hospitality providers a consistency of experience, convenience through technology and alliances and personal benefits through loyalty programmes. But it is not just the business traveller who seeks a common experience. Today's youth culture is increasingly globalized through television, music and the impact of Hollywood. The opportunities to market across international boundaries have therefore never been greater and are outlined in Figure 8.1.

International strategic marketing planning

Marketing across international boundaries requires a specific set of strategic planning skills. As chains and brands extend from their domestic market base, a new set of challenges emerges. Global regions are at different cycles of tourism development and levels of competitive intensity. Within countries a set of strongly entrenched domestic companies are waiting to tackle the interna-

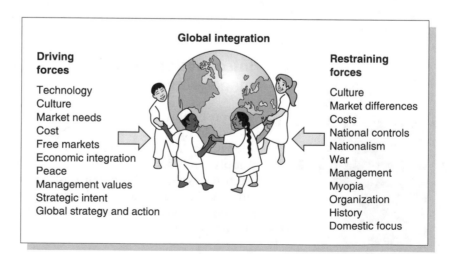

Figure 8.1 Forces affecting globalization. Source: adapted from Keegan (2002)

tional newcomers. Yu (1999) asserts that, unlike marketing in domestic markets, international hospitality marketing faces a different environment in foreign countries. The differences and challenges are reflected in the different political, legal, economic and cultural systems of the host countries. International hospitality firms have to learn the different culture of the customers in each host country, and adjust or modify their products and services to meet the needs of local markets. International strategic marketing planning is framed against long-term and short-term ambitions. Take Marriott's Mission statement emphasizing the global perspective, 'we are committed to being the best lodging and management services company in the world by treating employees in ways that create extraordinary customer service and shareholder value' (Marriott International, 1998). This chapter addresses the specific challenges to strategic marketing planning in an international context. To do this a number of specific issues are addressed. The structure followed mirrors that outlined by Calver (1994b) shown in Figure 8.2.

Scanning the international environment

The strategic marketing planning process begins with a detailed assessment of the business environment facing the organization. This is a particular challenge for international organizations. The process of systematically assessing the internal and external environment is known as scanning. To conduct effective environmental scanning to identify market gaps and approaches, international firms use International Management Information Systems. These systems are designed to aid the flow of information from both internal and external sources of information in each international market.

Internal sources

- Encompass data from company sales, financial and accounting needs as reported by overseas properties and foreign franchises. Market analysis and special research reports can be used as international sources. Surveys of sales representatives, in-house guests and members in the channel of distribution can generate valuable market information for managers.

External sources

- Government reports, World Tourism Organisation reports, World Travel and Tourism Council reports, International Hospitality Consulting firms (e.g. Pannell Kerr Foster, Arthur Andersen).

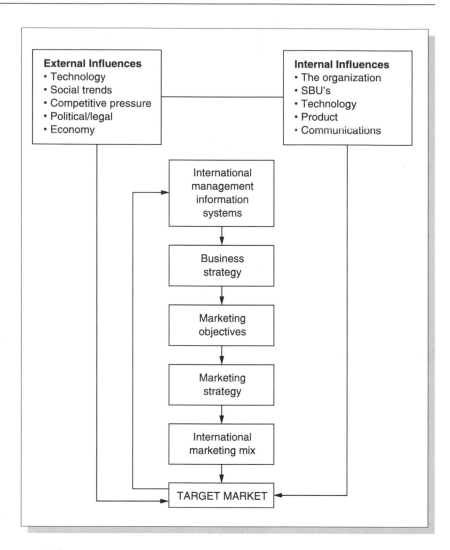

Figure 8.2 Influences on strategic marketing planning. Source: adapted from Calver (1994)

In terms of assessing the external and internal influences the scope of environmental scanning of the international environment is critical. Dev and Olsens' (2000) matrix (see Figure 8.3) offers a useful starting point for international marketers to prioritize their scanning process. The model proposes that the marketer needs to place greatest resources to address issues that are both important, in terms of their potential impact on the business, and require urgent attention of management. Least focus should be placed on issues that are low in importance and urgency.

Business and marketing strategy

As part of an international think-tank, co-sponsored by the International Hotel and Restaurant Association (IH&RA) and

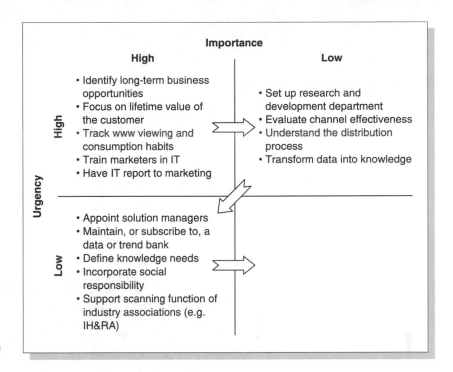

Figure 8.3 Urgent/ importance matrix of marketing. Source: Dev and Olsen (2000: p. 46)

the Hospitality Sales and Marketing Association, Dev and Olsen (2000) identified several key challenges to the marketing function in the hospitality sector.

Manage distribution costs

A key trend observed in international markets today is *disintermediation*, namely the bypassing of traditional intermediaries such as tour operators and travel agents by customers. New technology, especially the Internet, has led to a surge in travel portal sites offering customers the opportunity for 'one-stop' shopping for travel and hospitality services (Murphy *et al.*, 1996; O'Connor and Frew, 1998). While the extent to which customers will want direct access to book room stock is not entirely clear there will be a desire on their part, and that of companies, to streamline the distribution process.

Analyse customers

Companies need to have a deeper understanding of the issues associated with customer buyer behaviour. While there is a lot of data on observable pheneomena such as occupancy and demographics, there is a lack of impartial assessment of the more qualitative aspects that affect behaviour. As marketers take brands across international borders this need for depth of customer insight increases.

Rethink the business model

A litany of factors points to the poor state of marketing today in companies – declining satisfaction scores, diminishing loyalty, increasing commoditization of the product, disgruntled franchisees.

At the most recent Marketing Think Tank held by the International Hotel and Restaurant Association a number of key forces shaping the future of Marketing internationally were identified (IHRA, 1999).

Destination-focused marketing

Despite the current emphasis placed upon global distribution systems (GDS) and company central reservation systems (CRS), the traveller will begin to rely upon destination-marketing systems to select hotels, restaurants, and attractions once the destination is determined (Hill, 1999). This may, in the long run, have the effect of diluting the value of the hotel brand and lead to bypassing the current GDS and CRS. Destination-marketing systems will typically have some level of National or Regional Tourism board ownership, such as www.visitbritain.com for the British Tourist Authority or Bermuda Tourism www.bermuda-tourism.com. This becomes a more realistic possibility because of technological advances and the growth of the Internet. Whereas hotels and other providers of hospitality experiences were previously dependent upon GDS and CRS to sell their products and services, the changes occurring in the distribution system will now make it possible for providers in destinations to avoid those channels. Riley *et al*. (2001) argue that accurate measurements of loyalty need to be developed at the level of the destination. Increasingly we are likely to see this incorporate both measures of destination loyalty and traditional measures of loyalty to hospitality organizations.

Permission marketing

Permission marketing refers to the process where marketing communications are sent to recipients who have given prior consent to receiving such material. Such communication could be via telephone, mail or increasingly e-mail. In essence customers are invited to raise their hands to learn more, rather than be bombarded with unsolicited offers (Leopold, 1999). Permission marketing's expansion has been seen as critical in an era where the customer is bombarded with competing messages. In this scenario, customers are viewed as giving permission to marketers to send advertising messages to them. In return for this permission, the customer will expect to be paid to receive them. It is already quite common today for customers to receive free wireless telephones and computers in return for listening to, or observing a few minutes of advertising messages. Customers are also willing to provide information in exchange for frequent flyer miles or other loyalty programme rewards.

One-to-one marketing

The concept of *one-to-one* marketing has grown out of technological developments and the belief by the customer that it is possible to treat them as individuals. New communication technologies, most notably the Internet, facilitate a huge increase in the frequency and personalization of communication with customers. This communication can be conducted as efficiently on a global scale as in domestic markets. They are learning to expect customization in response to the growing trend of individualism. They seek greater freedom of choice and seem willing to pay for it. They want to make their choices on their time, meeting their desire for convenience and personalization. As this customer gains more experience from their travels, they will demand a wider range of experiences that they can personally bundle together based upon their travel desires and plans. This need is what underpins the belief that destination marketing will become more important in the near future since contemporary GDS and CRS are unable to bundle a wide range of experiences for every possible destination the traveller is headed (HSMAI, 1999).

The international marketing mix

Relationship marketing

The move to one-to-one marketing has led to the concept of relationship marketing becoming more centre stage in marketing. Relationship marketing refers to the establishment and maintenance of relationships with customers and other partners, involving an exchange of value to both participants.

The globalization of the hospitality industry is a factor driving relationship marketing. The transaction approach to marketing is primarily based on the mass marketing of package consumer goods in the USA. However, when we move these concepts to overseas markets, particularly service based ones, we find that they may not be applicable under a different culture, tradition, economic structure, legal system or institutional setting. Table 8.1 sets out the main shifts in emphasis characterizing the move from traditional to relationship marketing.

Traditional marketing	Relationship marketing
Orientation to single sales	Orientation to customer retention
Episodic customer contact	Continual customer contact
Focus on product features	Focus on customer value
Short-term horizon	Long-term horizon
Little emphasis on customer service	High customer service emphasis
Limited commitment to meeting customer expectations	High commitment to meeting customer expectations
Quality concerns only production staff	Quality concerns all staff members

Source: adapted from Bowen and Shoemaker (1998).

Table 8.1 Traditional versus relationship marketing

The benefits to companies retaining more of the customer base are potentially large. One US study pointed to a 100% profit boost to those companies that could retain just 5% more customers (Reichheld and Sasser, 1990).

Relationship marketing is particularly important to the hospitality industry as most hotel segments are mature and competition is strong. Often there is little differentiation among products in the same market segment. This is leading to increased concern that the product is becoming commoditized, with the inevitable consequence being a retreat to a damaging price-led basis of competition. Relationship marketing is seen by chains as a possible antidote to this commoditization as it is based on factors other than pure economics or product attributes (Bowen and Shoemaker, 1998). These reasons suggest that it is beneficial for hospitality companies to build true relationships with guests. Customer retention, price discounting and database – guest history – programmes are methods used by hoteliers to enhance relationships with customers (Yesawich, 1991). Bowen (1996) emphasizes that the usefulness of such strategies lies in their ability to draw on the true lifetime worth of the customer, namely the total spend with a company over a customer's life, citing the example of Ritz Carlton who calculate that the lifetime value of their typical customer is $100 000. This concept will become even more relevant as the scope and opportunity for spending with one company increases.

Payne (1997) has summarized the approach to relationship marketing (Figure 8.4). As the emphasis moves from traditional transaction marketing to relationship marketing the process for companies involves cross-functional approaches – marketing and operations and IT departments will have to cooperate more in order to manage the relationship with customers. This

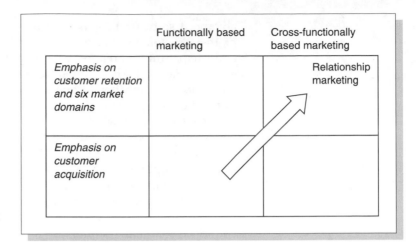

Figure 8.4 The transition to relationship marketing. Source: Payne (1997: p. 30)

challenge will be particularly acute with the international business traveller segment. Additionally, the relationship model reflects an approach that addresses a total of six key markets, not just the traditional customer market (see Figure 8.5).

Customer relationship management

By harnessing advances in information technology and communication channels, companies are endeavouring to deliver customer satisfaction at every point of contact. *Customer relationship management* (CRM) is being promoted as the means to guarantee business survival and success. CRM is a broad term, which encompasses not only applications, but also a business ethos and culture. In simple terms, the objective of CRM is to retain customers and cement consumer loyalty. It involves the use of

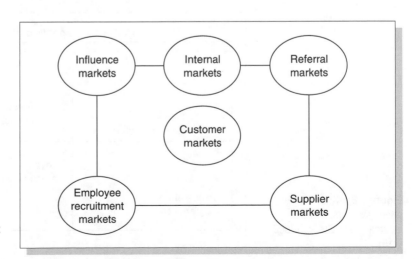

Figure 8.5 Relationship markets. Source: Payne (1997: p. 30)

advanced software to make the most of businesses' knowledge of their customers' behaviour in order to personalize services and predict future preferences. International software companies such as Siebel, SAP and Oracle have development programs with most leading hotel companies to integrate CRM systems in their operations. At the end of the day, CRM programs will not tell companies what people will do but it does build up behavioural models of customer types and provides powerful statistical methods. The use of CRM may not guarantee loyalty but it does optimize communication with customers, while generating information to forecast sales (O'Reilly, 2000). Estis Green (2000) has developed a model (see Figure 8.6) to illustrate the relationship between CRM programs and more traditionally employed marketing strategies.

International marketing alliances

Bowen (1996) argues that the international reach and scale of today's hospitality corporation is such that there is a pressing need for collaboration on a number of fronts, rather than out-and-out competition. Alliances, with a strong marketing rationale, are becoming commonplace, both within the hospitality sector, and with other complementary sectors. The Hilton International and Hilton Hotels Corporation marketing partnership, initiated in 2000, enables travellers to choose between more than 200 new hotels worldwide. Communications were simplified via the creation of a single logo with a common architectural model. A common advertising campaign was created, 'It happens at Hilton'. A common sales force was created, as was a loyalty programme with over 10 m members. The worldwide reservation centre handles

Figure 8.6 Knowledge/ interactivity spectrum. Source: Estis Green, (2000: p.15)

more than 30 million calls a year and a common Internet site, www.hilton.com, has been developed.

As another example of marketing alliances, in August 2001, the luxury international hotel groups Le Meridien and Nikko Hotels International announced an expansion of the global strategic alliance they formed in 2000 to now include all Nikko hotels in Japan and China. This enlarged the two groups' worldwide network to encompass 169 properties in 63 countries and territories. The addition of the 22 properties – 21 throughout Japan and one in China – became effective from 3 August, 2001.

Le Meridien and Nikko Hotels International signed their historic global sales, marketing and reservations alliance on 3 April, 2000, initially encompassing all Nikko Hotels properties outside of Japan – in Europe, North and Central America and Asia Pacific. Since then, Le Meridien has recorded a 30% increase in its business from the hospitality industry's important Japanese market. The increase has resulted from several sales and marketing initiatives Le Meridien implemented shortly after the alliance began. These included printing a Japanese version of its hotel directory and distributing it to key corporate accounts and leisure operators in Japan; producing joint directories; and increasing its presence at travel trade shows and joint road shows in Japan. The two companies have also linked their web sites. The JAL Mileage Bank loyalty programme has also provided Le Meridien with a 42% increase in the number of Japanese stays at its properties in the UK, France, Italy and Spain (Hotel-Online, 2000).

Distribution systems

Distribution strategy is central to competitive success in international hospitality marketing. The use of intermediaries is important for the impact that it has on other elements of the marketing mix and also because it creates a partnership type arrangement with all participants. From a current base of 20% of reservations being made electronically in 2000, it is estimated this number will rise to 50% over the following 5 years with upwards of 75–85% reached by the end of the decade. (Estis Green, 2000). The Internet, which today accounts for about 10% of electronic bookings, continues to increase its share in exponential terms and is set to force traditional GDS companies dramatically to improve their Web capability. Some, such as Travelocity (from Sabre) and 1Travel (from Amadeus), have already moved to respond to the dramatic shifts. The new technologies are set to empower customers greatly and a real challenge will exist for hotels to ensure that they are visible and accessible to the customer. The emergence of two types of Internet site with global reach is also particularly noteworthy.

Mega-travel generalists such as Travelweb and Expedia will possess enormous negotiating power as their presence will be on a global scale and give them access to large levels of inventory.

Rate-driven sites such as auction sites and discount sites will prove very attractive to a large segment of the market that is not brand sensitive. A good example of a discount site is Priceline.com. This company offers customers the opportunity to stay in hotels at heavily discounted rates: while they guarantee to offer branded hotels the identity of these hotels is hidden to the booker until the sale is confirmed, thereby protecting the image of the brand. By way of contrast, a wholesaler site that offers branded alternatives is Greathotelprices.com. While international hotel chains will have a scale to enable them to develop their own powerful, database driven websites, the likelihood is that customers and agents alike will more easily locate all hotels in a destination via the type of destination sites discussed earlier. This in turn may serve to weaken the brand loyalty to the international chains. For smaller domestic chains, there will be an even greater challenge to manage the distribution opportunities through third party intermediaries. It seems unlikely in the medium term that even the biggest international chain will be able to generate enough bookings through its own website to rival the bookings it receives through its central reservation system or agency network, whether online or traditional. In view of this, international hotel chains will continue to try to improve all their distribution channels.

Among the highly rated systems are that of Spanish hotel chain Sol Melia whose call centre staff are all either bi-lingual or tri-lingual and are tourism specialists, in addition to having excellent hotel knowledge. The 24-hour centre receives more than 6000 calls daily. Accor's new reservation system is called Tars On-Line and offers 'real-time' connection and a Revenue Management System to allow the closing of rates and the measurement of length of stay.

Product management

Standardization versus customization

The debate on the extent to which international marketing activities can be standardized has been addressed by Alexander and Lockwood (1996) and Crawford-Welch (1991). Standardization may be considered to be the process of extending and effectively applying domestic target market dictated product standards – tangible and/or intangible attributes – to foreign markets (Medina, 1998). This is in contrast to the total adaptation perspective that stresses the persistent differences between nations and the competitive and regulatory necessity to customize marketing strategy to individual markets. Theodore Levitt (1983) in his seminal article, *The Globalisation of Markets*, argues the most compelling case for standardization of international marketing activities. He argues that technology in communication has homogenized markets around the globe. In addition to the customer-centred rationale, other benefits of standardization include the efficacy of cost savings in service delivery, planning and distribution. Particularly in the budget sector, there is a move toward the expansion of the highly standardized or 'hard branding' as it is sometimes termed.

Nevertheless, even in the budget sector, concessions have to be made to local market conditions. One example of this is the difficulty faced by Holiday Inn when rolling out the Express brand in Spain. As the brand standard decreed the presence of a shower unit rather than bath, this led to the assignment of a 2* classification. While this classification would not prove a problem in the UK and other markets, in Spain there was a general perception of 2* hotels as denoting motels serving the trucking community. Holiday Inn were forced to introduce rooms with baths in order to obtain a 3* classification. There are additional challenges in the standardization process. The need for regional sensitivity is evident to the Chief Executive of Six Continents (formerly Bass Hotels and Resorts), Tom Oliver who, when speaking on the company's headquarters move from Atlanta to London, said; 'when you are based in the USA, you do not have much appreciation of all aspects of the European market ... the basic organizational issue ... is the regional organization ... you need to have one person who is responsible for the whole aspects of the region'. Bender (1996) concurs and argues that increased awareness and understanding of different cultures – what could be termed 'intercultural competence' – can provide a company with a competitive advantage that can benefit its international marketing capabilities.

Mikula and Kye-Sung (1997) make the point that the phrase 'think-global – act local', while overly simplistic, does attempt to define a broad range of activities that international hoteliers use in their marketing efforts. Keeping track of worldwide trends requires the organization of information by developing a system of categories so that the information could be used in a manner expedient to the hotel.

To be successful in international marketing a manager must have the necessary information quickly and efficiently to outmanoeuvre the competition by creating his own rules. Mikula and Kye-Sung (1997) argue that the hotel industry is largely affected by the infrastructure of the travel industry with the following six components: airlines, tour wholesalers, tour operators, retail travel agents for all segments, travel journalists and other special interest groups.

International branding strategy

Kotler (2000) defines a brand as 'a seller's promise to deliver a specific set of features, benefits and services to buyers' with the best brands conveying a warranty of quality. In this era of corporate concentration, in the hospitality and tourism sector it is striking how often the spotlight is placed on global marketing solutions. It is on the basis of strong brand names, synonymous with a product reality and consistency from one property to another, that the hotel industry has built the foundations for its growth and subsequent maturity, market by market, country by country.

The backing of strong brands with world-renowned names sustained by global distribution systems, particularly in the shape of the Internet, provides consumers with an extra guarantee and serves as an excellent promotional tool for all concerned. Individual brands, such as Four Seasons, find this ideal for attracting new and highly targeted clienteles, while 'umbrella' brands, such as Marriott, which typically have subbrands, e.g Courtyard and Fairfield Inn in the case of Marriott, rely on strong networks to guarantee their reputations. The continuing explosion in tourism will undoubtedly lead to the creation of universal brands (Panayotis, 2000). According to Sangster (2000) the arguments in favour of branding in the hospitality sector include:

- the ability to charge a premium price over equivalent offers from rival companies

- the ability to gain market share against these rivals

- the ability to keep customers by building loyalty to the brand.

However, Hart (1999) argues that a major contributor to the importance of branding in international marketing has been the lack of a globally accepted system of hotel classification.

Aaker (1996) describes the key assets that make a brand strong. These assets when taken together constitute the brand equity or worth of the brand. The four brand assets that companies need to manage are:

Brand awareness – which refers to the strength of the brand's presence in the consumer's mind. International hotel chains use companies such as NOP (National Opinion Polls) to conduct international research to assess the awareness levels of leading hotels among business and leisure travellers.

Perceived quality – is one particular brand association that is critical. It has been shown to drive financial performance and is often a major (if not the principal) strategic thrust of a business. International research companies, such as Scher, specialize in conducting such international brand comparisons in quality terms.

Brand loyalty – retaining the business of customers is key to profitability. Customer defection is the term used to describe what happens when companies lose customers. As will be shown later in this chapter, such losses are high when the total spending of customers over their lifetime is considered. A number of strategies are employed by hospitality organizations to strengthen brand loyalty including frequent-user programmes, customer clubs and database marketing (Yesawich, 1991).

Brand associations – the worth of the brand is closely linked to its identity or image in the mind of customers. The positive brand associations of the Disney name with entertainment, fantasy and storytelling are ones that the company has exploited throughout the hospitality sector from theme parks to cruise ships. Through international media, hotel marketers seek to develop a common set of associations for global brands such as Four Seasons and Inter-Continental.

As industry consolidation continues apace, the consolidation of brands is happening in tandem. Rebranding – or rebadging as it is sometimes termed – is fraught with difficulties, primary among them being the alienation of customers in countries grown familiar with existing brands. Ensuring a consistent product offering is also a challenge as older properties have to be incorporated alongside newer properties in an expanded brand portfolio.

The Starwood Group has been rebranding some of its properties to the Sheraton, Westin, Four Points (formerly Sheraton Inns) and the new St Regis, presumably because they make a better cultural fit in another family. The new 'W' brand from Starwood is designed to denote only boutique hotels to the preference of top-end travellers.

Just to add to the confusion, the Starwood name itself was virtually unknown even to frequent travellers as recently as 1999. Hart (1999) recognizes that the need to promote the brand to institutional investors has been as important in the rise of such corporate branding, as has the need to build awareness among customers. Another company that is placing increased emphasis on its corporate brand identity is Accor. On all its properties and collatoral material the individual hotel brand logo is supported by the Accor Hotels sub-logo.

As Kotler *et al.* (1998) point out, brands often need to be repositioned, citing examples of Westin International becoming Westin and Hilton Hotels becoming Hilton Hotels and Resorts. The latter move being subsequently replicated by Radisson when they were rebranded as Radisson Hotels and Resorts to strengthen their image as a hotel chain with strong leisure as well as business credentials and to develop a more unified image ahead of international expansion.

For individual hotel properties or a small independent chain the challenges of international marketing have a unique character. As Hart (1999) points out the individual marketing efforts are small against the far greater budgets and reach of the major brands and, in particular, they lack a global reservation system and a consolidated customer database.

One way to address these drawbacks for smaller chains is through consortia. Edwin Fuller (President and Managing Director Marriott), cited in Hart (1999), contends that there will always be a place for the unique, stand alone hotel that over the years is able to cultivate a loyal following based on its uniqueness. But these jewel-like properties usually are not focused on catering to the volumes of sophisticated travellers, who demand exceptional and consistent service at a fair price, which the industry will serve in the years ahead. In addition to consolidating into major global chains, Fuller expects to see more properties affiliating with major lodging brands. Fuller estimated that, at the end of 1998, only 21.5% of about 13 million international standard rooms worldwide were affiliated with a major chain. The breakdown is shown in Table 8.2.

A lower figure of 15% for branded hotels is quoted by Sangster (2000) but this includes all room stock.

For its part, Marriott manages and operates what is probably the broadest brand portfolio in the industry and has been an example of how what is termed a 'multibrand' strategy can be effective in entering numerous international markets with several brands targeting specific market segments.

Conclusions

The globalization of the hospitality sector poses interesting challenges for marketers. Brand development and distribution system management issues have been at the core of the activities of international hospitality marketers. While well-established international brands have continued to exploit opportunities, once domestic brands, most notably in the budget sector, are now being rolled out to emerging markets. For the marketer the rationale of such expansion is rooted in the cost savings potential and the consumer acceptance of a more global hospitality experience. Domestic hotel chains and individual properties are increasingly turning to consortia and other marketing alliances as a means of

Region	% of International standard hotels that are affiliated
USA/Canada	70
Europe	44
Asia/Pacific	28
Latin America	18

Table 8.2 Affiliation of international standard hotels

defence against the encroachment of international chains. Paradoxically, in a period of industry consolidation and standardization, the impact of new technologies engenders a greater potential than ever to provide a uniquely personalized communication with and service delivery to the customer. The growing sophistication of the international traveller, coupled with a desire to seek out that which is unique, will ensure the job of the international marketer will grow in complexity.

Summary

- International marketing strategy in the hospitality industry is being heavily influenced by a number of challenges including the 'disintermediation' of existing distribution channels, the growing 'commoditization' of the hotel product and the rising importance of destinations as drivers of customer demand.

- International marketing strategists will have to address the impact of technology on marketing, especially in the area of relationship marketing.

- There is considerable evidence that marketing alliances will increase in importance in international marketing activity and that these alliances will be both intra- and inter-hospitality industry in nature.

- The Internet's importance in international marketing will be particularly acute in the area of distribution management and will lead to growing power among established online intermediaries.

- There continues to be academic and practitioner debate about the extent to which international marketing activity can be standardized across geographic markets. In general, companies seek to exploit opportunities for global efficiencies, while simultaneously responding to local market conditions where consumer behaviour is diverse.

- One area where companies have sought to globalize their operations is that of branding. Coupled with increasing consolidation of hotel chains, there is a concerted effort to develop global hotel brands. US and French companies have been to the fore in this effort.

Review questions

1. Assess what the phrase 'think global – act local' means in the context of international hospitality marketing.
2. How will the Internet impact on the distribution strategy of international hospitality companies?

3. Which elements of the marketing mix require most adaptation to local market conditions?

4. Examine the restraining forces to global adaptation (see Figure 8.1) in the context of the international marketing of hospitality organizations.

5. Discuss whether CRM is mainly used as a technology application by hospitality companies rather than as a means of more effective relationship building.

6. How can independent, domestic chains, differentiate themselves from international brand entrants?

7. Distinguish between global marketing and global standardization.

8. Discuss the challenges and drivers to international marketing activity.

References

Aaker, D. (1996) *Building Strong Brands,* The Free Press, New York.

Alexander, N. and Lockwood, A. (1996) Internationalisation: a comparison of the hotel and retail sectors, *Service Industries Journal,* **16**, (4), 458–473.

Bender, D. (1996) Intercultural competence as a competitive advantage, *HSMAI Marketing Review,* **19**, (3), 8–15.

Bowen, J. (1996) Relationship marketing: a strategic perspective. In Kotas, R. *et al.* (eds), *The International Hospitality Business,* Cassell, London, pp. 366–373.

Bowen, J. and Shoemaker, S. (1998) Loyalty: a strategic approach *Cornell Hotel and Restaurant Administration Quarterly,* **39**, (1), 12–25.

Calver, S. (1994) Formulating strategy for the hospitality industry. In Teare, R. *et al.* (eds), *Marketing in Hospitality and Tourism: A Consumer Focus,* Cassell, London, pp. 285–311.

Crawford-Welch, S. (1991) International marketing in the hospitality industry. In Teare, R. and Boer, A. (eds), *Strategic Hospitality Management,* Cassell, London, pp. 166–193.

Dev, C. and Olsen, M. (2000) Marketing challenges for the next decade, *Cornell Hotel and Restaurant Administration Quarterly,* **41**, (1), 41–48.

Estis-Green, C. (2000) The information revolution in hospitality: a guide to intelligent marketing, HSMAI Foundation Research Review. *HSMAI Marketing Review,* **17**, (2), 1–19.

Hart, J. (1999) *Global Hotel Strategies: Investment and Marketing in a New Millennium,* Financial Times Business Ltd., London.

Hill, R. (1999) Hotels competing with DMC's: an industry trend worth watching, *HSMAI Marketing Review,* **16**, (1), 44–46.

Hotel Online (2001a) Le Meridien and Nikko Hotels International Expand Marketing and Reservations Alliance August 3, Internet

Reference   http://www.hotel-online.com/Neo/News/PR2001 _3rd/Aug01_NikkoMeridien.html.

IHRA (1999) *Vienna Marketing Think Tank*, International Hotel and Restaurant Association.

Kotler, P., Bowen, J. and Makens, J. (1998), *Marketing for Hospitality and Tourism*, 2nd ed., Prentice Hall, New Jersey.

Kotler P. (2000) *Marketing Management: Millennium Edition*, Prentice Hall, New Jersey.

Leopold, G. (1999) The evolution of relationship marketing into permission marketing, *HSMAI Marketing Review*, **16**, (1), 16–18.

Levitt, T. (1983) The globalisation of markets, *Harvard Business Review*, May–June, **61**, 92–102.

Marriott International (1998). *The Spirit to Serve*, Marriott International Annual Report, Bethesda.

Medina, J. (1998) Standardization vs. globalization: a new perspective of brand strategies, *Journal of Product and Brand Management*, **7**, (3), 227–243.

Mikula, J. and Kye-Sung, C. (1997) International hotel marketing in the age of globalisation, *International Journal of Contemporary Hospitality Management*, **9**, (1), 31–33.

Murphy, J., Forrest, E., Wortring, E. and Brymer, R. (1996) Hotel management and marketing on the Internet, *Cornell Hotel and Restaurant Administration Quarterly*, **12**, (2), 70–82.

O'Connor, P. and Frew, A. (1998). The evolution of hotel electronic distribution, *EuroCHRIE/HSMAI Conference Proceedings*, Spring, Oslo.

Oliver, T. (2000) Marketing is a battlefield, *HTR – Hotel Tourism Restaurant Magazine*, MKG Conseil, Paris, November, p. 49.

O'Reilly, A. (2000). Uniting force: the value of customer relationship management, *Marketing Institute of Ireland — Marketing News*, **12**, (3), 2–5.

Panayotis, G. (2000) *HTR – Hotel Tourism Restaurant Magazine*, MKG Conseil, Paris, **74**, December.

Payne, A. (1997) *Advances in Relationship Marketing*, Kogan Page, London.

Reichheld, F. F. and Sasser, W. E. (1990) Zero defections: quality comes to services, *Harvard Business Review*, September–October, 105–111.

Riley, M., Niininen, O., Szivas, E. and Willis, T. (2001) The case for process approaches in loyalty research in tourism, *International Journal of Tourism Research*, **3**, 23–32.

Sangster, A. (2000) European hotel branding, *Travel and Tourism Intelligence*, **6**, 63–83.

Yesawich, P. C. (1991) Getting to know you, *Lodging Hospitality*, **47**, (6), 64.

Yu, L. (1999) *The International Hospitality Business: Management and Operations*, Haworth Press, New York.

Further reading

Czinkota, M. and Ronkainen, I. (1998) *International Marketing*, 5th ed., Dryden, Fort Worth.

Doyle, P. (2002) *Marketing Management and Strategy*, 3rd ed., Pearson Educational, Harlow.

Molenaar, C. (2002) *The Future of Marketing*, Pearson Educational, Harlow.

Strauss, J. and Frost, R. (2001) *E-Marketing*, 2nd ed., Prentice-Hall, New Jersey.

Shimp, T. (1997) *Advertising, Promotion and Supplemental Aspects of Integrated Marketing Communications*, Dryden, Fort Worth.

International hospitality managers: past, present and future

Judie M. Gannon

Chapter objectives

When you have read this chapter you will be able to:

- Identify the key characteristics and skills of unit managers working in the international hospitality industry.

- Discuss how and why the skills and experiences demanded by international hospitality companies have changed.

- Explain the difficulties faced and barriers to be overcome by managers aspiring to international unit management positions within the hospitality industry.

- Discuss some of the challenges hospitality companies encounter when developing international human resources.

- Recommend and justify strategies and activities international hospitality companies and managers could deploy to achieve successful international growth in the future.

Introduction

There is a widespread rhetoric across the international hospitality industry about the importance and challenges of supplying an adequate quality and quantity of human resources to meet its growing demands (Gee, 1994; Go and Pine, 1995; Jones, Thompson and Nickson, 1998). Drawing on research into the human resource development practices of international hospitality companies, this chapter focuses on the challenges facing those who employ international hotel managers and aspirants to such positions. Analysis of questionnaire responses, interviews and documents from six international operators, over a 3-year period in the late 1990s, suggests that there have been shifts in the requirements of managerial resources. From the earlier chapters in Part One you should be familiar with the context of sectors of the hospitality industry and how these shifts in human resource demands reflect the dynamic nature of the industry itself. We will focus here on the personal attributes of aspirant unit general managers (UGMs), the skills and knowledge they must develop to achieve UGM status and how international hospitality companies have managed and coordinated the quality and quantity of managers.

Time for change?

> The GM we have today does not have, or will not have, sufficient business nous to be successful in 5 to 10 years time. So we need a different type of person with different skills from what is currently a classic GM profile now.
> Human Resources Executive, Company D

The mid-1990s were a period of great change within the international hospitality industry, especially in the hotel sector. The initial objective of the research this chapter is based on was to determine what becoming an international UGM entailed and how companies managed this process. Senior human resource executives and their teams were visited and interviewed, and human resource documentation collected to build a picture of how managers were selected and developed in six of the most prominent operators in the international hotel sector (Gannon and Johnson, 1995, 1997). Table 9.1 summarizes some of the key features of the companies concerned, including the number of countries they operated in (1997), their wider hospitality and tourism business interests, their parent company's home continent, the type of hotel properties (in terms of market service levels), and the modes of entry used in their expanding portfolios.

	Parent company's home continent	Number of countries	Wider business interests	Type of hotel properties	Predominant modes of market entry
Company A	Europe	75	Travel and tourism operators, and range of other hospitality concerns	Upmarket business and leisure to budget brands	Extensive franchising, management contracts, and some unit ownership
Company B	Europe	40	Range of other hospitality concerns	Luxury class to budget brands	Management contracts, some unit ownership
Company C	Europe	60	Brewing and leisure interests	Luxury class to budget brands	Franchising, some management contracts and limited ownership
Company D	North America	38	Timeshare and some leisure interests	Luxury class and upmarket business and leisure brands	Management contracts
Company E	Asia	45	Retailing	Luxury class and upmarket business and leisure brands	Mainly management contracts, some ownership
Company F	Europe	48	Leisure and gaming interests	Luxury class and upmarket business and leisure brands	Management contracts, limited ownership

The data in this table are based upon information collected in mid-1997.

Table 9.1 International hotel operators

One of the strongest and most consistent messages which emerged from the fieldwork and subsequent analysis highlighted how the growth of each company and the competitiveness of the industry had meant that future managers would have to differ greatly from the managers of today and yesterday. Later in this chapter we will examine the extent of these transformations in light of the executives' discourses on past, present and future UGMs. It is first pertinent to review the existing literature on unit managers' development within the international hospitality sector.

International hospitality managers

Research on the development of hospitality managers has proceeded steadily over recent decades, though in common with most insights on the industry the hotel sector dominates the literature (CHME, 2001). There has also been, until recently, a tendency for the research to be based on national contexts. As such the origins of managers becomes an important consideration here. Typically there are:

- Parent country nationals (PCNs) – managers who are working outside their home country, for a company with the same nationality as themselves. For example a French national working for a French company in the Czech Republic.

- Host country nationals (HCNs) – managers who are working inside their own home country which is playing host to a foreign company's subsidiary (a French national working in France for a company from Sweden).

- Third country nationals (TCNs) – managers who are working outside their home country for a company operating outside its home country (a French national working for a Swedish company in the Czech Republic).

Another widely used term in the literature is expatriates and this covers PCNs and TCNs, i.e. those working outside their home environments. However, as we shall see from the literature and research findings, HCNs may face many similar challenges to their foreign colleagues. In fact to reach unit level management positions within international hospitality companies HCNs are likely to have taken a management position abroad with their international employer. The literature reviewed in this chapter introduces some of the key themes in the research on international hospitality manager characteristics and their development. However, due to the magnitude of the literature in this field as a whole the following themes have been selected as they address the most pertinent issues. The four selected areas of focus are managerial characteristics, departmental experience, career paths and mobility, and company interventions. An extensive research and literature tradition exists in the generic international management field and a selection of these sources is suggested in the further reading references.

Managerial characteristics

If as Kriegl (2000: 64) suggests, 'Hospitality companies' success abroad depends largely on the availability of qualified managers who are able to export, translate and maintain their companies' operational standards and service consistency overseas', it is vital that we know what type of individual constitutes a competent manager. A range of studies have been conducted on unit level managers in the hospitality industry, though most have concentrated on the hotel sector. Typically the samples for such research have been based on managers operating in one country, although they have often included respondents who originate outside that nation (Gilatis and Guerrier, 1994; Nebel *et al.*, 1995; Gilbert and Guerrier, 1997; Ladkin and Riley, 1996; Ladkin and Juwaheer, 2000). Respondents were predominantly male, and tended to be college educated. There was a general dearth of female unit managers, with Nebel *et al.* (1995) noting a distinct drop in female unit managers in the luxury class of hotels participating in their research. This suggests that while the number of female managers at junior and middle management levels continues to increase, few in-roads have been made at the senior unit management level within the hotel sector (Guerrier, 1999).

Several studies have examined the average time it takes for a manager to reach their first UGM position. Ladkin and Riley's (1996) study of UK hotel general managers indicated that it typically took between 10 and 11 years. The investigation of UGMs in Mauritius by Ladkin and Juwaheer (2000) suggested that the average time taken to reach a UGM position was between 16 and 13 years. Nebel *et al.*'s (1995) examination of hotel general managers in the USA suggested that the average age of GMs for upscale and luxury hotels was 43 years. Managers were aged around 33 when they became UGMs, ordinarily taking between 7 and 10 years to reach this level.

The national context also influences the extent of opportunities available for individuals to reach UGM level. For example, where countries are experiencing growth in specific hotel markets (luxury versus mid-scale properties) and the overall maturity of the sector will impact upon the demand for, and career opportunities available to, managers.

We are also concerned about the range of skills and personal characteristics of aspirant UGMs. Gilbert and Guerrier (1997) examined how British managers perceived how managers' roles had changed between the 1970s and 1990s. Broadly they found that managers in the 1990s prioritized education and qualifications, interpersonal and relational skills, and the adoption of democratic and consultative management styles. Their 1970s predecessors, they felt had relied on their knowledge and expertise in craft skills and autocratic management approaches. Ladkin and Juwaheer's (2000) work in Mauritius suggested that managerial skills were indeed being gradually prioritized over traditional technical skills.

For those planning international careers in the hospitality industry there clearly seems to be evidence for preference in interpersonal, intercultural and commercial competencies. Shay and Tracey (1997) identified that the most desirable attributes for expatriate managers were people skills and adaptability, flexibility and tolerance, followed by emotional maturity, industry experience, and self-confidence. However, they admitted that, as in other business sectors, hospitality managers were often selected for international assignments on the basis of their technical and craft competencies rather than their social skills. This is despite evidence that soft skills are more important when identifying individuals who are likely to succeed in an international assignment. Feng and Pearson's (1999) study of expatriates in China found they prioritized the ability to adjust and adapt, develop relationships, manage culturally stressful situations and develop their knowledge of the culture.

A recent study of graduates from the Cornell Hotel School, following international careers, found that the skills of greatest importance were interpersonal skills, cultural sensitivity, flexibility and adaptive leadership, and motivation and interest (i.e. individuals must be driven to work hard and succeed). Intercultural competence and international etiquette, demonstrating an understanding of international business matters, the ability to work with limited resources and effectively manage stress were judged to be relatively important, while functional and technical skills were rated as the lowest priority for managers working in the international hospitality industry.

Evidence from Gilatis and Guerrier (1994), Shay and Tracey (1997) and Kriegl (2000) suggests that building a manager's cross-cultural skills may be far harder but more consequential than developing their functional and technical skills, in an international hospitality organization than another international business context. This is because the hospitality industry demands that a high level of interpersonal and relational skills are demonstrated in a context where the host country culture and the needs of a diverse customer base must be understood and catered for.

Departmental experience

Alongside the debate between 'soft skills' and 'hard technical skills' there is also interest in the pattern of functional jobs managers undertake en route to becoming an UGM. Several of the most prominent researchers in the field (Nebel *et al.*, 1995; Ladkin and Riley, 1996; Ladkin and Juwaheer, 2000) found their UGM respondents spent the majority of their careers in the food and beverage function. While research respondents suggested management skills were of increasing importance to their career success, food and beverage skills and experience featured in the top half of the ranked skills. The rooms department was the only other operational area where those on their way to UGM positions had worked (Nebel *et al.*, 1995). This study also measured the variety of departments experienced by UGMs, concluding that 40% had worked in only one department prior to becoming a UGM. Within a department respondents were likely to have three different assignments, at different management levels or in different sizes of departments, suggesting a substantial absence of variety in their all-round hotel management expertise. It is important to note here that female aspirants to UGM positions are particularly disadvantaged as senior level food and beverage management experience is still seen as a male enclave (Nebel *et al.*, 1995).

When exploring the differences between older and younger GMs these researchers found that younger GMs (those under 43 years) were actually more likely to have operational experience in rooms or food and beverage departments. The authors' highlight how, between the average time taken to reach UGM status (9 years), the average time spent as an executive assistant manager (EAM) (3 years), and the typical time spent in their main department (5.25 years), there is very little room for managers to develop cross-functional expertise. The ability to reach EAM level, and subsequently the UGM level, is therefore dependent upon a manager's performance in one department. However, until the EAM level is achieved very few UGM aspirants will have gained expertise or exposure to the rest of a hotel's departments (Nebel *et al.*, 1995).

In addition, it is vital to assess whether all hotel departments are accessible to managers aspiring to become international UGMs. Gilatis and Guerrier (1994) argue that host country managers take up specific posts – personnel managers, financial managers and chief engineers – due to the need for knowledge of local languages, laws, suppliers, resources, and culture. However, expatriates often undertake these positions in the short term, when a new unit is being developed to ensure company standards are met.

Career paths and mobility

Hotel manager's careers are highly mobile, with incumbents moving between management levels, employers and locations (Nebel *et al.*, 1995; Ladkin and Riley, 1996; Ladkin and Juwaheer, 2000). One study of UK general managers indicated that they changed jobs every 3–4 years, typically holding seven positions before becoming UGMs (Ladkin and Riley, 1996). The study of UGMs in Mauritius found that the average length of time in jobs was between 2 and 5 years (Ladkin and Juwaheer, 2000). Similar results were also found in a cohort of US UGMs (Nebel *et al.*, 1995) with managers normally serving between 9 and 14 years with their present employer. It was also found to be extremely unusual for managers not to have been EAMs with the same company prior to their first UGM position. This indicates that long tenure with the same employer is an important feature of UGMs' careers providing opportunities for a manager's talent to be spotted at the departmental level before wider exposure at the EAM level.

Most moves are self-initiated rather than company directed, with the majority of managers seeking transfers within their present employer's portfolio rather than outside it (Nebel *et al.*, 1995; Ladkin and Riley, 1996). However, the study of UGMs in Mauritius did show a slight domination of external company moves over internal company moves (Ladkin and Juwaheer, 2000). This is interesting when it is observed that this sample included a significant proportion of PCNs and TCNs. Where companies did initiate international moves for their managers, human resource executives reported few problems with managers accepting such career opportunities, as there was widespread acknowledgement of the high level of mobility required of hotel professionals (Gilatis and Guerrier, 1994).

The length of assignments is an important factor to consider, with Dowling *et al.* (1999) finding that the average length of international assignment for Japanese expatriates was between 4 and 5 years. However, American managers were typically on assignment for between 2 and 3 years, despite evidence that longer assignments facilitate better adjustment to the foreign situation. Shorter assignments tended only to be used as developmental opportunities for junior or trainee managers.

International hospitality company approaches

International transfers may be used for a range of reasons, including the opportunity to solve specific staffing problems, develop the present cohort of managers, transfer knowledge and expertise across the company, and maintain managers' levels of satisfaction and motivation (Gilatis and Guerrier, 1994; Adler, 1997; Dowling *et al.*, 1999). These arguments can be seen to be of mutual benefit to managers and companies. While there are presently more developed country nationals (PCNs or TCNs) managing units in developing countries it is important to emphasize that HCNs can gain great benefits from international transfers.

The arguments for the localization of staff at all levels in international business mean that more creative approaches to foreign assignments should be deployed (Gee, 1994; Go and Pine, 1995; D'Annunzio-Green, 1997; Dowling *et al.*, 1999). However, as Jones *et al.*, (1998) have argued, local managers are disadvantaged in their careers by processes of socialization, which derive not just from the parent company's home country culture but the associated occupational and organizational identities. In fact they warn that 'Companies need to look carefully at the tacit assumptions which shape decisions about managerial career progressions and to be aware of the extent to which they are informed by notions of acceptability forged within the parent country context', (Jones *et al.*, 1998: 1060).

Having briefly examined why companies may use international managers across their businesses, it is worthwhile considering some of the challenges international hospitality operators face in controlling and coordinating their managerial resources. High expatriate failure rates, i.e. managers returning to their home country prematurely due to poor work performance, have been a major concern for companies for many years (Adler, 1991). Shay and Tracey (1997) investigate this phenomenon and suggest there is a 30% perceived failure rate for hotel expatriates. This compares with expatriate failure rates across generic businesses of between 25 and 45%, with figures substantially higher (70%) for American expatriates in developing countries.

Researchers argue that service sector expatriates must engage further with the local culture, languages and customs than their manufacturing sector peers. As such, international hospitality human resources should be provided with effective support systems to ensure the success in their overseas experiences. However, only a quarter of the respondents had engaged in cross-cultural training, and they suggested similar reasons to generic research studies on why expatriates often fail. The two most prominent reasons were spouses' inability to adjust and the manager's inability to adjust to the host culture. However, a manager's lack of personal or emotional maturity was also emphasized as a likely explanation (Shay and Tracey, 1997).

Many other authors have commented on the difficulties facing managers and their families when international moves are made (Gilatis and Guerrier, 1994; Dowling *et al.*, 1999). Support for these groups is rather patchy with only just over 10% of the spouses from Shay and Tracey's sample receiving company sponsored support to participate in any pre-departure training. The international managers in the Gilatis and Guerrier's (1994) research found they were more likely to receive training and support only when they were moving to a developing country. Those transferring to a developed country were often expected to make all necessary housing and travel arrangements themselves. Many respondents admitted to using the coping strategy of seeking refuge in their work environment upon arrival at their new unit. However, this approach was again likely to have an adverse effect on their family's adjustment (Gilatis and Guerrier, 1994; Gee, 1994).

Effective coping strategies, and those easily supported by international employers, included learning the local language (even though the day-to-day work language is English), and the importance of keeping an open mind with regard to cultural differences. There was limited evidence of best practice in preparing and supporting international assignees with some use of international briefing centres, and cross-cultural training opportunities (Gilatis and Guerrier, 1994, D'Annunzio-Green, 1997; Shay and Tracey 1997; Kreigl, 2000). It was suggested that minimal training had been provided because of limits on time, high costs of provision and the move to localizing management cohorts. Given the relatively extensive use of international managers and the commercial opportunities in developing countries, it is disturbing that the number of participants receiving training in cross-cultural and international adaptation skills was so dismally low (Gilatis and Guerrier, 1994; Yu and Huat, 1995; D'Annunzio-Green, 1997; Shay and Tracey, 1997; Kreigl, 2000). It is clear that the most effective training techniques, such as overseas study and internships, international travel, foreign language studies and international management studies, need to be developed and available to a wider audience of workers in international hospitality companies.

This brief overview of the literature suggests that aspiring international UGMs in the hospitality industry have an arduous path to achieve their career goals. First, they must achieve the right balance of managerial and technical skills and expertise, achieve and update formal qualifications, and develop a suitable range of interpersonal skills. They then need to develop departmental expertise, most likely in the food and beverage or rooms functions, and ensure they achieve recognition for their efforts so opportunities for EAM level positions are available. Achievement of the right combination of departmental management experience will require them to be highly mobile. However, they must seek out and initiate the majority of moves themselves, rather than relying on their employer's development and training policies. Where they move overseas they are unlikely to be offered pre-departure, language or cross-cultural skills training and support by their employers. In short they must demonstrate mobility, departmental expertise and business acumen, cultivate a network of contacts to aid their career development, learn foreign languages and become culturally sensitive and adaptable in an industry where the pace of change itself is difficult to comprehend. It is little wonder that UGMs claim their career successes are achieved through dogged determination, personal investment and self-sacrifice (Le Sueur, 1998).

Past, present and future general managers

The attention of this chapter now moves to the results from six case studies of international hotel companies' approaches to developing international UGMs. Picking up on the themes from the literature review the observations of senior human resource executives from these companies are examined and balanced against their experiences of the shifting demands for UGMs.

Past unit managers

One of the clearest indications of change in the international industry was the way the human resource executives talked about the individuals who had previously held unit management positions. Among these managers there was a conspicuous absence of formal qualifications and all round business expertise. The overwhelming majority had risen through the ranks, from operational positions, predominantly through the food and beverage side of the hotel industry. As such many of the human resources specialists bemoaned the UGMs' level of business acumen and strategic thinking, and ability to manage units without extensive standard practice manuals. Their career successes were seen to be based upon patronage from senior unit managers, and very little formal assessment had taken place to ascertain their credentials for managing units. For example the Human Resources Executive from Company E said,

> Traditionally a manager became an EAM, then GM if their own boss thought well of them ... A lot of EAMs got there because they looked the part and were liked. Historically they would have gone on to become GMs without there ever being any critical evaluation of whether they had what it took to be a successful GM in the future.

Overall the human resource executives recounted tales of unit managers with superior social skills, who acted as 'mine host' and imbued fine dining traditions, but lacked the strategic acumen of their peers in other sectors. Prior to the 1990s the international development of the hospitality industry had relied on managerial resources being highly mobile throughout their careers, but in particular their late twenties and early thirties. The human resources executives remarked that this meant managers had tended not to start families until their mid- or late thirties. However, family life did not reduce the level of mobility among this cohort because such managers were unlikely to be part of dual career families or have sophisticated concerns about their children's education.

Present unit managers

Those who held UGM positions in the mid-1990s were more likely to have formal qualifications than their predecessors and often achieved UGM positions at an earlier age. The average age for a UGM across the sample was 35–38 years; however, younger UGMs were being appointed, in particular to budget and mid-range hotel brands, which tended to be smaller units. The Human Resources Executive from Company A commented that,

> The average age of the UGMs differs according to the size and brand of the hotel, though our managers are achieving such positions earlier. A GM of brand T (budget) could be 28 years old, but there will never be a 28-year-old manager of brands Y or Z.

These shifts are coupled with the growth of hospitality and business education courses and the emergence of multiple branded, hospitality and hotel portfolios. The human resources executives articulated particular concerns regarding their present managers' management styles. They were seen as conformist and reactive in their approaches to managing units. The executive who said 'our guys presently think like they're number two's rather than the guy at the top' typifies this concern. An absence of sufficient strategic thinking among UGMs in the mid-1990s is particularly interesting. It was during this period that the positive contribution of strategic business unit (SBU) thinking became prominent, and the frustration of the human resource executives regarding their UGMs' lack of strategic business acumen is telling (Olsen, 1991).

Wider social changes also had an impact on the development and progress of UGMs and their aspirants. Managers were still seen to be highly mobile early in their careers but problems were being encountered with managers in their late thirties and early forties. The human resource executives recounted how dual career families were now limiting the mobility of their more experienced UGMs. This became a particular source of aggravation to those responsible for appointing UGMs to properties where owners demanded more experienced and, as such, older managers, creating a 'sandwich effect' on mobility. This can be summarized by comments from the executive from Company C,

> The more experienced and older managers bring their own problems of partners and children, and we have to respect their domestic situation. Unfortunately the younger managers do not have the experience and as such can't fit into the empty shoes.

Future unit managers

The human resource executives spoke with great enthusiasm about the UGMs of the future. Given the concerns highlighted earlier, the human resources specialists could see managers achieving UGM positions even earlier in their careers, hence overcoming some of the problems related to mobility. The development of more local managers was also mentioned as a route to overcome this problem. However, only brands aimed at local customer markets could be seen to operate without any expatriate management in the longer term.

The six companies operate international brands at all market levels, so the elimination of expatriates is unlikely. The value of younger managers as UGMs was not solely based on their mobility but on what were felt to be the characteristics of a new breed of managers. Such individuals would have to be college educated, and meet demanding formal selection criteria in rigorous assessment centres, unlike the majority of their predecessors. As such they would be far more competent earlier and able to take on the exacting challenges of international unit management. Across all the human resource specialists there was a view that these young managers should be more proactive, entrepreneurial and creative in their management approaches. The ability to exploit commercial opportunities across a range of markets is seen as a minimum requirement of future UGMs.

The clear contrast between past, present and future managers in international hotel companies can be charted through four layers, identified in Table 9.2, between individual managers and the international hotel companies, which determine the likelihood of achieving senior unit management positions.

Level 1	Level 2	Level 3	Level 4
Personal characteristics of managers	*Managers' skills*	*Interface factors*	*Company factors*
Age	Business acumen	Mobility	Growth plans
Sex	Languages	International orientation	Operating conventions
Nationality	Networking ability	Human resource	Brands
Education	Department expertise	management practices	Types of units
Single/attached	Leadership and people	and procedures	Management
	skills		structures
	Innovation and		Human resource
	entrepreneurship		strategies and policies

Table 9.2 Levels of factors influencing international managers' careers

Level one – managers' characteristics

The first managerial level contains characteristics that managers cannot, or are unlikely to, change to achieve career success. These are predetermined factors that influence career success. For example, age is such a factor, as across the sample human resource executives identified that more individuals were achieving UGM positions in their late twenties and early thirties. A manager's nationality or sex can determine which countries can provide career opportunities. For example female managers find it very difficult to achieve senior management positions in most Muslim countries.

Level two – managerial skills

This level corresponds to factors individuals can change in order to achieve career success. It is apparent at this level how hotel companies inform and influence managers' skills and competencies. The transformation in management skills in the past, present and future analysis highlights the trend across all companies to value broader business skills rather than specific hospitality management expertise. The human resources executives stressed the move away from reliance on food and beverage expertise as a prerequisite for general management, in preference to sales and management, finance and rooms management experience. However, the evidence from the literature suggested that many UGMs had built their careers upon expertise developed in food and beverage or rooms management.

The extent to which managers acquire the other skills at this level would appear to depend upon their own company's priorities and future plans. Aspiring managers will need to ascertain the importance of these skills by identifying suitable role models and mentors from across their company. They could also use formal (selection criteria, performance measures and reward structures) and informal (company communications, brochures, employee newsletters) aspects to guide the development of the appropriate skills set for their employer or one of its competitors.

Level three – human resources interface

The third level is, arguably the most interesting level of analysis, as these factors cannot be attributed clearly to either the company or individual manager levels. Instead this level is the interface between the players; both determine the extent to which mobility, international and operating orientation are prioritized. For example, managers' mobility is determined not only by an individual's skills and personal characteristics but also by their company's growth plans, management structures, and operating conventions. At this level managers must demonstrate their desire and ability to move further up the organization. Managers must make sure their achievements are recognized and rewarded, or formally request a transfer. Simultaneously companies need to have systems that communicate forthcoming opportunities to managers. The use and promotion of role models, career histories and career counselling provide the basis for such an interface between the company's human resources goals and its ambitious employees.

Level four – international hospitality company

The fourth level relates to the international hotel employers themselves, which the human resource executives identified as influencing their managerial resource requirements. Key movements in the international hotel industry resulted in the respondents' reporting that branding and restructuring have impacted upon their demands for unit managers. Each company acknowledged that stronger brand definitions, the result of increasing industry competition, had meant career opportunities had been opened in some cases and closed in others, to managers with specific skills and backgrounds. Careful consideration of the long-term implications of all strategic decisions on the quality and quantity of managers is essential with systems in place to ensure human resource strategies and policies are conscientiously implemented and evaluated. Currently companies' approaches to developing managerial resources are distinctive with respect to their international market entry modes, growth plans and portfolio of units developed. However, such approaches may stifle career opportunities for some managers. For example, in the case of Companies A and C, both recalled difficulties with encouraging owners to accept women as senior managers while their own franchisees operated many more hotels with women as UGMs.

Conclusions

Having explored the literature and recent research on what it takes to become an international hospitality manager, it is apparent how difficult it is to achieve such a career goal. The chapter has summarized the factors influencing the opportunities open to managers and companies into four levels. Included are tentative suggestions regarding the activities managers can engage in to develop their skills and career opportunities. Similarly international hospitality companies are counselled to consider the ramifications of their strategic and operational approaches to international growth on the long-term quality and quantity of international managerial resources. It is apparent that the fast pace of change in the industry is not reflected in advances in the management of managerial resources. A particular concern identified by the literature and respondents includes how to achieve real equality of opportunity given the complexity of supporting employee development from a distance with only limited resources.

Above all we need to consider that managers are products of our time, and our understanding of what it means and takes to be a manager varies. It is therefore imperative that our conceptions of management are continually revised and that the incumbents of management positions are encouraged to explore the boundaries of their roles and careers.

Summary

- Aspiring UGMs face many challenges en-route to achieving their career goals. They will need to be mobile, develop an appropriate skills set, management expertise in a suitable department and effective cross-cultural coping techniques.

- International hospitality companies provide only limited support to managers (and their families) taking up international assignments.

- The skills demanded of international hospitality managers have shifted over recent decades in line with wider industry, economic and social changes.

- Our views of what it takes to be a manager continue to change and it is imperative that aspiring managers and forward thinking companies encourage managers to push back the boundaries of their occupation.

Review questions

1. What do you think have been the significant influences on the demand for international hospitality managers?
2. What skills and experiences would you encourage an aspiring international hospitality manager to acquire?
3. What sort of support and training should international hospitality operators be developing and offering to their human resources?
4. What barriers might some aspiring UGMs experience in their attempts to develop international hospitality careers?
5. What influences the degree of mobility a manager may experience in their career?
6. What are some of the challenges facing human resource executives when they transfer managers on international assignments?

7. What are the challenges managers and their families face when they accept an international assignment?
8. Why may the EAM level be such an important management position to aspiring UGMs?

References

Adler, N. (1997) *International Dimensions of Organizational Behaviour* 3rd ed., South-Western College Publishing, Ohio.

Council for Hospitality Management Education (CHME) (2001) *Getting ahead: graduate careers in hospitality management*, Report commissioned by the Higher Education Funding Council for England (HEFCE).

D'Annunzio-Green, N. (1997) Developing international managers in the hospitality industry, *International Journal of Contemporary Hospitality Management*, **9**, (5/6), 199–208.

Dowling, P. J., Welch, D. E. and Schuler, R. S. (1999) *International Human Resource Management: Managing people in a multinational context*, South-Western College Publishing, Ohio.

Feng, F. and Pearson, T. E. (1999) Hotel Expatriates in China: selection criteria, important skills and knowledge, repatriation concerns, and causes of failure, *International Journal of Hospitality Management*, **18**, (2), 309–321.

Gannon, J. and Johnson, K. (1995) The global hotel industry: the emergence of continental hotel companies, *Progress in Tourism and Hospitality Research*, **1**, (1), 31–42.

Gannon, J. M. and Johnson, K. (1997) *Managing the International Hotel Manager: the HRM Challenges in the International Hotel Industry*, EuroCHRIE and IAHMS Conference Proceedings, Sheffield UK, November, pp. 79–84.

Gee, C. (1994) Selection and preparation of international hotel executives, Chapter 9 and International human resource management, Chapter 10. In *International Hotels: Development and Management*. Educational Institute of the American Hotel Motel Association, East Lansing, Michigan.

Gilatis, N. and Guerrier, Y. (1994) Managing international career moves in international hotel companies. In Cooper, C. P. and Lockwood, A. (eds) *Progress in Tourism, Recreation and Hospitality Management*, **5**, Belhaven Press, London, pp. 229–241.

Gilbert, D. and Guerrier, Y. (1997) UK hospitality managers: past and present, *Service Industries Journal*, **17**, (1), 115–132.

Go, F. M. and Pine, R. (1995) *Globalisation Strategy in the Hotel Industry*, Routledge, London.

Guerrier, Y. (1999) *Organizational Behaviour in Hotels and Restaurants: An International Perspective*, John Wiley & Sons, Chichester.

Jones, C., Thompson, P. and Nickson, D. (1998) Not part of the family? The limits to managing the corporate way in international hotel chains, *International Journal of Human Resource Management*, **9**, (6), 1048–1063.

Kriegl, U. (2000) International hospitality management, *Cornell Hotel and Restaurant Administration Quarterly*, **41**, (2), 64–71.

Ladkin, A. and Juwaheer, T. D. (2000) The career paths of hotel general managers in Mauritius, *International Journal of Contemporary Hospitality Management*, **12**, (2), 119–125.

Ladkin, A. and Riley, M. (1996) Mobility and structure in the career paths of UK hotel general managers: a labour market hybrid of the bureaucratic model? *Tourism Management*, **17**, (6), 443–452.

Le Sueur, A. (1998) *Running a Hotel on the Roof of the World: Five years in Tibet*, Summersdale Publishers, Chichester.

Nebel, E. C., Lee, J. and Vidakovic, B. (1995) Hotel general manager career paths in the United States, *International Journal of Hospitality Management*, **14**, (3/4), 245–260.

Olsen, M. D. (1991) Structure changes: the international hospitality industry and firm, *International Journal of Contemporary Hospitality Management*, **3**, (4), 21–24.

Shay, J. and Tracey, J. B. (1997) Expatriate managers: reasons for failure and implications for training, *Cornell Hotel and Restaurant Administration Quarterly*, **38**, (1), 30–35.

Yu, L. and Huat, G. S. (1995) Perceptions of management difficulty factors by expatriate hotel professionals in China, *International Journal of Hospitality Management*, **14**, (3/4), 375–388.

Further reading

Black, J. S., Gregersen, H. B., Mendenhall, M. E. and Stroh, L. K. (1999) *Globalizing People through International Assignments*, Addison-Wesley, Reading, Massachusetts.

Cullen, J. B. (1999) *Multinational Management: a Strategic Approach*, South-Western College Publishing, Ohio.

Le Sueur, A. (1998) *Running a Hotel on the Roof of the World: Five years in Tibet*, Summersdale Publishers, Chichester.

Useful websites

http:// www.imd.ch/
http:// www.worldculture.com/
http:// www.rici.com/
http:// www.shrm.org/hrlink/intl.htm
http:// www.ilo.org

Financial management

Paul Beals

Chapter objectives

When you have read this chapter, you should be able to:

- Discuss the importance of the unit-level economics of lodging operations to their financial success.

- Analyse the difficulties lodging operations encounter and will continue to encounter in controlling labour costs.

- Identify that entity and capital structures influence the financial viability of hotel investments.

- Explain the role of management contracts as the vehicle for aligning the interests of hotel owners and operators.

- Evaluate the increasing importance of technology and e-commerce as a means of gaining competitive advantage and improving lodging firms' financial performance.

Introduction

A number of the lodging-industry executives consulted in the preparation of the present chapter observed that their industry, while evolving at a steady pace, has a fair distance to go to rival other retail industries in the sophistication of its financial and marketing models. As little as 35 years ago, the worldwide hotel industry was an artisanal, disparate sector where hoteliers practised a time-honoured craft but valiantly resisted efforts to transform their distinctive trade into a mere business. In some parts of the world, the craft model of hostelry still exists and provides an opportunity for hotel companies to rationalize and standardize – detractors would say homogenize – operations. To a wide extent, however, the transformation of the industry is well under way. This chapter will attempt to identify the principal financial issues that mark this transformation, as well as presuming to predict how various financial factors will impact the industry in the future.

The events of 11 September, 2001

The present chapter is inevitably influenced by the events of 11 September, 2001, for neither this writer nor the hospitality-industry executives consulted in its preparation could ignore the immediate impact of the attack on the USA. However, there was general agreement that the negative effects on travel and tourism would prove, in the longer view, transitory. Especially among North Americans and Europeans, a common observation held that the situation of late 2001 was far less unsettling than the 1990–91 period. In both North America and the Pan-European market, inflation is tame, debt levels are more conservative, and interest rates markedly lower, with London Interbank Offering Rate (LIBOR) at approximately 4.5% versus more than 10% a decade ago. The current situation is thus evaluated as being far less detrimental to the long-run prospects of the industry than might be suggested by the precipitous decline in occupancies and Revenue Per Available Room (RevPAR) in the principal cities of the Northern hemisphere during the last quarter of 2001.

In Asia and Australia, the impact of reduced travel from North America is a far less significant factor than the oversupply of hotel rooms that constrains all market participants' pricing power and financial performance. Ultimately, the long-term prospects for Asia depend more on bringing market discipline to the economies of the region, thus bridling development while demand catches up with supply.

Overview

Branded lodging facilities across the world demonstrate a tendency toward a more efficient, more rational design to accommodate the economic realities of the hospitality industry. Increasingly, this attention to the fundamental economics translates into a wariness of food-and-beverage operations, with the conventional business hotel becoming, as one executive put it, a 'bed-breakfast-bar' operation rather than a traditional full-service hotel. The degree of this transformation follows a vector from west to east, commencing in North America where limited-service hotels are widespread, through the Pan-European market with its slow but steady transformation to a simpler style of operation, to Asia, where the concentration of branded operations is the least, but where only the rigidity of the financial system slows the inevitable emergence of a more efficient operational model.

Following the same vector, we can observe an increasing emphasis on branding, with North America leading, the European and Middle Eastern markets following suit despite a lag, and Asia with the largest potential for increased branding opportunities. Investors perceive branding as a means of reducing risk, not only because a franchise affiliation connects their individual properties to a potentially robust distribution channel, but also because they recognize that their customers seek the assurance of a brand when making purchase decisions. Thus as owners in the European, Middle Eastern, and Asian markets gain greater experience with lodging investments and appreciate better the volatility attendant on their operating leverage, it is logical for them to seek the safe harbour of branding to reduce risk.

The potential for consolidation in the industry adheres to a pattern more cultural than geographic. Anglo-Saxon companies, such as the UK's Six Continents Hotels, take the lead in absorbing competitors, rationalizing their operations, and consolidating entities, often into multibrand firms that, while complex, can yield significant efficiencies. Latin companies, with exceptions such as France's Groupe Accor, are less inclined to consolidation and standardization, while Asian firms are often the creations of strong, iconoclastic individuals who resist mightily any efforts that might remove their personal stamp from their holdings.

Not surprisingly, the degree of financial sophistication and transparency follows the same cultural pattern. Greater involvement of the public markets and the analyst community, greater transparency of reporting, more complex financial structures, and attention to stakeholder interests are the hallmarks of most Anglo-Saxon companies, but far less the preoccupation of the management of Latin or Asian firms. As economic exigencies require these firms to adopt different operational models, we can also expect that their financial models will evolve, and that they will be led to accept the constraints imposed by the public markets.

Unit-level economics

Historically, lodging-industry operating executives have demonstrated a greater aptitude for cost control than they have for revenue generation. Certainly, the downturn of 1990–91 called upon operators to reduce costs deeply, and much of the re-engineering accomplished in the early 1990s has yielded lasting benefits.

Despite these efforts, cost control remains a priority, although revenue generation has also emerged as an emphasis of nearly equal importance for operating executives.

Cost control

Between 1990 and 2000, operating profit (measured under the Uniform System of Accounts for the Lodging Industry as income before fixed charges and management fees) increased on average by some 10 per cent across all US lodging segments (Raleigh, 2001). Although 1990 was a difficult year and 2000 a strong year during which many properties enjoyed impressive pricing power and significant increases in average daily rates, the evolution clearly represents a long-term change in operating efficiency. Notwithstanding these gains, the onset of recession in 2001 has resulted in calls for even greater cost reductions. Moreover, the emphasis is likely to continue, even after the industry recovers in, as estimated by most pundits, late 2002 or early 2003. This will be the result of greater pressure from lodging-company shareholders and hotel owners as they attempt to compensate for returns lost during the recession, pressure to realize savings from investments in technology, and the continuing efforts of larger firms to shed non-strategic assets while maximizing the productivity of those properties remaining in their streamlined portfolios.

The Pan-European market saw an increased emphasis on cost control in the 1990–95 period before entering a period marked by aggressive merger and acquisition (M&A) activity. Although meaningful M&A activity is likely to resume at some point in the coming decade, in Europe the emphasis has shifted to cost control. Cost control is expected to continue as a priority for the decade to come, both because private equity sources have become more sophisticated in their understanding of hotel operations and thus demand more of hotel operators, and because the increasing consolidation of hotels in publicly-traded companies subjects the industry to greater scrutiny from both debt and equity analysts.

In Asia, the impact of the financial crisis of 1997 and the generally overbuilt lodging market promises to extend, by most estimates, upwards of ten years. Although the scrutiny of the public markets is far less intense because of the more widely dispersed ownership of hotels, Asian owners have inevitably turned to cost control as a means of reducing their losses. In an environment where the alternatives for revenue enhancement are limited because of the oversupply of hotel rooms, cost control becomes the only means of improving cash flow from operations, and promises therefore to be the most important emphasis until demand and supply are brought into equilibrium.

Labour costs

In numerous geographical markets, labour cost is the principal operating expense of lodging properties. The relative importance of labour as an operating expense tracks not geography, however, but the degree of socialization of the economy where lodging properties operate. Thus, North American labour costs are significant, but not nearly as onerous as those in most countries of the European Union (EU) or Japan and, to a somewhat lesser extent, Korea.

The shortage of workers willing to make long-term careers in the hospitality industry further exacerbates an already challenging situation. For example, despite relatively high levels of unemployment, France's lodging sector is perpetually in need of 50 000 to 60 000 additional full-time employees, while Germany consistently experiences approximately the same shortfall. In North America, hoteliers are laying off thousands of service workers, many of them new entrants into the labour force through governmental welfare-to-work programmes. The experience is painful, not only on humanitarian grounds, but because hoteliers recognize that, when the recovery commences, it will likely prove difficult to rehire staff whose first employment in the industry proved disappointingly short-lived. In Asia, this labour is more available and, especially in Southeast Asia, typically less costly than in the Northern Hemisphere. However, employee efficiency and retention continue to challenge the region's hoteliers, making it difficult for individual properties to develop a competitive advantage in an overcrowded market.

Thus, across the world operators face the same fundamental problem: identifying, recruiting, and retaining an adequate work force. Labour costs therefore promise to remain an intractable problem, either because the price of employees is elevated by social charges and market conditions or because employees, while available, are unproductive and transitory, driving up the overall cost of operations.

Although elevated labour costs will persist, there is incremental progress on several fronts, and similar opportunities promise to surface in the coming decade. The sharing of certain back-of-the-house functions (e.g. laundry, accounting, human resources management) across multiple operations, including those of different brands within a portfolio, often yields substantial savings. Similarly, e-based procurement effectively allows separate operations to share the expertise of procurement specialists and consolidate their purchases to achieve lower costs. Outsourcing of selected functions (e.g. housekeeping, ground keeping, maintenance) promises to continue to provide economies of scale and flexibility, reducing individual property's costs. A similar flexibility is gained in seasonal resorts when employees accept to annualize their hours worked in exchange for fewer overall contractual hours. By avoiding overtime and the cost of engaging extras, the employer achieves increased productivity for his labour expenditure and the employee effectively increases his compensation per hour worked.

Finally, the reduction in the number of ex-patriot managers is likely to continue. Hotel owners will increasingly resist the additional cost of specialized non-nationals, while local managers will enhance their qualifications through exposure to international operations implanted on their soil and through readier access to formal training in hospitality management.

Revenue generation

The most significant development in the arena of revenue enhancement has been the adoption of a revenue-optimizing model to replace the simplistic capacity-maximization approach of 'putting heads in beds'. Yield management systems that focus operators on the financial contributions – both to rooms and other departments – from individual market segments at different points on the demand curve represent a tremendous step forward for the lodging industry (Kimes, 2001). Already well established in North America, yield management systems are penetrating Europe, frequently as a feature of the franchisor's added value. In Asia and Australia, the utility of yield management systems is currently less evident because widespread discounting leaves hoteliers little pricing power. However, in the longer term, the adoption of yield-management systems is inevitable as the absorption of supply increases and international companies gain a greater presence.

In an increasingly competitive global market, operators are forced to 'think outside the box', pursuing market segments and embracing distribution tactics they previously eschewed. A number of European resorts, for example, are actively seeking shoulder markets, booking a larger percentage of their room nights through tour operators, and launching e-commerce initiatives. Such responses can be expected to multiply and spread across global lodging markets as cost-saving efforts reach their limits, forcing operators to pay even greater heed to revenue generation to improve returns.

Investment, trading and owner-operator issues

As a hybrid operating and real estate endeavour, lodging is as dependent on operating factors for its success as it is on the strategic orientation of monetary and fiscal policymakers, investors, and management boards. Indeed, the future of the industry is as dependent on these non-operating factors as it is on the fundamental unit-level economics. The evolution of these factors, and their impact on the value of lodging assets, therefore deserve careful examination.

Greater transparency

Except in Asia, lodging-industry executives agree that financial reporting on lodging operations and investment performance is steadily evolving toward greater transparency. Relatively speaking, North American and UK-traded companies provide exemplary reliability in their reporting, while also fostering communications between professional analysts and corporate executives. European-based companies are following suit, frequently recognizing that Anglo-Saxon versions of their financial statements are required to gain the attention of the wider markets. However, they are slower to engage in the same dialogue with the analyst community that is commonplace in Anglo-Saxon markets.

Notwithstanding the general trend toward greater transparency, the complexities of international reporting require careful attention. For example, companies operating within the Euro-zone may well report in their local currency, Euros, and US dollars. Similarly, although the Uniform System of Accounts for the Lodging Industry has been widely adopted by international companies, it purposely allows users significant flexibility to customize the basic model to specific circumstances. Thus full interpretation of detailed financial statements frequently requires currency translations, adaptation to differing accounting models, familiarity with multiple terminologies, and an understanding of the operating characteristics of the properties under examination.

Entity structures and tax considerations

Thoroughly tax-driven projects and entity structures are not widespread in the global market, as they have been at other times (e.g. North America in the 1980s). However, in specific circumstances specialized structures are employed to gain tax advantages and financial flexibility.

In Europe, for example, sale-leaseback transactions offer opportunities for companies to preserve cash yet gain control of lodging assets. Although the lodging asset remains on the balance sheet of the purchasing entity (typically a bank), the lessee-operator effectively amortizes the capital cost of the asset and the interest cost of financing the acquisition because he enjoys full deductibility of the lease payments. The same tax-shelter benefits would, of course, be available to the operator if he purchased the property using conventional debt, but the amortization of the operator's capital cost would be spread over a significantly longer period than the 20–25 year term of sale-leaseback agreements. Moreover, some sale-leasebacks are structured for periods as short as 12 years, thus accelerating the deduction and providing greater tax efficiency.

In addition, the same transaction may be structured so that the asset is conveyed at its book value, saving the operator capital gains taxes on the sale of the asset.

Equity analysts and rating agencies regularly interpret sale-leasebacks as debt, and evaluate the risk of hotel companies accordingly. However, even the most critical of analysts will agree that sale-leaseback transactions preserve cash and permit hotel companies to expand their distribution rapidly – not an insignificant advantage in an era of branding. Groupe Accor, for example, has used sale-leasebacks frequently, enabling it to expand the reach of its brands without the requirement to raise large amounts of capital.

Other scattered instances of tax-favoured treatments can be enumerated. Developers in selected Eastern European countries receive exemptions from taxes during the hotel's start-up period as an incentive to realize projects. Specific destinations in the EU are eligible for similar tax incentives in order to increase their competitiveness and spur development. In Ireland, a significant proportion of a hotel's assets qualify for accelerated depreciation, while in Spain acquired goodwill can be amortized over a relatively short ten years, thus increasing the tax efficiency of acquisitions.

Finally, in most jurisdictions, lodging companies can gain tax advantages by the familiar tactic of acquiring entities with outstanding losses and carrying these losses forward to offset the acquirer's corporate profits. In general, however, the essential rule of tax strategy observed by today's hotel companies is: make all acquisitions and dispositions with an eye to the tax consequences, but determine the merit of the transaction based on its fundamental economics and strategic fit.

Management contracts

The strategy of separating lodging operations from ownership has proved viable over the last thirty years. Today most 'hotel companies' are primarily operators rather than owners, deriving the bulk of their rooms inventory from managed hotels. This trend promises to continue as most hotel companies emphasize distribution, lean balance sheets, and steady growth in earnings. Moreover, the increasing importance of branding will lead more operating companies to expand their distribution systems, using either franchising or management contracts, according to the requirements of the deal – as long as incremental rooms are added to the system.

Across the world, hotel management companies are seeing the end of the ascendancy they enjoyed in the 1970s and 1980s (Beals, 1995). Although even the most inexperienced owner quickly comes to appreciate the importance of branding and professional day-to-day property management, the days when an operator could open negotiations by presenting a form contract and assuming a 'take it or leave it' stance are over. Even management-company executives agree that owners are increasingly sophisticated, either through hard-won experience or because they have purchased the expertise, engaging consultants or asset managers to represent their interests. In North America and Europe, where owners have the longest experience dealing with operators, it is not unusual for owners to influence significantly, in the words of one executive, the 'feel and touch' of a property, involving themselves in myriad operational decisions.

Greater owner activism is reflected in the fee structures negotiated with management companies (Barge and Jacobs, 2001). Base fees remain modest percentage (two to four) of revenue, although the overall tendency is to pay operators slightly more in base fees than they received in the crisis years of the early 1990s. Incentive fees, however, are increasingly calculated as a percentage of cash flow after debt service and a guaranteed return to ownership. Similarly, performance clauses and termination provisions shift an increasing proportion of the risk to operators. In a competitive market with numerous hotel companies seeking to expand their distribution, owners will continue to consolidate their negotiating power. With the exception of certain Latin countries, where local custom prevails, management agreements are becoming increasingly complex, prescribing more aspects of the operator's responsibilities, and the trend is expected to continue.

Above all, the increasing strength of owners is reflected in the financial contributions they are able to secure from management companies. Some owners, especially in North America, will not contemplate taking on a management company as a minority equity partner because the security interest an equity stake confers on the operator can prove problematic if the majority owner wishes to sell the property, or if he becomes disenchanted with the operator's performance and seeks to remove him. There are other North American owners who believe that even 'sliver' equity from the management company provides sufficient alignment of interest between owner and operator to make the risk tolerable. In other parts of the world, however, majority owners are better protected from claims originating with minority interests, especially non-nationals. In these circumstances, owners more readily seek equity contributions, and the trend is increasing as owners become more knowledgeable and adept at negotiating management agreements.

Other forms of financial contributions from operators align their interests with owners without engendering the potential complications of an equity interest. For example, operators may contribute furniture, fixture, and equipment or operating capital to the project (Eyster, 1988).

To secure contracts, management companies may be led to provide unsecured loans of varying kinds, from non-interest-bearing, non-amortizing loans to interest-bearing amortizing loans. Most loans are for terms of 5–10 years, and those that bear interest are typically at below-market rates. Sometimes used in Europe, 'key money' resembles non-interest-bearing debt but may ultimately become a cash contribution without an equity interest. Operators who advance cash in the form of key money receive no return on their capital, but may receive a return of their capital if the contractual arrangement founders before the end of its term. If, however, the project is successful, the owner retains the key money and the operator has effectively purchased an annuity – the fee stream received over the contract's term.

Finally, operators may demonstrate their alignment with owners' interests by offering various types of guarantees. Such pledges put operators at risk and reassure owners of their commitment to the project. A common guarantee provides a 'cure', requiring the operator to advance funds if the cash flow from operations does not reach predetermined levels. Funds advanced by the operator may or may not be reimbursed, depending on the specific terms negotiated by the parties, and operators rarely (if ever) receive a return on the capital paid in to the project under cure provisions.

As lenders have become more conservative in the loan-to-value (LTV) ratios they permit for mortgages, so-called mezzanine financing – high-coupon subordinated debt that is tantamount to equity – has become a means for owners to increase a project's or portfolio's gearing. Larger hotel companies, such as Marriott International, will frequently provide credit enhancement for mezzanine debt, guaranteeing to make debt service payments if the cash flow from operations is insufficient. (Although the potential liability is revealed only in the hotel company's footnotes, credit rating agencies and financial analysts have proved quick to spot the attempt at off-balance-sheet financing and routinely add the obligation to the firm's liabilities.)

Owners have learned that the management contract can prove far more than, as one investor described it in the 1990s, 'just another document to sign at the closing'. Indeed, valuations in numerous markets prove that a lodging property operated under an existing management contract is, in fact, an encumbered asset. Owners, acutely aware of their dependence on management companies to realize value from their assets, will continue to utilize contract terms such as those discussed above, as well as other innovations, to ensure that the owner's and operator's interests coincide.

Investment in technology

Lodging companies' managements and the owners they serve currently take the same 'go slow' approach to technology investments that many consumers exhibit. As one lodging-fund executive with Goldman Sachs observed, 'We [owners] don't want to be left out, but we'd like sure proof of the benefits before we leap'. Certainly this caution is likely to persist until lodging markets in numerous parts of the world recover. However, in the longer term the efforts already underway promise to increase, ultimately yielding a much more widespread adoption of technology at the property level and an increased use of e-commerce.

Research in North America, where the use of e-commerce is reasonably advanced, suggests that lodging customers are not entirely enamoured of the hotel industry's efforts to date (Jeong, Oh and Gregoire, 2001). For the lodging companies that have already embraced e-commerce, continued progress will require diligence and an ongoing commitment from the boardroom. For the fledgling attempts at e-commerce to succeed, these companies must achieve critical mass, yielding an efficient channel of distribution. Moreover, companies must devise tactics to share the cost savings of their e-commerce applications with consumers, thus inciting their participation in the channel and their long-term loyalty.

Whatever the challenges of employing e-commerce effectively, the effort is worth the proverbial candle. To the extent that lodging companies can escape their dependence on travel agents, GDS systems, tour operators and, more recently, Internet auction sites, they will own the distribution system. The current emphasis of lodging companies is to expand by increasing their distribution – i.e. the geographic dispersion of their physical properties. This is a requisite condition for market dominance in a brand's individual market segment(s), but ultimate success – and the largest financial payoff – can only be achieved when the brand also controls its distribution channels.

The increasing importance of branding bodes well for the wider use of technology at the property level. As one executive at Six Continents Hotels observed, '[technology] vendors left a vast middle ground of hotel operators poorly served'. As branding increases – and as franchisors incorporate more technology services and requirements into their brands – progress in the use of technology will inevitably result, increasing customer satisfaction and enhancing unit-level financial performance.

Capital availability

Although there are some exceptions (e.g. China, Korea), in general, investment capital is not flowing into the lodging sector, and the situation promises to persist until 2003. Some speculate that 2001's dramatic downturn in North American lodging activity and valuations will permanently quell investors' willingness to provide capital to the lodging industry. Most, however, concur that the current situation is no more deleterious than other cyclical declines and that the sector will recover, once again attracting investment capital. In Europe, where the declines are marked but less severe, merger-and-acquisition activity is expected to resume as the lodging industry recovers in 2003. Most Asian markets will require a much longer period of recovery as demand slowly increases and comes into better balance with supply. There will, however, be some refinancing activity, and as long as Asian banking practices continue without reform, capital will, in selected instances, flow into lodging.

Although hotel-operating companies may record impressive earnings and earnings growth, hotel property companies will struggle perpetually to attract capital because their accounting earnings cannot rival the results achieved by other more readily understood sectors. Moreover, as the aftermath of 11 September demonstrates, lodging's high degree of operating leverage spells volatility when volume fluctuates, and this is daunting to most participants in the capital markets. Because of these factors, private equity has been and will continue to be an important source of capital for the lodging industry.

Banks in the Pan-European and Asian markets will also continue to be a source of both debt and equity capital. Securitization of debt will continue as a means of tapping the public markets in North America and Europe and can be expected to gain increasing acceptance in Asia. The financial structures of individual projects and the balance sheets of publicly traded hotel operators and lodging property companies will become increasingly complex. Investment banking houses, ever ready to generate fees by creating new products, will 'take to market' innovative hybrid securities that exploit the special characteristics of the lodging industry.

Real Estate Investment Trusts (REITs) are slowly developing in selected European countries. These tax-favoured mutual funds will not grow in importance, however, until a set of common Pan-European statutes governing their creation, administration, and tax treatment is developed. In addition to allowing REITs to gain the efficiency of owning multiple properties across Europe, enabling statutes must permit REITs greater control over the operation of the assets in their portfolios, as recently enacted legislation in the USA does. If not, REITs will stall because of the inherent dilemma peculiar to lodging real estate: creating value depends on successful operation of the lodging asset, but to retain their tax-free status, REITs must be passive investors, and are accordingly forbidden from operating the assets in their portfolio.

Insurance companies and pension funds were once ideal capital sources for hotels because the maturities of their obligations could be matched to the life cycles of hotels in their portfolio. In today's far more volatile market, however, insurance companies and pension funds across the world make only limited direct investments in hotel projects. Those who desire an exposure to the lodging sector are more inclined to purchase the securities of hotel operating and property companies, preferring a readily traded instrument to the illiquidity of hotel ownership or a permanent mortgage on a distressed property. As the securitization of hotel investments increases, insurance companies and pension funds are likely to satisfy their appetite for lodging investments by continuing to hold securities, rather than through direct investment or whole loans.

Conclusions

The apocrypha of the lodging industry holds that numerous renowned hoteliers – from César Ritz to E. M. Statler, Conrad Hilton and Kemmons Wilson – issued the sage advice that the most important determinant of success is 'location, location, location'. If the modern hotel industry has a personage the equal of any of the preceding four, he might observe that the key to success today is 'performance, performance, performance'.

Performance at the unit level is the fundamental engine of the lodging industry. The pressure on hoteliers to view every operating decision in light of the underlying economic model, instead of tradition and competitive practice, will continue unabated. Similarly, pressure to market the lodging product more effectively will be an inevitable component of an increasingly competitive marketplace. Performance in reaching the consumer and influencing his purchase decision to maximize yield will be the hallmark of successful lodging companies. Finally, the thinking of lodging executives must continue the evolution from an operations mindset to a strategic orientation. The financial re-engineering resulting from this shift will meet the final performance test, ensuring that fairly priced capital is available and that the financial structures of lodging companies are optimized.

Acknowledgement

Note: the author wishes to thank the members of L'Association des Anciens de l'Institut de Management Hôtelier International (Cornell-ESSEC) who contributed valuable insights to the research reported above.

Summary

- The lodging industry is well underway in its transformation from a craft orientation to a business enterprise, as witnessed by the greater attention to unit-level economics.

- A pattern of increased rationalization of operations and increased branding can be observed, beginning in North America and progressing eastward.

- Although revenue generation is increasingly an objective of operating managers, cost control remains an important tactic for operating managers seeking to improve unit-level financial performance.

- High labour costs promise to remain an intractable problem, either because the price of employees is elevated by mandatory social charges and market conditions or because employees are transient, making for an unproductive workforce.

- Yield management systems are the most significant development in hoteliers' revenue-generation efforts.

- Specialized tax situations can impact on the economic viability of lodging projects, and a limited number of them are available to hotel owners in various parts of the world.

- The separation of operations and ownership continues to be the predominant paradigm, making management contracts an important vehicle for aligning the interests of hotel investors and operators.

- Technology and e-commerce are underutilized tools in the lodging industry, but they hold great promise as a means for lodging companies to gain competitive and financial advantages.

- Private equity will remain an important source of capital for the lodging industry, but increasingly sophisticated instruments will also be used to direct public debt and equity capital to the industry.

Review questions

1. Which geographic areas of the world seem to exhibit the highest degree of branding and rationalization of day-to-day operations? Can you suggest reasons why this pattern exists?
2. What distinguishes Anglo-Saxon lodging companies?
3. How are Latin lodging companies different from Anglo-Saxon lodging companies?
4. Historically, hoteliers have been more adept at cost control than at revenue generation. How is this changing as hoteliers are called upon to improve operating results?
5. Discuss the relative importance of labour costs to hotel operations. What determines the level of labour costs for hotel operations in various geographic regions?
6. What is a yield management system? When hoteliers employ a yield management system, what are they attempting to accomplish?
7. What types of special tax situations are favourable to hotel development?

8. Why is the use of management contracts expected to be the principal means by which hotel companies expand the number of rooms in their chains?
9. What is the greatest benefit lodging companies can enjoy if their e-commerce efforts are successful?
10. Why is private equity likely to continue to be an important source of capital for the lodging industry?
11. What are the three types of performance necessary for success in the lodging industry today?

References

Barge, P. and Jacobs, D. (2001) Management agreement trends worldwide. In *Hotel Topics: Issue No.7*, June, available at www.joneslanglasalle.com

Beals, P. (1995) The hotel management contract: lessons from the North American experience. In Harris, P. (ed.) *Accounting and Finance for the International Hospitality Industry,* Butterworth-Heinemann, Oxford.

Eyster, J. (1988) *The Negotiation and Administration of Hotel and Restaurant Management Contracts.* Cornell University School of Hotel Administration, Ithaca, NY.

Jeong, M., Oh, H. and Gregoire, M. M. (2001) *An Internet Marketing Strategy Study for the Lodging Industry.* American Hotel and Lodging Foundation, Washington.

Kimes, S. (2001) *The '4-C' Strategy for Yield Management.* Center for Hospitality Research at Cornell University, Ithaca, NY.

Raleigh, L. E. (2001) Hotel investments: back to the future? *AAHOA Hospitality*, November, pp. 34–35.

Further reading

Eyster, J. J. (1997) *Hotel Contracts in the U.S.: The Revolution Continues and Twelve Areas of Concern: A Supplement to the Negotiation and Administration of Hotel and Restaurant Management Contracts.* Cornell University School of Hotel Administration, Ithaca, NY.

Raleigh, L. E. and Roginsky, R. J. (1999) *Hotel Investments: Issues and Perspectives*, 2nd ed. Educational Institute of the American Hotel and Motel Association, East Lansing, MI.

Rushmore, S. and Baum, E. (2001) *Hotels and Motels: Valuations and Market Studies.* The Appraisal Institute, Chicago.

Rushmore, S., Ciraldo, D. M. and Tarras, J. (2001) *Hotel Investments Handbook 2002.* The West Group, New York.

Themes and prospects

Bob Brotherton

Introduction

The primary purpose of this final chapter is to provide a thematic synthesis of the material contained in the previous chapters, highlight some issues, questions and problems arising from these, and to be somewhat more speculative concerning the future prospects for the international hospitality industry. Given the range and diversity of the topics and issues covered in Chapters 1 to 10, this may appear to be a rather daunting, if not foolhardy, venture. However, it is possible to identify some recurrent themes in this material that are also reflected in the extant literature.

When you have studied this chapter you will be able to:

- Identify key themes pertaining to the industry as a whole.

- Discuss the underlying reasons for the existence of such common themes.

- Analyse how the industry, and its constituent sectors, may evolve in the future.

- Evaluate the future prospects for the industry.

- Provide alternative views of how, and why, the industry may develop in the future.

Themes

My analysis of the material contained in the previous chapters suggests that it is possible to group the recurrent themes and issues raised by the authors into two basic categories. First, there are issues that may be described as *structural and/or strategic* in nature. These are derived from the structural and competitive characteristics of the industry, the global versus local dilemma and the expansion or growth of the industry. Second, there are issues I would categorize as essentially *operational* in nature, though a number of these either are derived from strategic concerns or are likely to have strategic implications for international operators. Among these, those associated with the application and use of information technology, the significance and value of branding, the development of more extensive and durable customer relationships and the critical importance of people (both staff and management) would appear to be pre-eminent. These are all value drivers and key sources of competitive advantage. In addition to these two basic categories a further, perhaps less substantive, one of comparability may be added. Comparing industrial structures, company performance, service quality, facility and product design etc. across different cultures and countries has its own inherent problems and it is important to be aware of these to avoid the production of inaccurate and misleading conclusions.

Structural/strategic

One clear commonality across the sectors of the international hospitality industry is the *many dominated by the few* structural characteristic often found at individual country level, though this does vary in its incidence and prominence in different regions/countries due to variability in 'local' market development. As the authors of Chapters 1 to 3 clearly indicate, the size structure of the international hospitality industry is highly fragmented, with a large number of small, often independently owned and managed, companies constituting the bulk of those operating in the hotel restaurant and contract foodservice sectors. By contrast the dominant players in each of these sectors are extremely large international, if not global, corporations with a significant operational presence in a range of different countries. This invariably generating for them substantial shares of the national markets they operate in and, by a simple process of aggregation, giving them a similar position within the international arena.

However, here lies one of the problems in attempting to define the parameters or boundaries of the international, as opposed to a national, hospitality industry – this being the interface between the international and the national. One the one hand, it would be relatively simple to define the parameters of the international industry by only including hospitality companies that have operations in more than one country. While this may be acceptable for a company to be regarded as 'international', it would not reflect the reality of the international industry, as these companies operate and compete in markets containing hospitality companies that are not international by way of a presence in more than one country, but are in that they derive custom from international travellers and compete with international companies for domestic business.

Unfortunately, the logical extension of this line of argument would tend to suggest that virtually all hospitality businesses should be considered as constituents of the international hospitality industry! This would clearly be rather problematic, both conceptually and empirically. Nevertheless, the problem remains; where should the line between a given national hospitality industry and the international industry be drawn, and on what basis? The 'black' and 'white' extremes of this conundrum are clear, i.e. international hospitality companies being the black and domestic hospitality businesses not in direct competition with international hospitality company operations in their country being the white. The problem lies in the 'grey' between these two extremes.

There are no easy answers or solutions to this issue. One possibility would be to include companies who are in direct competition with international hospitality companies and those who have a high proportion of their business generated from international travellers. However, this would be difficult to establish in practice and would not really be applicable to many domestic contract foodservice companies competing against their international counterparts. Another aspect of this problem is what may be termed the 'hidden' hospitality businesses that operate in the international environment but tend to be excluded from any definition of the industry as they are not part of international hotel, restaurant or contract foodservice companies. Among these, the hotel properties owned by major tour operators and cruise line accommodation operations would figure strongly. Some tour operators now have their own hotel divisions with substantial portfolios of properties and the largest cruise operators collectively provide significant numbers of bed nights on their vessels.

Perhaps Jones (1999) is right when he observes that some commentators suggest the international hospitality industry does not exist as a 'single entity'. On the other hand, the very fact that we refer to an international hospitality industry does suggest that it is possible to identify its boundaries in terms of inclusion/exclusion in order to define what is, and what is not, to be included in the definition of the industry. If we cannot do this there is little point in describing it as an industry. Clearly, much more thought needs to be given to this issue.

A second strategic theme is the extensively debated *global versus local* dilemma. This being a strategic choice issue of whether to pursue a standardized strategy or one that is more variable, customized and contingent upon local circumstances and conditions. However, this choice is not always one of such a 'zero sum' nature. Popular phrases such as 'think global – act local' and 'glocalization' are embedded within the concept of 'mass customization' (Pine, 1993; Gilmore and Pine, 1997). This suggests it is possible to standardize many, if not all, of the company's internal business functions, production processes and product components while simultaneously offering customized product/service packages to different markets and segments. Jones (1999: 435) provides a simple example of this in the case of American hotel chains having to 'adjust full room service provision to reflect the British practice of having tea making facilities in the room'. In a more expansive context Watson (1997) suggests that McDonald's, a truly global hospitality organization, views itself as a 'multi-local' operator, with local partners, suppliers and menu variations to reflect local tastes and customs. The global aspect of McDonald's being its vision, corporate values and systems (Brotherton and Adler, 1999).

This is a serious strategic problem for international hospitality companies as the market environments and segments within which they operate are highly heterogeneous, yet amenable to branded operations. For example, local circumstances may necessitate some variation in the brand's components for the offer to be acceptable to a particular domestic market, but these may be the very components that customers from other countries value the most. The tension here is to retain the original value embodied in the brand while modifying its format and delivery in particular locations. Where the demands and priorities of different groups of customers are broadly similar this can be achieved fairly easily, where they are not it is a much more fundamental problem. This is essentially the internal–external dilemma referred to by Brotherton and Hopping (1997) and Brotherton and Adler (1999), who suggest that the additional dimension of culturally-based market differences creates a strategic tension between the 'internal' desire to clone a successful brand in other countries and the 'external' desire to ensure market acceptability via some degree of customization. In turn, this implies an immutable 'core', that cannot be significantly modified without threatening the original value, and a 'periphery' that can be customized without threatening the integrity of the brand. The challenge is to identify the boundary between the two.

A third theme is the *growth and expansion* of the industry and individual companies operating within it. As one might expect, the expansion of the industry in general is governed by prevailing economic and travel conditions. In short, the more buoyant the world economy and the greater the volume of international travel the greater the incentive for hospitality companies to expand. However, we must be careful here not to leap to some rather questionable conclusions. Simply to assume a direct and positive relationship between the health of the world economy, international travel volumes and the growth of the international hospitality industry *per se* would be misleading. Though this may be true in the case of international hotel companies and, perhaps to a slightly lesser extent, for international restaurant operators, there is a much lower level of correlation between these factors in the case of contract foodservice, especially international travel.

The key issue here is the extent to which the companies concerned are dependent on international, as opposed to, national markets. Although international hotel companies are dependent upon the health of individual national economies/markets for a proportion of their business, they are perhaps more dependent overall on international business and leisure travel. This being clearly evidenced by the enormous negative effects on the revenues, profits and expansion plans of international hotel companies due to the dramatic reductions in such travel as an immediate consequence of the 11 September 2001 terrorist attacks in the USA. By contrast, the restaurant and contract foodservice sectors in general are less dependent upon international travel-related business. Of course they are not immune to the effects of a travel downturn or global economic recession, as both of these tend to be aggregate reflections of difficulties in a number of significant national economies. Neither are they totally isolated from these aggregate effects as some aspects of contract foodservice are travel-related, i.e. in-flight and airport catering, and many restaurant operators, especially in large and/or capital cities receive substantial business from international travellers.

On the other hand, they are generally less exposed to the vagaries of the international travel market and perhaps have more opportunities to secure substitute business from the domestic/local markets they operate within. For example, contract foodservice companies may continue to expand in the face of such negative macro conditions by focusing on welfare (educational and health service related) catering opportunities that are unlikely to be strongly affected by these conditions. Similarly, restaurant and contract foodservice operators often have greater operational scale and location options than hotels. The development of 'micro-unit' and/or 'home delivery' formats and utilization of 'host environment' locations (Jones, 1999) provide, perhaps with the exception of the latter, alternative growth options not available to hotel companies.

In terms of the growth strategies adopted by international hospitality companies it is clear there has been a general move on the part of hotel and contract foodservice companies to favour acquisitive horizontal integration strategies, either of a takeover or merger nature, to achieve expansion over the last two decades. This is a process that has led to the creation of a number of significant, multibrand international hotel chains and global contract foodservice companies who now possess considerable economies of scale and market power. Allied to these acquisitive strategies are others, especially in the hotel sector, that have served similar purposes. In particular the use of strategic alliances with local partners, management contracts and franchising have all served to extend the global presence and market reach of the major international hotel companies. By contrast, the restaurant sector has tended to favour more organic expansion, though franchising has been particularly significant in the fast food part of the sector.

The growth of the industry as a whole has been facilitated by relatively low barriers to market entry across the sectors and national economies. Though clearly some countries are more difficult to enter and operate within, because of politico-legal constraints and/or strong cultural differences, the economic power of the largest players and the desire, especially among developing countries and emergent economies, to secure income from international tourism has helped to generate this growth. Indeed, the latter have often provided financial and other incentives to attract such inward investment. Notwithstanding these opportunities, the success of such expansion has not always been as large as the companies might have expected. Local constraints and rigidities, in combination with intense competitive environments, have conspired to make life rather challenging for many entrants. This has been particularly the case for smaller, independent business chains that tend to lack the supportive resources of the larger corporate chains.

Operational

One key theme to emerge from many of the chapters in this book is the increased, and increasing, importance of *information technology* (IT) application and use in all sectors of the international hospitality industry. In part this is a strategic issue by virtue of the fact that IT not only has operational implications for individual property and/or brand configurations and performance, but also for the structure, organization and competitive posture of a company. However, the decision has been taken here to identify IT as an operational issue because it is at this level that many of the issues surrounding it become more transparent and pertinent. At a strategic level, IT and associated communication technologies have already transformed the global business environment, the ways companies conduct their business and how business functions are organized and operate. In turn, this has not only led to changes in operational structures and processes, in terms of improving on past practice, but is beginning fundamentally to change the mindsets of hospitality service managers, deliverers and customers. As Peter O'Connor and Gabriele Piccoli and Alex Gibson amply demonstrate in Chapters 5 and 8, this process will revolutionize operational thinking and practice in the future as the technology develops further and becomes embedded in the operational function and service product reflecting its centrality in the lives of hospitality customers.

I will comment further on some of the future aspects of this in the final part of this chapter but perhaps we need to be careful about overstating its impact on operational structures and processes to date. O'Connor and Piccoli have already indicated the somewhat conservative nature of IT adoption and utilization within the industry and Jones (1999: 436) makes the most astute observation that 'If Cesar Ritz or any other famous hoteliers of the nineteenth century were to be reincarnated, they could walk into any of the world's top luxury hotels and recognize how work was organized, what jobs workers were engaged in, and the way the hotel business was conducted. At unit level, both in hotels and foodservice, organizational form and behaviour have changed little'. Whether this will persist into the future is another matter to be commented on later. Nevertheless, the point here is that IT has not revolutionized the operational environment to date. The extent to which it will in the future is arguable, even though the extent to which it could is potentially revolutionary, as we shall see later in this chapter.

A second key issue is that of *branding*. There is no doubt that the last two decades in particular bear witness to the increasing dominance of branded hospitality operations in the international arena. Whether companies have followed a single or multibrand path, the power of the brand has been a significant factor in driving forward the international industry. Brands are invariably regarded as 'known' entities that reduce the purchase risk involved for the customer and enable the company to defend its position in the marketplace against competing brands. This being reflected in a brand being the customer's 'product of choice', repeat purchase, loyalty etc., and the company's market share.

While it is undeniable that these benefits do accrue, this whole perspective is a rather negative one. It is essentially defensive in nature. Does the customer buy because the product delivers the best value for them, as the marketing literature would have us believe, or because it is the least risky option? Do companies really use their brands to build long-term relationships with their customers or merely employ them as a short-term hedge against various kinds of risk? As Muller (1999) points out, the creation of a quality product/service and its flawless delivery are important but the real leverage a brand offers is its potential for becoming 'resident in the consumer's mind'. In short, the creation of an enduring emotional attachment rather than a simple habit. This is the 'positive' dimension of the hospitality brand, the offensive approach that lays the foundation for the possibility of lifetime loyalty and revenue streams. Is this really the approach that most, if not all, international hospitality companies have taken in the establishment and development of their brands? The evidence appears to suggest it is not.

Another key theme is the importance of *people*, and in particular *customer relationship management (CRM)*. This tends to be evident in discussions concerning the importance and value of pursuing customer retention/loyalty and/or developing relationship marketing. Among countless others, Shoemaker and Lewis, (1999) and Muller (1999) make it clear that all the technology in the world will not deliver any significant advances in these areas, though the technologies will be significant enablers in that they provide the potential for developing both the informational and communications architecture required successfully to operationalize these concepts. However, the point here is that database marketing and frequency or loyalty programmes are not synonymous with CRM or relationship marketing. Indeed, they are not necessarily the logical precursors for these developments in the sense that CRM and relationship marketing are not simple linear extensions of, or developments from, these activities. They involve different mindsets, alternative business models and fundamental changes in the company's philosophy and operational orientation. They are truly holistic 'customer-focused' and 'knowledge-based' activities that demand a different *modus operandi* and are revolutionary rather than evolutionary in nature.

While the customer focus referred to above addresses one side of the people equation involved in the intangible elements of the hospitality service transaction, it is becoming increasingly evident that international hospitality companies are realizing, albeit perhaps rather late in the day compared to other international industries, that managers and employees also require much greater attention. If relationships with customers are so crucial to competitive advantage and success, and few if any would dispute this, it is not just the product they are supplied with or the data held on them to help customize the offer that ultimately drives effective performance in this respect. Beyond a 'satisfying' level of product/service provision, embodied in the company's standard offer, it is the quality of the management and staff which provides added value and, in turn, generates the possibility of retaining and developing relationships with customers that raise their switching costs to a level that significantly inhibits the propensity to transfer their business to another provider. In one sense there is nothing new in this. All service businesses know that if there is a baseline consisting of a desirable product that can be made readily and easily available, the basic foundations are in place for success. However, regardless of this, success will not be achieved, certainly not in any lasting sense, if the delivery of the offer by the staff is not consistently good and if the management do not act appropriately to create the support this requires.

An over concentration on the application of new technologies to improve the infrastructure and efficiency of the hospitality operations environment is an imperfect substitute for the 'Human Moment ... an authentic psychological encounter that can only happen when two people share the same physical space' (Hallowell, 1999: 59). As Muller (1999) adeptly points out in the context of restaurants, technology can deal admirably with those aspects of the offer that are amenable to commoditization, but it cannot replace 'the restaurant experience itself'. This is reinforced by Shoemaker and Lewis (1999) who, while not denying the vital role technology plays in establishing a prerequisite informational foundation to enhance customer satisfaction and loyalty, make the point that the realization of this potential is crucially dependent on the company's human resource policies and practices. Moreover, they suggest that the type of 'value-added' and/or 'value-recovery' potential existing within the intangible maze of customer–employee and manager–employee relationships is frequently not realized 'because top management has failed to see the link between customer loyalty and employee satisfaction, and employee satisfaction and profits' (Shoemaker and Lewis, 1999: 356).

Comparability

Comparability is always a problem when different entities are analysed to identify similarities and/or differences. The basic 'comparability problems' are the same whether the comparison is one undertaken at a relatively local, homogeneous level or one that is cross-national, cross-cultural or international in nature. That said, the introduction of different linguistic and cultural traditions, politico-legal systems, economic and business practices, statistical definitions and data collection procedures and social norms into the analytical melting pot considerably complicates the issues.

The fundamental comparability problems are 'equivalence' and 'representativeness' (Brotherton, 1999, 2000, 2002). Both are concerned with the validity of comparisons. Equivalence minimizes any potential internal bias in the comparisons being made, while sufficiently representative samples from the comparative contexts enhance the external validity of the comparisons. At the international, cross-national/cultural level serious equivalence and representativeness problems often arise because of inter-cultural/national differences and the scale of the entities being compared.

Unfortunately, the hospitality management literature tends to suggest that practice is variable on both these issues. In the case of equivalence, the study by Burrell et al. (1997), into equal opportunities for women employees in the hospitality industry in four European countries, makes no attempt to address the obvious issues of conceptual or lexicon equivalence associated with the design and implementation of the questionnaire. The study does not even make it clear whether the questionnaire was translated into the different languages of the countries concerned, or whether it was implemented in English alone! The study by Pizam *et al.* (1997), into the relationship between national and industry cultures and managerial behaviour, employed a survey questionnaire to elicit information from 192 hotel managers in Hong Kong, Japan and Korea, but does not contain any comment on whether the questionnaire was implemented in one or more languages or whether it was evaluated for conceptual equivalence prior to its use. Indeed, as the Cronbach's alpha reliability coefficients reported in the study ranged from a low of 0.32 to a high of 0.69, it might be assumed that it was not! Similarly, when the study by Moutinho *et al.* (1995), comparing the future development of the hotel sector, was extended beyond the predominantly English speaking countries of Scotland, England, Wales and Ireland to be replicated in Spain, the authors offer no information about how such equivalence problems were addressed in the design or implementation of the questionnaire survey in this different context.

By way of contrast, the study by Armstrong *et al.* (1997), of cross-cultural expectations in relation to the measurement of service quality perceptions, constitutes a model of good practice. Not only was the wording of the SERVQUAL instrument adapted for the hotel industry context, to ensure contextual equivalence, but lexicon equivalence was addressed as: 'The instrument was translated and back-translated from English to Japanese and Chinese by different language experts at Hong Kong based universities' (Armstrong *et al.*, 1997: 186). Similarly, the study by Brotherton *et al.* (2002), of critical success factors in UK and Dutch hotels, is also a model of excellent practice. Here the original UK questionnaire was back-translated by two independent bilingual colleagues and pilot-tested with a small group of Dutch hoteliers. This process highlighted some literal and conceptual differences that were dealt with to ensure conceptual equivalence before the instrument was used in Holland.

Regarding the sample representativeness issue, Hallam and Baum's (1996: 46) study of the 'internal and external factors that may cause hotels to contract out portions or all of their food and beverage operations', within the contexts of the USA and UK, suffered from representativeness and comparability problems arising from the small samples achieved (34 in the UK and 28 in the USA). Van Hoof *et al.* (1996: 87) 'compared the perceptions of lodging managers in the United States, Canada, and the United Kingdom about computer technology and their opinions on technology needs, competency, and levels of automation', and again the size and variability of the samples achieved (237 in the USA, 131 in the UK and 43 in Canada) gives rise to the same concerns as the Hallam and Baum study.

A further example of some of these 'representativeness' problems can be found in the 1999 Worldwide Hotel Industry Study, produced by Horwath International in collaboration with the International Hotel & Restaurant Association and Smith Travel Research. The worldwide trends and results contained in this publication are based on data from 'more than 3000 hoteliers' representing 720 000 rooms. First, what does 'more then 3000 hoteliers' mean? Was it 3001 or 3999, or something in-between? Why does this matter? Well, if it had been 3999 rather than 3001, the sample would have been approximately one third larger in size. A not insignificant difference when the sample size is rather small in relation to the size of the population, as you will see below! Secondly, how representative is 720 000 rooms? At first glance this would appear to be a substantial number. However, other data in the report indicate that the mainland USA has 3 300 000 rooms alone, with the People's Republic of China having almost the same number of rooms as the sample! Furthermore, as David Litteljohn indicated in Chapter 1, World Tourism Organisation (WTO) statistics showed the existence of some 15.5 million hotels and similar establishments existing in 1998 and cited Todd and Mather (2001) who suggest that the top 20 corporate hotel chains controlled 1.8 million rooms in 2001.

In addition, the report presents the results of the survey data by Price, using the categories of luxury, first class and mid-price/economy, and by size (under 100 rooms, 100–300 rooms and over 300 rooms). Unfortunately, the report does not indicate the criteria used to define the price categories but, more significantly, for comparative purposes, also does not specify the number of hotels or rooms contained in any of the price or size categories! This of course raises the question of whether we are comparing like with like. If the sample as a whole is dominated by large numbers of hotels in one of the price and/or size categories, we may be comparing very unequal groupings and generating dubious conclusions. On the other hand, if the distribution across each of the sub-sample categories is reasonably balanced we would not. The problem is we simply do not know which of these situations is the case. The report also states that 'all values are presented as means'. While there is nothing inherently problematic in this, the fact that we are not provided with the 'n' for each category, or for the different regional data, and have no indication of the dispersion of each distribution (i.e. the range, standard deviation etc.), is problematic. Without this information we have no way of knowing whether any between-group comparisons we may wish to make will be based on similar distributions or otherwise.

Prospects

Though future predictions tend to be subject to the 'one man's meat is another's poison' syndrome, the longer-term prospects for the industry would appear to be potentially encouraging, not-withstanding the fact that many challenges lie ahead. Indeed the analyst Paul Slattery (Director of Corporate Finance, Dresdner Kleinwort Benson), speaking at the International Hotel & Restaurant Association's 1999 Annual Congress, suggested that the potential for growth in the hotel sector is 'awesome' (Hamelin, 1999). A doubling of hotel rooms to 30 million, with several chains having over 1 million rooms, and a tenfold increase in turnover to over 2 trillion dollars is estimated. It is also expected that the major hotel chains will lead the way in this process as they could increase their room stock by a factor of four, while non-chain companies are expected to exhibit zero growth. However, Slattery also goes on to indicate that all of this would require access to investment capital of $30 billion per year and a profound increase in the effectiveness of corporate management in the hotel chains, with the latter being a prime driver to secure the former. With the share prices of many leading UK and US hotel companies under per-forming and standing at deep discounts in relation to their stock markets it will be more difficult to raise the necessary capital and realize the growth potential. There are strong echoes here of Paul Beal's contention in Chapter 10 that the future mantra for interna-tional hospitality companies will be 'performance, performance, performance' rather than 'location, location, location'!

This raises the issue of the challenges facing international hospitality companies in the near future. If all this potential is to be realized there will need to be a sea change in management thinking and practice (Olsen, 1999, 2001) and, as Judie Gannon has previously indicated in Chapter 9, this will require the recruitment of people with different managerial skills than in the past. It will also require a fundamental re-evaluation of the human resource management (HRM) function as Woods (1999: 447) suggests that 'little has changed in HR over the past 40 years or so'. Woods also contends that 'HR is at a cross-roads and has two likely futures. Either HR will evolve and adapt and become much more important to organizations [or] HR as we know it will disappear and be replaced by a combi-nation of outsourcing and technology' (1999: 443–444). This dichotomous choice is a possibility, but a more likely scenario is a combination of these two with some of the more 'traditional' and administrative HRM functions being outsourced or technol-ogy driven along with a re-orientation of other HRM functions to add real measurable value.

A similar trend can be identified in relation to other functions. For example, the revolutionary potential offered by information and communication technologies is immense. Over the coming years this technology will offer tremendous opportunities for international hospitality companies fundamentally to revise their marketing and distribution functions, the way they are structured, their business processes and their managerial mindsets. However, while these developments offer the potential for significant improvements in operational efficiencies, they also carry an imperative for increased investment in the human and intellectual capital embodied in their employees and managers. Many commentators indicate that the longer-term impact of the technology driven opportunities will be to commoditize the hospitality product, or at least significant elements of it. Olsen (1999) suggests that the brand will disappear, yield management systems will become obsolete, knowledge-based robots and personal software agents will take control away from companies and re-locate it among customers. Therefore, where will international hospitality companies look for sustainable sources of competitive advantage?

If significant elements of their product/process nexus can only be traded on a commodity basis they have a problem with traditional answers to this question. As price is the only competitive factor in a commodity market this would imply a concentration on cost reduction to become the least cost/price supplier. This is a possibility but, as the cost reduction technologies are available to all, is it sustainable? In addition, labour market conditions and dynamics may mitigate against this even more in the future (Olsen, 1999). A more attractive alternative, though this is not a zero sum choice, would be to secure advantage in those aspects of the hospitality product that are highly valued by consumers and more difficult for competitors to copy. In short, the intangible, relationship aspects of the hospitality experience, the real 'feel good' factors that generate high levels of customer satisfaction, emotional attachment and loyalty that tend to transcend the monetary value of the transaction and create real value for the customer.

Beyond providing safe, secure environments and demonstrating a concern for wider issues of social responsibility, the real source of sustainable advantage is the relevance and quality of the personal service that can be delivered. Of course the technology provides a platform for this, via customer databases, data mining, and product/process enhancements etc., but this potential will remain unrealized without the development of high quality personal service. Customers are not, and increasingly will not be, significantly influenced by marginally better room comfort, food, check-in procedures, billing efficiencies etc. A reasonable level of provision/performance is expected in these basic elements and the hospitality customer in general probably has a relatively wide quality tolerance band, at least in the short term. What is really important to customers are things that make their life easier, reduce inconvenience, take decisions and tasks away from them, save them time, make them feel good etc. Much of this can only be achieved through considered and intelligent human interaction. Most people are creatures of habit, they don't like surprises or change, they value familiarity, they want their lives to be less stressful, they want to be valued and obtain greater value from their life experiences. The same applies to employees as well as customers. Unfortunately, until hospitality companies really start to see employee satisfaction and loyalty as an essential precursor to customer satisfaction and loyalty the industry will remain in the 'same old, same old'. Whether future competitive dynamics will really revolutionize thinking in this respect is yet to be seen. If the past is any guide to the future it will not!

Conclusions

The international hospitality industry is a vibrant and very diverse industry full of interesting paradoxes and dilemmas. It has seen great success overall over the last two decades and there have been many significant strategic and operational changes as it has evolved to its present form. Nothwithstanding its diversity and complexity, the astute observer should be able to identify common themes, problems and failures, as well as essential differences between its component sectors. There are identifiable patterns and trends that tend to transcend national/cultural influences. However, we must never forget that there are also important differences across nations and cultures. The secret here is to disentangle the generic from the specific. In this respect both academics and practitioners have much work to do.

Summary

- The structure of the international hospitality industry is one characterized by 'the many dominating the few'.

- Defining the international hospitality industry is problematic.

- International hospitality companies are all grappling with the 'global versus local' dilemma.

- The industry has grown considerably over recent years and has the potential for even greater growth in the future.

- Company growth has arisen largely as a consequence of horizontal integration strategies and 'collaborative' arrangements.

- Information and communication technologies have impacted on the industry and hold the potential for even more radical transformation in the future.

- Branding has been a significant factor in the development of large international hospitality companies.

- Customer relationship management and relationship marketing are becoming increasingly important as a source of differentiation and to increase customer loyalty.

- Making comparisons across companies and cultures is problematic and care must be taken to ensure equivalence and representativeness.

Review questions

1. What problems are encountered in attempts to define the international hospitality industry?
2. How would you define the industry?
3. How can smaller, independent hospitality businesses survive in the face of the enormous power wielded by the corporate giants?
4. Under what circumstances would you advocate a global standardization strategy or a locally customized strategy?
5. Is mass customization the answer to the global versus local problem?
6. Do you believe that the industry will continue to expand at its present rate?
7. To what extent will new information and communication technologies prove to be revolutionary in the industry?
8. What are the main comparability problems encountered in the international context and how can these be minimized/ eliminated?
9. What are the key challenges facing international hospitality companies over the next 5–10 years?
10. What do you believe is the key source of competitive advantage for international hospitality companies?

References

Armstrong, R. W., Mok, C., Go, F. M. and Chan, A. (1997) The Importance Of Cross-Cultural Expectations In The Measurement Of Service Quality Perceptions In The Hotel Industry. *International Journal of Hospitality Management*, **16**, (2), 181–190.

Brotherton, B. (1999) Comparative Research. In Brotherton, B. (ed.) *The Handbook of Contemporary Hospitality Management Research*, John Wiley and Sons Ltd, Chichester, pp. 143–172.

Brotherton, B. (2000) The Comparative Approach. In Brotherton, B. (ed.) *An Introduction To The UK Hospitality Industry: A Comparative Approach*. Butterworth-Heinemann, Oxford, pp. 1–22.

Brotherton, B. (2002) *Is Your Mirror the Same as Mine? Methodological Issues in Undertaking and Interpreting Cross-Cultural Studies*. Paper presented at the EuroCHRIE conference, ESADE, Barcelona.

Brotherton, B. and Adler, G. (1999) An Integrative Approach To Enhancing Customer Value and Corporate Performance In the International Hotel Industry. *International Journal of Hospitality Management*, **18**, (3), 261–272.

Brotherton, B. and Hopping, B. (1997) Culture And Corporate Strategy In The International Hotel Industry: Towards A Synthesis? Abstract published in the *Proceedings of the Seventh Annual CHME Hospitality Research Conference*, Glasgow Caledonian University, pp. 256–258.

Burrell, J., Manfredi, S., Rollin, H., Price, L. and Stead, L. (1997) Equal Opportunities For Women Employees In The Hospitality Industry: A Comparison Between France, Italy, Spain And The UK. *International Journal of Hospitality Management*, **16**, (2), 161–179.

Gilmore, J. H. and Pine B. J. (1997) The Four Faces of Mass Customisation. *Harvard Business Review*, **75**, (1), 91–101.

Hallam, G. and Baum, T. (1996) Contracting Out Food And Beverage Operations In Hotels: A Comparative Study Of Practice In North America And The United Kingdom. *International Journal of Hospitality Management*, **15**, (1), 41–50.

Hallowell, E. M. (1999) The Human Moment at Work. *Harvard Business Review*, **77**, (1), 58–66.

Hamelin, H. (ed.) (1999) *Creating Value Through People and Partnership – A Report on Human Resources Management for the Hospitality Industry*, IH&RA, Paris.

Jones, P. (1999) Operational Issues and Trends in the Hospitality Industry. *International Journal of Hospitality Management*, **18**, (4), 427–442.

Moutinho, L., McDonagh, P., Peris, S. M. and Bigne, E. (1995) The Future Development Of The Hotel Sector: An International Comparison. *International Journal of Contemporary Hospitality Management*, **7**, (4), 10–15.

Muller, C. C. (1999) The Business of Restaurants: 2001 and Beyond. *International Journal of Hospitality Management*, **18**, (4), 401–413.

Olsen, M. D. (1999) Macroforces Driving Change into the New Millennium – Major Challenges for the Hospitality Professional. *International Journal of Hospitality Management*, **18**, (4), 371–385.

Olsen, M. D. (2001) Hospitality and the Tourist of the Future. In Lockwood, A. and Medlik, S. (eds) *Tourism and Hospitality in the 21st Century*, Butterworth-Heinemann, Oxford, pp. 206–215.

Pine, B. J. (1993) *Mass Customisation: the New Frontier in Business Competition*. Harvard Business School Press, Boston, MA.

Pizam, A., Pine, R., Mok, C. and Shin, J. Y. (1997) Nationality vs Industry Cultures: Which Has A Greater Effect On Managerial Behaviour? *International Journal of Hospitality Management*, **16**, (2), 127–145.

Shoemaker, S. and Lewis, R. C. (1999) Customer Loyalty: The Future of Hospitality Marketing. *International Journal of Hospitality Management*, **18**, (4), 345–370.

Van Hoof, H. B., Verbeeten, M. J. and Combrink, T. E. (1996) Information Technology Revisited – International Lodging-Industry Technology Needs And Perceptions: A Comparative Study. *The Cornell Hotel and Restaurant Administration Quarterly*, **37**, (6), 86–91.

Woods, R. H. (1999) Predicting is Difficult, Especially About The Future: Human Resources in the New Millennium. *International Journal of Hospitality Management*, **18**, (4), 443–456.

Further reading

Beyond the chapters in this book perhaps the single best source of material relating to contemporary themes and future issues is the special edition of the *International Journal of Hospitality Management*, Vol. 18, no. 4, that explores many aspects of the topics dealt with in this book. In addition, the publications produced by the International Hotel & Restaurant Association (IH&RA), especially the output from their 'Visioning The Future' workshops, are very useful to access the views of both academic and industry experts.

Index